Think/Point/ Shoot

Media Ethics, Technology, and Global Change

Annette Danto and
Mobina Hashmi

In collaboration with
Lonnie Isabel

Routledge
Taylor & Francis Group

NEW YORK AND LONDON

First published 2017
by Routledge
711 Third Avenue, New York, NY 10017

and by Routledge
2 Park Square, Milton Park, Abingdon, Oxon, OX14 4RN

Routledge is an imprint of the Taylor & Francis Group, an informa business

Library of Congress Cataloging in Publication Data
Names: Danto, Annette, author. | Hashmi, Mobina, author. | Isabel, Lonnie, author.
Title: Think-point-shoot : media ethics, technology and global change / Annette Danto and Mobina Hashmi; in collaboration with Lonnie Isabel.
Description: Abingdon, Oxon; New York, NY : Routledge, 2017.
Identifiers: LCCN 2016008877 | ISBN 9781138847958 (hardback) |
ISBN 9781138847965 (pbk.) | ISBN 9781315726267 (ebk)
Subjects: LCSH: Mass media—Moral and ethical aspects. | Digital media—Moral and ethical aspects. | Journalistic ethics.
Classification: LCC P94.D37 2017 | DDC 175—dc23
LC record available at https://lccn.loc.gov/2016008877

ISBN: 978-1-138-84795-8 (hbk)
ISBN: 978-1-138-84796-5 (pbk)
ISBN: 978-1-315-72626-7 (ebk)

Typeset in Times New Roman
by Keystroke, Neville Lodge, Tettanhall, Wolverhampton

Printed in Canada

Think/Point/Shoot

Think/Point/Shoot gives students a thorough overview of the role of ethics in modern media creation. Case studies emphasize the critical issues in global media ethics today in all stages of media creation from preproduction research and development to production and post-production. This volume features practicing filmmakers, journalists, and media creators who provide insight into dealing with real-world ethical dilemmas.

For this era, digital imagery, sounds, and web communication have opened doors to sharing thoughts and ideas instantaneously with potentially vast audiences. This presents exciting opportunities, but also serious ethical, legal, and social challenges. The cases and exercises found in this book are applicable to the current media field while still remaining grounded in strong ethical theory. *Think/Point/Shoot* explains the challenge of communicating a story to a worldwide audience while maintaining ethical standards.

A companion website provides additional resources for students and instructors:

- Chapter summaries and case studies
- Important forms.

Instructors will also find:

- Classroom exercises
- PowerPoints
- Video from the "Global Media Ethics" conference of March 2013.

Annette Danto is a filmmaker and Professor in the Department of Film at Brooklyn College. A three-time awarded Fulbright Scholar in Filmmaking, she holds degrees from McGill University, Columbia University, and New York University's Tisch School of the Arts Maurice Kanbar Institute of Film, Television and New Media.

Mobina Hashmi is an Assistant Professor in the Department of Television and Radio at Brooklyn College, and the Director of the Center for Global Television. She has a BA from Dartmouth College, and a PhD in media and cultural studies from the University of Wisconsin at Madison. Her work has been published in *Economic and Political Weekly* and in *South Asian History and Culture*.

Lonnie Isabel is a reporter and former Deputy Managing Editor of *Newsday* and Newsday-Laventhol Visiting Professor at Columbia University's Graduate School of Journalism. Isabel is a 30-year veteran of the newspaper business and has worked as a political reporter, investigative reporter, and editor for *Newsday, Boston Globe, Boston Herald*, and *Oakland Tribune*. Isabel joined the newly created CUNY Graduate School of Journalism in 2005.

Conversations, questions, and debates with students have been integral in shaping our understanding of the central issues regarding media ethics. With sincere thanks, this book is dedicated to our students in the United States, the United Kingdom, and India at the following institutions: Brooklyn College, CUNY Graduate School of Journalism, Columbia University's Graduate School of Journalism, Hunter College, Brooklyn College's India Documentary Production Program (2010–2015), Maurice Kanbar Institute of Film, Television & New Media at New York University, British Film Institute's New Filmmaker Program (2015), Bangor University's Media Production Program (2015), MOP Vaishnav College for Women, University of Madras' Communications Department, L.V. Prasad Film and Television Academy (2005–2015), Asian Institute of Journalism, Suchitra Film and Drama Academy, Indian Institute of New Media and Journalism, and Mahindra École Centrale (2015).

Contents

Acknowledgments

RESEARCHING, writing, and editing a book is like making a movie. Collaboration encompasses unpredictable challenges involving diverse craft specializations, simultaneous activities, and the cumulative effects of decisions.

Inspired by the documentary *Reflections on Media Ethics* (Danto, 2011, www.forward intime.com), *Think/Point/Shoot* grew out of a conference on global media ethics in New York in 2013 and the discussions that followed from it.

First, my gratitude is extended to those interviewed in the documentary *Reflections on Media Ethics*: Noam Chomsky, Amy Goodman, Jon Alpert, and Baroness Mary Warnock. The late Albert Maysles and George Stoney were also pivotal to this project; both true pioneers of documentary cinema. While at the National Film Board of Canada and throughout his career, George Stoney exemplified ethical documentary practice.

On March 13–14, 2013, Mobina Hashmi and I, along with Lonnie Isabel, sponsored a conference, "Global Media Ethics," held at Brooklyn College and the CUNY Graduate School of Journalism. The proceedings of that conference gave rise to this publication. Appreciation is extended to the following institutions and individuals for their support of the conference: Brooklyn College, CUNY Graduate School of Journalism, New York Women in Film and Television, Loreen Arbus Foundation, and the Pulitzer Center for Crisis Reporting. Special gratitude is owed to the following individuals: Maria Conelli, Dean of Visual Media and Performing Arts at Brooklyn College; Stephen Shepard, former Dean of the CUNY Graduate School of Journalism; Terry Lawler, Executive Director of New York Women in Film and Television; Loreen Arbus; Stuart MacLelland of the Department of Television and Radio at Brooklyn College; Tracy Lovett from the Television Center; Jay Kim of Brooklyn College's Department of Film; George Casturani, Director of Broadcast and A/V Systems at the CUNY Graduate School of Journalism.

For the publication of *Think/Point/Shoot*, I would like to extend major appreciation to Mobina Hashmi for her ongoing collaboration on various media ethics initiatives since 2010. Our complementary strengths have made the completion of this book a reality. Thank you Lonnie Isabel for bringing a journalist's perspective to the Global Media Ethics conference and this volume.

Gratitude to all the contributing authors, specifically Christine Choy, Tami Gold, Yoruba Richen, Jon Alpert, and Samir Chopra—all of whom participated in the Global Media Ethics

Conference and have written chapters for this book. Equal gratitude is extended to contributing authors: John Gurrin, K. Hariharan, Terilyn Shropshire, and Scott Sinkler.

I am indebted to Jaime Wolf for his generous advice and contributions to the copyright ethics chapter. Appreciation to Neil Rosini and Stephanie Black for their participation.

Thank you to the editors at Routledge/Taylor & Francis for ongoing guidance and feedback: Ross Wagenhofer, Nicole Salazar, Deirdre Byrne, Brianna Bernel, Linda Bathgate, Katy Morrissey and Bonita Glanville-Morris.

Major appreciation is also owed to Mick Hurbis-Cherrier, Sandra Robinson, Alex Makhlin, and the Research Foundation of CUNY.

Mick Hurbis-Cherrier, Professor of Film & Media Studies at Hunter College, was instrumental in making this book a reality, not only by introducing us to Routledge/Taylor & Francis, but also for his ongoing wise guidance.

Sandra Robinson, Professor of Asian Studies at Sarah Lawrence College, provided critical feedback and generous advice for the entire book. Her constructive suggestions were central to each stage of the project, from the initial proposal to editing of the final manuscript.

Alex Makhlin of the Brooklyn College Library offered conscientious assistance in the final stages of manuscript preparation. Gratitude to the Research Foundation of CUNY for funding support granted to *Think/Point/Shoot.*

Additional acknowledgments are extended to the following: British Film Institute's New Filmmakers Program (2015), and especially Prof. Dyfrig Jones, Bangor University, Wales, U.K.; Prof. Uma Vangal, the Daniel Pearl Foundation, and the U.S. Consulate in Chennai for inviting me to highlight media ethics at the Daniel Pearl Film Festival in Chennai, Bangalore and Trivandrum in October 2015; and Prof. Lynne McVeigh for reading selected chapters, offering insightful comments and ongoing encouragement.

In this volume I refer to various past productions. In particular I would like to acknowledge my key collaborators from *Shanti's Story* (Danto, 2004) and *Portraits of Two Women from Burkina Faso* (Danto, 2002). I am most grateful to Dr. Vijaya Srinivasan, former Director of the Belgaum Pathfinder Office; Prof. Dorothy Rompalske; Ilango Samuel Peter; K. Prabhakar; and Adjaratou Lompo of Burkina Faso.

On behalf of the co-editors, we are most grateful to Asif Raza for his expert and timely assistance with the photographs in this book.

Our sincere appreciation to all the photographers whose work is found in this volume, including Ilango Samuel Peter, Mary Edith Mardis, Nathan Weber, David and Joanne Kagan, Alexander Milne, Balakrishnan Anat, Jan McLaughlin, Stephanie Black, Takeshi Fukunaga, and the late Ryo Murakami.

Annette Danto

East Hampton, NY

January 10, 2016

I want to echo Annette's sentiments and extend my gratitude to all the persons and institutions who have helped us along in this journey, especially Lonnie Isabel. In addition to those listed above, my deepest thanks to Shazia Iftkhar, Daniel Marcus, Irene Sosa, and Liv Yarrow for their support, advice, and encouragement at various stages of this project.

Above all, I want to express my appreciation of all that Annette Danto has done to make this project possible. She has been the guiding force at every step of this project and has been a wonderfully generous, patient, and fun collaborator. As she has noted, it takes a lot of support from a lot of people to complete a book. It is a testament to Annette that so many have gladly shared their insight, experiences, and knowledge with us; and I thank her for inviting me to join her in this endeavor.

Mobina Hashmi
Brooklyn, NY
January 14, 2016

Contributors

CO-EDITORS

Annette Danto is a filmmaker and Professor in the Department of Film at Brooklyn College. A three-time awarded Fulbright Scholar in Filmmaking, her work has been used by international non-profit organizations including Pathfinder International, United Nations Development Fund for Women, and the Gates Foundation to strengthen educational outreach campaigns addressing women's health, economic development initiatives, and girls' education. Her recent documentary *Reflections on Media Ethics* (2011) is distributed by forwardintime.com., along with *The Never Ending Path* (2005), which is in permanent collections of 125 academic institutions worldwide. Danto has been an invited lecturer on media ethics at national and international venues including: British Film Institute (U.K.), Bangor University (Wales), Daniel Pearl Film Festival (India), U.S. State Department and Fulbright initiatives in Washington, D.C., Chennai, Delhi and Bangalore. Danto holds degrees from McGill University, Columbia University, and New York University's Tisch School of the Arts Maurice Kanbar Institute of Film, Television and New Media.

Mobina Hashmi is Assistant Professor in the Department of Television and Radio at Brooklyn College, and the Director of the Center for Global Television. She has a BA in film and computer science from Dartmouth College, and a PhD in media and cultural studies from the University of Wisconsin at Madison. She is currently working on a book, *Work and Television in Global America*, which analyzes how U.S. television programming negotiates the impact of labor globalization on the raced, gendered, and classed hierarchies of citizenship, and on an analysis of the formation of television news publics in Pakistan. Her work has been published in *Economic and Political Weekly* and in *South Asian History and Culture*.

Lonnie Isabel is a reporter and former Deputy Managing Editor of *Newsday* and Newsday-Laventhol Visiting Professor at Columbia University's Graduate School of Journalism. Isabel is a 30-year veteran of the newspaper business and has worked as a political reporter, investigative reporter and editor for *Newsday*, *Boston Globe*, *Boston Herald*, and *Oakland Tribune*. As Deputy Managing Editor at *Newsday*, he was responsible for directing the post-September 11 coverage, the Iraq War, the Second Gulf War, President Clinton's impeachment, and several presidential campaigns. He joined the newly created CUNY Graduate School of

Journalism in 2006, where he started the International Reporting Program that has trained more than 75 journalists to cover international issues, and the International Journalist in Residence program that brings an endangered, targeted, or threatened journalist each year to study and work at the school.

CONTRIBUTING AUTHORS

Jon Alpert is a journalist and documentary filmmaker known for his use of cinema verite. He has traveled widely as an investigative journalist and has made films for NBC, PBS, and HBO. Over the course of his career, he has won 15 Emmy Awards and three DuPont-Columbia Awards. He has been nominated for two Academy awards: in 2010 for *China's Unnatural Disaster: The Tears of Sichuan Province*, and in 2012 for *Redemption*. Alpert has reported from Vietnam, Cambodia, Iran, Nicaragua, the Philippines, Cuba, China, and Afghanistan. He has interviewed Fidel Castro several times and was one of the few Western journalists to have conducted a videotaped interview with Saddam Hussein since the Persian Gulf War. While employed by NBC, Alpert was the first American journalist to bring back uncensored video footage from the first Persian Gulf War. The footage, much of it focusing on civilian casualties, was canceled three hours before it was supposed to be aired, and Alpert was simultaneously fired. In 1972, Alpert and his wife, Keiko Tsuno, founded the Downtown Community Television Center, one of the country's first community media centers.

Samir Chopra is a Professor of Philosophy at Brooklyn College and the Graduate Center of the City University of New York. He has a BA in Mathematical Statistics from Delhi University, an MS in Computer Science from the New Jersey Institute of Technology, and a PhD in Philosophy from the City University of New York. His academic interests include pragmatism, Nietzsche, the philosophical foundations of artificial intelligence, philosophy of law, the legal theory of artificial agents, and the politics and ethics of technology. He is co-author of *A Legal Theory for Autonomous Artificial Agents* (University of Michigan Press, 2011). He blogs at samirchopra.com and at The Cordon at ESPNcricinfo and is on Twitter @eyeonthepitch.

Christine Choy is a filmmaker and Professor at New York University's Tisch School of the Arts Maurice Kanbar Institute of Film, Television and New Media. She has produced and directed over 70 documentaries in various forms, receiving over 60 international awards. Among them are numerous fellowships such as the John Simon Guggenheim, the Rockefeller, and the Asian Cultural Council, as well as an Academy Award Nomination for the documentary film *Who Killed Vincent Chin?* Many of her works examine the dynamics of Chinese and Korean communities and the relations between black and Asian communities in the United States.

Tami Gold is a filmmaker and Professor of Film and Media Studies at Hunter College. She is a recipient of Rockefeller, Guggenheim, and AFI Fellowships. Her work has screened at the New York Film Festival, the Tribeca and Sundance Film Festivals, as well as international labor, women's, and LGBT film festivals. Broadcast screenings include: HBO, PBS, the

Learning Channel, and community-based venues throughout the world. Her work focuses on injustice, the lives of feminists, and the boundaries of gender conformity.

John Gurrin is an artist, sound engineer, filmmaker and Professor at New York University's Tisch School of the Arts Maurice Kanbar Institute of Film, Television and New Media. His work has been shown internationally and reviewed in *The New Yorker* and *The New York Times*. He has been the sound designer on notable projects including Metallica's long form video *The Unforgiven*; CD recordings include Momenta Quartet's *Similar Motion*; and production sound on many documentaries and narrative films notably Andrew Jarecki's *Capturing the Friedmans*.

K. Hariharan is a filmmaker, Academic Dean of Mahindra École Centrale in Hyderabad and former director of L.V. Prasad Film and Television Academy in Chennai, Tamil Nadu, India. He was born in Mumbai, Maharashtra where his father was the vice-president of Eastman Kodak. Hariharan's films have received top awards nationally and internationally. He has directed films for the Children's Aid Society of India and received the National Film Award for Best Tamil Feature Film, as well as the Golden Prize at the Moscow International Film Festival. Hariharan has written numerous articles for various publications in India, including *The Hindu* and *The Times of India*. He is a regular guest lecturer at universities worldwide, and has been a visiting faculty at the University of Pennsylvania.

Yoruba Richen is a filmmaker and Director of the Documentary Program at the CUNY Graduate School of Journalism. Her most recent documentary, *The New Black*, won Audience Awards at AFI Docs, Philly Q Fest, and Frameline LGBT Film Festival; and Best Documentary at the Urbanworld film festival. *The New Black* opened theatrically at New York's Film Forum and aired on PBS's *Independent Lens*. Grants received include: Sundance Documentary Fund, Chicken & Egg Pictures, Ford Foundation, Creative Promise Award at Tribeca All Access. Richen was a Sundance Producers fellow, and is a TED speaker and a Guggenheim Fellow.

Terilyn Shropshire is a film and television editor with extensive feature film credits including *The Secret Life of Bees*, *Love and Basketball*, *Eve's Bayou*, *Black Nativity*, *Sparkle*, *Jumping the Broom*, *Diary of a Mad Black Woman*, the ABC series *Quantico*, and the *Lifetime Achievement Award tribute to Sidney Poitier for the 74th Annual Academy Awards*, for which she received an Emmy nomination. Additional awards include: American Cinema Editors (A.C.E.) Eddie Award for Best-Edited Motion Picture for Commercial Television for *Redemption: The Stan Tookie Williams Story*. She is a member of the Academy of Motion Picture Arts and Sciences, the Academy of Television Arts and Sciences and American Cinema Editors. She has been featured in *L.A. Weekly Magazine* and was on the *Essence Magazine's 2014 Hollywood Hot List*. She holds dual BA degrees in Broadcast Journalism and Cinema from the University of Southern California.

Scott Sinkler is a producer, director and Director of Photography based in New York City. He has worked on documentaries, arts programs, commercials, and corporate and non-profit film and video productions since the 1980s. His work as director of photography is notable and includes documentaries such as Katie Couric's *Fed Up*, PBS's *Ice Warriors* and HBO's

An Apology to Elephants, as well as for series like PBS's *Wide Angle*, *The Tony Awards Show*, *Egg: The ARTS show*, WNET's *City Arts* and *City Life*, and several series for Bloomberg Television. Sinkler's documentary *Inside Life Outside* was included in the Whitney Biennial and is in the permanent collection of the Museum of Modern Art. His films have received Emmy awards, as well as recognition at international film festivals. He has written, consulted, and has taught courses and master classes at New York University.

Introduction

Establishing Shot 1
Format and Practice

Annette Danto

DIGITAL technology has catapulted us into a continuously evolving revolution. Digital cameras are built into every phone, cameras are attached to high-flying drones, and wearable GoPros are capturing perilous feats. Interactive media are now embedded in everyday accessories—watches and other gadgets, toys, and appliances. Astonishing technologies are galvanizing media creators worldwide, generating new approaches at incredible speeds.

In all its variations, media has as its primary mission the challenge of communicating with audiences, whether through fiction, documentary, digital journalism, or social media.

Given the context of shared global communication, is visual media a universally accessible language? Are there gaps between messages sent and messages received? How much do the intentions of the media creator matter? Can we gauge whether communications are received as intended?

This is where media ethics comes in.

Visual communication is always an *unreliable* universal language given viewers' differing emotional needs, life experiences, cultural, religious, and educational backgrounds. Applying a "one size fits all" model does not work—neither in global cultural politics, nor in aesthetics.

Images do not simply record factual existence: they interpret. As we make conceptual and technical choices, we remain part of a culture and work within a contemporary cultural code. We are therefore influenced in our creative and technical choices, often subliminally. This calls for greater mindfulness and scrutiny by media-makers.

Existing ethical frameworks have evolved in the context of older media such as film and television. When we encounter Web 2.0 platforms like Twitter, Facebook, Instagram, YouTube or Tumblr, we are faced with images, sounds, and advertisements that can shock, entertain, inform, and confuse us.

For media-makers, this presents added challenges and obligations. The impact of what we create, how it is created, how it circulates, and where it is seen can create ethical

FIGURE A.1   Images do not simply record factual existence, they interpret. Vegetable seller in a Hanoi marketplace. Courtesy of Mary Edith Mardis.

predicaments. Forecasting pitfalls and designing solutions requires thought and a little crystal-gazing. As you will learn from the filmmakers, journalists, editors, and others in this book, even the most seasoned media-makers grapple with ethical complexities.

LIVING WITH IMAGES

Visuals have immediacy, an emotional and powerful impact on today's high-speed society. The brain processes images faster than text. Images are easily shared online, generating "buzz" and sparking conversation.

Visual technology offers each of us extraordinary opportunities for freedom of expression. It allows control over how we chronicle and remember events in our lives. An ethical challenge is reconciling individual freedom of expression with ethical representations of peoples, issues, and controversies. What do we do when conflicting priorities become apparent? How can we determine whether or not an image is unjustly abrasive? Global communications today require that we pay special attention to this last question.

The circulation of these political cartoons [see Box 1] and the controversy they generated brings home the complexity of media ethics in a cosmopolitan, digital age. The cartoons found an audience far larger—and much different—than the one anticipated by the Danish

BOX 1   DANISH NEWSPAPER AND CONTROVERSIAL CARTOONS

In September 2005, an editor at the Danish newspaper *Jyllands-Posten* asked newspaper cartoonists to draw the prophet Mohammed as they saw him. A few days later, 12 different cartoonists submitted their depictions which were published in the paper. The images initiated controversy immediately because of the sensitive and sacred subject being presented in an insensitive and offensive manner. The publication of the cartoons was soon followed by burnings of the Danish flag, protests, boycotts of Danish products, and violence. The cartoons became famous around the world because of the amount of controversy they stirred up.[1]

newspaper, and they became the catalyst for a broader debate about Europe's colonial legacy, multiculturalism, and immigration.

Shocking imagery and controversial content can lead to different interpretations when they travel to different contexts. The resulting controversies tend to be reproduced for reasons of sensationalism, provocation, or boredom, or by an individual seeking the limelight.

Context matters! People's sensitivities vary according to location, time, race, class, gender, and generation. Instead of simply focusing on individual freedom of expression as an absolute value, media producers need to reflect on their broader ethical obligations to their audiences. Viewers, as well, have ethical responsibilities and need to be critical of all sources of visual information.

Even if an image seems familiar, the ethical requirement for each of us is to learn more about it before we fold it into our work, recirculate it, or try passing it off as representative of a specific culture, history, or circumstance.

FROM TEXT TO IMAGE

Our literacy skills have changed over time.

What writing was to earlier generations, image creation has become to this generation. Writing expanded our capabilities, enabling the development of law, philosophy, grammar, literature, poetry, and history. In ancient societies, literacy was limited to privileged classes.

Over time the reach of the alphabet meant that more people could learn to read. This altered the world rapidly. Because it expanded communication of thoughts and ideas to people in other locations and generations, the alphabet was central in our advancement as a civilization.

Writing evolved with papyrus and paper, the pen, the printing press, mass production of newspapers and magazines, and the typewriter. Technological developments altered not only how things were written and the medium through which the written word was reproduced, but also the content of the writing and for whom it was written.

FIGURE A.2   "Nearly 80 per cent of children in the United States between the ages of 0 and 5 use the internet on a regular basis" (Kessler, 2011). Credit: Maria Uspenskaya.

Today, communicating complex ideas, thoughts, and emotions requires a new literacy involving multimedia skills. Communication is quick and abbreviated. Characters are now formed by the press of a key rather than the physical motion of the hand. The internet has changed our styles of social interaction and communication.

In the mid-1980s only a select group of scientists and programmers had a working knowledge of the internet. Today, two-year-old children are learning how to use digital tablets.

For this generation, digital imagery, digital sounds, texting, and web communication have opened doors to sharing thoughts, ideas, and feelings instantaneously to potentially vast audiences. This presents exciting opportunities, but also serious ethical, legal, and social challenges, such as:

• Representation of underserved and vulnerable populations.
• Issues of privacy, censorship, and surveillance.
• The blurring of the observer and observed in an age of ubiquitous social media.
• Defining and defending the public interest against commercial desires.
• The uses and abuses of artistic imagery including issues of consent.

BOX 2   CHILDREN AND THE INTERNET

"Nearly 80 per cent of children in the United States between the ages of 0 and 5 use the internet on at least a weekly basis" (Kessler, 2011). "Digital media has become a regular part of the media diet of children 0–8 years old, with half (52%) of all 0 to 8 year-olds [surveyed] having access to a new mobile device such as a smartphone, video iPod, or iPad/tablet" (Common Sense Media, 2011). A 2015 survey of 2,658 tweens and teens, ages 8–18, found that young people use an average of six to nine hours of entertainment media daily (Common Sense Media, 2015).

BOX 3   REPRESENTATIONS OF UNDERSERVED AND VULNERABLE POPULATIONS

In South Hutchinson, Kansas, two 18-year-old employees of a nursing home were accused of taking pictures of an 83-year-old woman's genitals with a cell phone camera. The nursing home reported the incident to police after the two women—both certified nurse's aides—showed the digital image to a fellow employee, who reported it (Reeves, 2006).

BOX 4   PRIVACY, CENSORSHIP, AND SURVEILLANCE

Cyberbullying came to national and international attention when Tyler Clementi, an 18-year-old student at Rutgers University in Piscataway, New Jersey, jumped to his death from the George Washington Bridge on September 22, 2010. On September 19, his roommate and a fellow hall mate used a webcam without Clementi's knowledge, to record Clementi kissing another man. Students at Rutgers and Twitter followers were encouraged to watch via webcam.

BOX 5   THE BLURRED BOUNDARY BETWEEN OBSERVER AND OBSERVED IN AN AGE OF UBIQUITOUS SOCIAL MEDIA

A Florida man posted a horrifying photo of his wife's body on Facebook after he allegedly murdered her in the kitchen of their South Miami townhouse. The disturbing photograph was on his Facebook page after he had shot his wife and made a bizarre confession on the site (Ovalle, 2013).

BOX 6   DEFINING AND DEFENDING THE PUBLIC INTEREST AGAINST COMMERCIAL DESIRES

Calvin Klein received a great deal of attention when they used a very provocative image of an underage Brooke Shields in their advertisements. This controversy led to a great deal of free publicity for Calvin Klein from news organizations covering the story.

BOX 7   SHOCKVERTISING: THE USES AND ABUSES OF ARTISTIC IMAGERY

A Diesel jeans advertisement depicted a gun pointed at the viewer with a caption: "How to teach your children to love and care." A Benetton spokesman commented on the ad, stating: "If you are a jeans maker you can't run with the pack and expect to get any attention. Jeans are about sex and danger." (Horovitz, 1993, p. D1)

In an era of information overload and incessant public exposure to media, how far should one go to get noticed? In advertising, creating jarring, eye-opening images that startle, surprise, and sensationalize content is one way of drawing attention to a specific message or product. But should there be limits?

This sparks our discussion of media ethics.

MEDIA ETHICS: ABSOLUTISM AND RELATIVISM

Are there behaviors involving use of media that are always wrong, regardless of context?

- A documentary on the poor state of public education in New York City includes interviews with students at failing schools. All of the students interviewed are black and Latino. There are also Jewish and Asian students attending these schools, but they are not interviewed. Is this footage feeding into negative stereotyping?
- Two Indonesian death squad leaders are given an opportunity to re-enact mass murders. Are there ethical concerns when highlighting graphic violence and murder as a form of entertainment (Oppenheimer, 2012)?
- A group of Syrian refugees manages to infiltrate the Hungarian border. If you conduct interviews with the refugees, should your editor blur their faces and distort their voices before the footage is broadcast?

Moral absolutism is the ethical view that particular actions are intrinsically right or wrong. Theft, for example, is viewed as always wrong—even if done for the well-being of others. Robin Hood would be arrested for stealing regardless of his intentions.

FIGURE A.3   In an era of information overload and incessant public exposure to media, how far should one go to get noticed? Credit: Alex Malikov.

Moral absolutism emphasizes rules and commitment to duty. There are clear guidelines for human behavior and living life. Moral absolutism allows for predictability of ethical behavior—regardless of circumstance. Using deception to gain access to a celebrity for a story, or using deception to infiltrate an animal shelter abusing animals is wrong. Gratuitous sex or violence added to a short film to increase ratings and popularity would always be wrong under this frame of reference.

This is in contrast to moral relativism or situational ethics. Relativists believe that what is right or good for one person might not necessarily be right or good for another—even under similar circumstances. A situational approach would hold that right and wrong for anyone depends upon the circumstances. From this perspective there is no absolute right answer to ethical dilemmas that would hold true in all instances. Robin Hood might not be arrested if a moral relativist were handing down the punishment. Robin Hood would be able to justify theft on the grounds of his intentions to feed the poor.

In media production, a documentary pretending to be a documentary while actually consisting of a series of staged and orchestrated events can be rationalized as ethical if the filmmaker is inspired by this approach. Relativists tend to highlight particular circumstances and believe that right and wrong vary according to cultures and situations.

For people working with media, understanding the differences between these two opposing points of view is a necessary first step in media ethics education.

ALTERNATIVE MODES

Think/Point/Shoot explores media ethics in contexts ranging from preproduction to production, postproduction, and distribution. It also highlights ethical issues raised by new media such as alternative modes of production and content creation, interactivity, and real-time distribution.

Diverse media operate at different speeds and for different durations. The time factor introduces unique ethical challenges. For example, a feature filmmaker may work on a screenplay for years. This allows time to ponder story elements. Blogging, and especially livetweeting, on the other hand, requires instantaneous decision-making with little or no time to consider ethical pitfalls.

New media transmits content through connection and conversation, often in real time. It enables people around the world to share, comment on, and discuss a broad range of content. Unlike past technologies, new media is based on an interactive community.

Distribution of real-time media introduces its own range of ethical dilemmas. For example, a citizen journalist covering a political event can blog or post footage on various websites immediately, without release forms or copyright clearances. This would not be the case for a video journalist working at *The New York Times* where a series of gatekeepers scrutinize each and every story.

FIGURE A.4   Critical thinking and self-reflection are useful before attempting to represent a culture other than one's own. Courtesy of David and Joanne Kagan.

The prevalence of repurposed content presents distinct ethical challenges. Repurposing content involves the rearranging of sources for new audiences, sometimes in ways that the original author did not plan or consider possible. For the original author, and often for internet sites circulating the material, this may present copyright predicaments.

The ethical requirement for each of us is to learn more about repurposed content before we fold it into our work, re-circulate it, or imply that it is representative of culture, history, or circumstance.

Working with new media can be done in solitude, which raises issues of anonymity and accountability. Since there are no gatekeepers, responsibility falls on the individual to self-monitor and self-regulate.

The following three guidelines may be helpful:[2]

1. Understand the importance of compassion and empathy for others. Avoid seeing people as tools for self-promotion and self-gain.[3]
2. Acknowledge being a global citizen; a member of a heterogeneous world with awareness of differences as well as shared human needs.
3. Practice self-reflection and critical thinking about your own traditions and behavior.

While the scope of our book is wide-ranging, our message is simple and straightforward: all stages of media creation and all forms of media require careful consideration of ethics. Above all, values such as truth, honesty, respect for all persons, and fairness are not specific to technology. Core ethical values transcend technological innovation.

PLAN OF THIS BOOK

Think/Point/Shoot is designed for those who create or want to create media. You will not find a full review of the scholarly literature on theories of media ethics here. Instead, we offer fundamental theoretical insights that are related to practical aspects of media creation. Similarly, although you will not find here a technical manual, *Think/Point/Shoot* offers a unique translation of media ethics theory as it applies to technical and craft specialization.

This book is divided into three sections. Each section represents a stage of media creation:

- *Think* = Preproduction
- *Point and Shoot* = Production
- *Postproduction* = Editing, Copyright, and Distribution.

Highly acclaimed producers, directors, cinematographers, editors, journalists, and scholars share insights and examples of media ethics dilemmas. Respected filmmakers such as Jon Alpert, Christine Choy, Tami Gold, and Yoruba Richen challenge audiences with timely media controversies and generate innovative frameworks suited to the new media environment.

A list of key take home points is offered at the conclusion of each chapter. Highlighting the essential content of each chapter, these take home points are guideposts leading you toward developing fundamental ethical strategies for how to proceed in all stages of media creation.

A companion website includes discussion questions, additional case studies, a list of resources including a complete filmography, and interactive exercises.

Following are summaries of the three sections.

Think: this section examines the initial stage of preproduction, research, and development from an ethical perspective. It identifies ethical choices critical to moving forward with any media project. Such choices relate to the birth of a concept or story, competing funding agendas, authenticity, representing the underserved and vulnerable, and ethical issues related to representing minority identities. Working toward ethical practice, media-makers should emphasize collaboration and transparency with participants during this preliminary stage of media preproduction.

Point and Shoot: this section focuses on the ethical challenges of production: technical framing, cinematography, and sound recording. Ethical dilemmas may need to be resolved instantaneously by the cinematographer and, at times, the sound recordist. What guidelines help in making on-the-spot technical decisions? When it comes to covering sensitive, tragic, or painful content, are there preferred approaches that are more ethical? Safeguarding identities of interviewees presents serious ethical responsibilities; how best to approach this? Technical options include shot size, camera angle, composition, and eye line. How do these variants operate on an audience member's emotions? Media "ambush" tactics or surveillance techniques might be more effective in certain circumstances. How do we navigate the ethical dilemmas that are inevitable in these situations?

Postproduction: dealing with ethical dilemmas in the editing room can include manipulation of emotion and creating stories that may not be evident from existing footage. What approaches can editors take when confronting conflicting directives? What about media regulation and censorship? Might there be times when media censorship is an ethical option? There has been a historic struggle over ownership of creative work. What is copyleft and when is fair use justifiable? How can media creators protect their work through copyright laws? Distribution of media is no longer reserved for the privileged few. Online companies such as Amazon, Vimeo, Netflix, iTunes, and YouTube offer media-makers access to global audiences.

Technology can both improve and undermine. It can quickly turn from being a friend into an enemy. *Think/Point/Shoot* sets forth a framework for media preproduction, production, and postproduction that is simultaneously creative, effective, and principled. Ideally, we can aspire to inhabit a media landscape that reflects the highest ethical standards.

All media-makers need a tool kit. Ethical principles are important tools belonging in that kit: tools that can enhance and enrich our media world in all its forms.

NOTES

1   See Powers (2008) and Anderson (2006) for variant discussions about the impact of the Danish Cartoons.

2   Following Martha Nussbaum's lecture on December 16, 2007 at Hebrew University in Jerusalem (2010), these values are here applied to a discussion of media preproduction, production, and postproduction. Martha Nussbaum's talk sheds light on the role educational institutions should play in recognizing ethical issues as necessary in the educational process.

3   Mohandas Gandhi's approach to economics incorporates ethics. Economics that hurts the well-being of a nation or individual is immoral. The value of any industry should be gauged less by the dividends it pays its shareholders than by its effect on the people employed in it. Gandhian economics represents an alternative to mainstream economic ideologies. It promotes economic self-sufficiency without an emphasis on material pursuits or compromising human development. Gandhi's emphasis on peace, "trusteeship," and co-operation has been promoted as an alternative to competition as well as conflict between different economic and income classes in societies. Gandhian focus on human development is also seen as an effective emphasis on the eradication of poverty, social conflict, and backwardness in developing nations.

BIBLIOGRAPHY

Alia, V. (2004). *Media ethics and social change*. New York, NY: Routledge.

Anderson, J. W. (2006, January 31). Cartoons of prophet met with outrage. *Washington Post Foreign Service*. Retrieved from: www.washingtonpost.com/wp-dyn/content/article/2006/01/30/AR2006013001316.html

Common Sense Media. (2011, October 25). Common sense media research documents media use among infants, toddlers, and young children. Retrieved from: www.commonsensemedia.org/about-us/news/press-releases/common-sense-media-research-documents-media-use-among-infants-toddlers

Common Sense Media. (2015, November 3). Landmark report: U.S. teens use an average of nine hours of media per day, tweens use six hours. Retrieved from: www.commonsensemedia.org/about-us/news/press-releases/landmark-report-us-teens-use-an-average-of-nine-hours-of-media-per-day

Crane, S. A. (2008). Choosing not to look: Representation, repatriation, and holocaust atrocity photography. *History and Theory, 47*(3), 309–330.

Day, L. A. (2006). *Ethics in media communication* (5th ed.). Belmont, CA: Thomson, Wadsworth.

Friend, C., & Singer, J. B. (2007). *Online journalism ethics: Traditions and transitions*. Armonk, NY: M. E. Sharpe.

Goldman, R., & Papson, S. (1996). *Sign wars: The cluttered landscape of advertising*. New York, NY: Guilford Press.

Goldstein, T. (2007). *Journalism and truth: Strange bedfellows*. Evanston, IL: Northwestern University Press.

Good, H. (2003). *Desperately seeking ethics: A guide to media conduct*. Lanham, MD: Scarecrow Press.

Good, H., & Dillon, M. (2002). *Media ethics goes to the movies*. Westport, CT: Praeger.

Gutnick, A. (2011, March 10). Always connected: The new digital media habits of young children. *The Joan Ganz Cooney Center*. Retrieved from: www.joanganzcooneycenter.org/publication/always-connected-the-new-digital-media-habits-of-young-children/

Hebrew University of Jerusalem. (2010, September 19). Prof. Martha Nussbaum on "humanistic education & global justice." Retrieved from https://youtube.com/watch?v=A_IR1CID3Ns

Helber, S., Ramsey,P., & Drew, J., The Associated Press. (2015, August 8). Reporter, cameraman killed on air; gunman dies. *The Daily Local*. Retrieved from www.dailylocal.com/article/DL/20150826/NEWS/150829836

Horovitz, B. (1993, May 11). Shock value helps an obscure jeans maker be not so obscure. *Los Angeles Times*, p. D1.

Kessler, S. (2011, March 15). Study: 80 percent of children under 5 use internet weekly. *USA Today*. Retrieved from: http://content.usatoday.com/communities/technologylive/post/2011/03/study-80-percent-of-children-under-5-use-internet-weekly/1#.VonwR7NunIU

Oppenheimer, J. (2012). *Statements*. Retrieved from *The Act of killing* (Film): http://theactofkilling.com/statements/

Ovalle, D. (2013, December 4). South Miami Facebook killer pleads not guilty to first-degree murder. *Miami Herald*. Retrieved from: www.miamiherald.com/news/local/community/miami-dade/article1958188.html

Papson, R. G. (1996). *Sign wars: The cluttered landscape of advertising*. New York, NY: Guilford Press.

Powers, S. (2008). Examining the Danish cartoon affair: Mediatized cross-cultural tensions? *Media, War and Conflict, 1*(3), 339–359.

Raskin, M. (2013, January 3). Managing your children's screen time. *The Washington Post*. Retrieved from: www.washingtonpost.com/lifestyle/style/managing-your-childrens-screen-time/2013/01/03/9c47cea2-2e84-11e2-89d4-040c9330702a_story.html

Reeves, G. (2006, August 2). Teen girls charged for pix of woman, 83. *Kansas City Star*. Crime Scene Kansas City.

Shedden, D. (2002, July 20). Media ethics bibliography. *Poynter*. Retrieved from: www.poynter.org/uncategorized/785/media-ethics-bibliography/

Underwood, D. (2002). *From Yahweh to Yahoo! The religious roots of the secular press*. Urbana, IL: University of Illinois Press.

Wire Reports. (2015, August 26). Killer played to Twitter age in on-air shootings in Virginia. *The Dallas Morning News*. Retrieved from www.dallasnews.com/news/headlines/20150826-killer-played-to-twitter-age-in-on-air-shootings-in-virginia.ece

Establishing Shot 2
Media Ethics Theory

Mobina Hashmi

> Society exists not only by transmission, by communication, but it may fairly be said to exist in transmission, in communication.
>
> John Dewey (Carey, 1989/2008, p. 11)

> What we got here is a failure to communicate.
>
> Luke, *Cool Hand Luke* (1967)

Communication and media studies is not a unified field of study. Scholarship on media comes from disciplinary traditions as diverse as psychology, journalism, anthropology, art history, law, documentary production, sociology, English, political theory, science and technology studies, political economy, and philosophy. This introduction synthesizes some of the most influential ideas from these disciplinary frameworks in order to offer a range of ways of thinking about the same core ethical issues in media: responsibility to the subjects and collaborators, awareness of the power of images and narratives to shape public opinion, and understanding our own position in relation to broader structures of power and privilege.

Media ethics is its own robust field of study, but our goal here is more to introduce you to the ethical commitments that inform a range of other fields of media studies. Cultural studies and critical media studies scholars, for instance, rarely discuss ethics explicitly, but their work is often fully committed to analyzing how lack of control over how one is represented is intertwined with social, political, and economic disenfranchisement. For example, scholarly analyses of popular television programs, such as *Hilmiyya Nights* (Egypt), *Cagney & Lacey* (United States), or *Yo soy Betty, la fea* (Colombia), explain how the meanings of race, gender, class, religion etc. in these programs influence how different groups are perceived in society (Abu-Lughod, 1995; D'Acci, 1994; Rivero, 2003).

At the most basic level, ethical uncertainty comes from the tension between absolutist or normative beliefs and relativist or situational practices. For example, is it *always* wrong to film someone without their consent? Or, is it wrong only in the *specific context* of filming those who are not in positions of power? The first part of the introduction to this book works through these questions with reference to specific examples while the following few paragraphs provide some additional context.

Scholars interested in developing absolutist or normative ethics often begin with Immanuel Kant's categorical imperative that we should follow only those principles that would also be acceptable to us as universal laws. In this paradigm of *deontological ethics*, filming someone without their consent would be ethical only if you were comfortable with it being true in all contexts including someone filming you without consent, and if it fulfilled a social duty or responsibility.[1]

Often grounded in Aristotelian ethics, ethical relativism emphasizes the context and conditions in which we act. If we cannot develop ethical norms that are universal, then we must ask the fundamental questions of what it means to live a good life and what it means to be a good person. In other words, what kind of society do you want to live in? What virtues distinguish a good member of this society? In the example above, if you want to live in a society based on mutual trust, respect for others might be a key virtue. Your decision to film with or without consent would then be based, not on an external rule, but on the extent to which you have cultivated that virtue in yourself and on your ethical evaluation of the context in which you have to make the decision to film or not to film.

The two approaches mentioned above dominate discussion of moral philosophy in the Western tradition. It is important to recognize that ethical principles are seen as legitimate only to the extent that they are backed by some form of authority that is widely accepted. In most societies and cultures, religion—the will of a divine being or beings or force—initially acted as this authority. For example, in the Judeo-Christian tradition, the ten commandments (e.g., to not kill, to not steal, to honor one's parents) are a set of moral principles backed by God's authority. Buddhist ethics include the avoidance of destructive actions and greed. Islamic ethics note that since responsibilities to people are as important as responsibilities to God, charity is one of the five pillars of the faith. There are, of course, many different traditions within each of these faiths. One source of ethical complexity today lies in the fact that in most societies, religious authority has been replaced—or at least modified by—secular forms of authority such as scientific knowledge or the "will of the people" as determined by democratic elections.

Thus, one of the main differences you will note between the different approaches discussed in this section is that they legitimize their ethical perspectives by appealing to somewhat different forms of authority. A second difference is that while some talk about the need for codes or rules of behavior, others emphasize that we need to cultivate an ethical self that will allow us to meet the challenge of identifying and understanding the complex confluence of factors involved in any ethical question.[2]

The fundamental ethical principles that we emphasize throughout this book are respect for others, the ability to see oneself not just as an individual but also as a member of larger communities, and the willingness to engage in critical self-reflection. Along with cultivating these ethical dispositions, the perspectives below enable you to develop a deeper understanding of the kinds of ethical challenges you might face.

The remainder of this chapter is divided into three sections: applied ethics; key media studies approaches to ethics; and a summary of key themes and issues across these different approaches with an emphasis on how theory and practice intersect.

APPLIED ETHICS

Applied ethics prioritizes understanding the specific situations and contexts in which ethical questions can arise. This section briefly describes a subset of applied ethics: codes of ethics developed by different professional organizations to address issues that are of specific relevance for their disciplinary practice.

Journalism

Leading news organizations such as *The New York Times* and National Public Radio (NPR) have their own ethics handbooks or statements of ethical principles. For example, according to NPR's ethics handbook:

> NPR is at its core a news organization. Our news content, whether on the radio, on the web, or in any other form, must attain the highest quality and strengthen our credibility. We take pride in our craft. Our journalism is as accurate, fair and complete as possible. Our journalists conduct their work with honesty and respect, and they strive to be both independent and impartial in their efforts. Our methods are transparent and we will be accountable for all we do.[3]

NPR lists accuracy, fairness, completeness, honesty, independence, impartiality, transparency, accountability, respect, and excellence as its ten ethical goals. *The New York Times* (2004) lists almost identical goals, and its guidebook even contains sample letters refusing gifts or unsolicited awards that journalists can use as they practice independence and impartiality.

Stephen Ward, a leading scholar of media ethics, puts it very simply and effectively: "Ethical thinking requires the guidance of rules but it should not be shackled to them" (Center for Journalism Ethics, n.d.). Professional codes of ethics like the two mentioned above are a means of publicly proclaiming a willingness to be held accountable. These organization-specific codes are also important for internal communication and are used to hold individuals accountable—to the point of being fired.

However, as the practice and role of journalism in society shifts, the codes of ethics need to be revised. The Society of Professional Journalists (SPJ), one of the leading professional organizations in the United States, revised its Codes of Ethics in 2014 specifically to address issues raised by the spread of digital journalism and the growing presence of "citizen journalists" who have not been professionalized either through academic programs or through employment. The preamble to the code now encouraged that the principles described for ethical journalism be used "by all people in all media" (Society of Professional Journalists, 2014). Although the four main principles—seek truth and report it, minimize harm, act independently, be accountable *and transparent*—remained essentially the same, the injunction to be "transparent" as well as accountable was added in recognition of the shifting economics of the news industry.

The new SPJ Code begins the same way as the old one: "Members of the Society of Professional Journalists believe that public enlightenment is the forerunner of justice and the foundation of democracy" (Society of Professional Journalists, 2014). Journalists might now blog, tweet, and shoot video on their phones rather than writing a story and ordinary people might now practice forms of journalism and the SPJ adapts to these changes, but as the quote above illustrates, it remains committed to its vision of the role of news as the "foundation of democracy."

Keeping this in mind, we could say that the real challenge to journalism ethics does not come from new technologies or new practitioners, but from very real changes in the *business* of journalism such that mainstream news organizations are now expected to be profitable. Such changes have encouraged the rise of opinion or commentary programs on 24-hour cable news channels and the blurring of gossip, news, information, and opinion on entertainment outlets. These new outlets are often simply not committed to the same equation between accuracy and independence and the cultivation of an informed citizenry as we see, for example, at NPR.

However, it is important to recognize that the search for the "truth" and objectivity in journalism is a deeply contested issue. Walter Lippmann (1995/1920), one of the key influences on modern journalism, for example, separated the informative "news" function of the press from the search for the "truth." Thus, another challenge to these codes comes from groups and organizations that have historically been excluded from the definition of the "public interest" and who feel that news organizations have simply not been invested in ensuring justice and democratic participation for them.

Cultural Anthropology

The American Anthropological Association (AAA) Statement of Professional Responsibility states:

> Anthropologists must be sensitive to the power differentials, constraints, interests and expectations characteristic of all relationships. In a field of such complex rights, responsibilities, and involvements, it is inevitable that misunderstandings, conflicts, and the need to make difficult choices will arise.
>
> (American Anthropological Association, 2012).

The principles listed in this statement center around ethical *relationships* rather than ethical *information* as for journalists. The AAA statement lists "Do no harm" as its very first principle; other principles include gaining informed consent from research participants, being open and honest, making one's research accessible, and keeping vulnerable populations in the fore of any consideration of competing ethical obligations.

The main research methodology for cultural anthropologists is *ethnography*, which involves a complex balancing act of immersion in the culture being studied while keeping a critical distance. For example, media scholar Vicki Mayer (2003) based her analysis of how young Mexican Americans engage with Mexican telenovelas on two years of weekly and, over the summer, daily interaction with different participants at a cultural arts center (see also, Mayer, 2008). The position of an ethnographer within the field of "complex rights, responsibilities, and involvements" mentioned above demands the cultivation of an ethical sensibility that is difficult to codify. Hence, instead of codes of ethics, we see ethical principles and additional institutional checks in the form of institutional review boards at universities and research centers that vet each research proposal.

Anthropology is particularly relevant for media scholars and practitioners because its ethical norms have had a huge influence on documentary production and because ethnography is one of the main ways in which scholars study how media becomes part of everyday life. These norms—the fundamental principle of doing no harm and the centrality of informed consent—are at their core about recognizing three key facts: first, the anthropologist/media practitioner often has more power than the people he or she is studying/representing since they can shape how their stories are told and to whom; second, by entering into the lives of others, they are necessarily altering those lives even if in only slight ways; and, third, they have entered into a relationship with their subjects and thus have ethical obligations to them.

FIGURE B.1 Early Western anthropologists have been criticized for their orientalist gaze; in this photograph, the subject—a woman from a Baka tribe in the Dzanga-Sangha Forest Reserve in the Central African Republic—gazes back at the photographer. Credit: Sergey Uryadnikov/Shutter stock.com.

Documentary and Fiction Media Production

Documentary production has clear connections to anthropology and thus shares the commitment to informed consent. The chapters in Section 1 of this book, especially those by Tami Gold and by Yoruba Richen, explore the ethical complexities of informed consent in documentary production. Documentary production also shares some ethical territory with journalism such as the commitment to honesty and accuracy. Noted documentary scholar Bill Nichols (2006) writes:

> A documentary ethics approaches a foundational level when it addresses the need to respect the dignity and person of subjects and viewers alike, as well as acknowledge that a struggle for power and the right to represent a distinct perspective are at issue.
>
> ("Conclusion," para. 1).

As Nichols' words indicate, respect and trust between the documentarian and the subject(s) as well as between the documentarian and the audience are at the heart of documentary production. But, unlike journalists, documentarians do not have to be neutral or objective. Indeed, many are advocates whose work, as Nichols (2006) says, "seeks to evoke feelings, alter or strengthen commitments and propose actions that are propelled by shared beliefs" ("Filmmakers and their audience," para. 1).

In this view, the role of documentary is to *motivate* and *persuade* the public and in this capacity it involves a degree of creativity that is different from journalism. The "truths" uncovered by documentary media can be closer to those in literature than in most forms of news reporting.

Fiction production, freed from explicit demands for accuracy, independence, and an explicit public interest role would seem to be a clear example of freedom of expression and an exercise in creativity. It thus potentially treads in murkier ethical waters because the media creator(s)' obligations to society are not as clearly defined. There is no professional "code of conduct" that prevents me from making a movie that glorifies the Ku Klux Klan. However, we can see professional codes come into play in a number of places. For example, fiction production is governed by explicit codes of conduct when it comes to workers on union shoots including creative "above-the-line" personnel and intellectual property rights. The MPAA (Motion Picture Association of American) and the NAB (National Association of Broadcasters) have each at various points in their history had a code (Hays Code and the Blue Book respectively) that set moral guidelines and obligations for what could be shown and how it should be shown. In addition, various ratings systems and public pressures from organization ranging from the NAACP to religious groups have forced a degree of ethical reflection about the stereotyping and exclusion of minority groups.

MEDIA STUDIES AND MEDIA ETHICS

This section will introduce you to the ethical issues central to three key areas in media studies: media and democracy, the politics of representation, and new media and everyday life.

Media and Democracy

The foundational premise of this body of scholarship is that an informed citizenry is essential for the healthy functioning of a democratic society and the media are the primary source of information in modern societies. Since "the people" are the ultimate source of authority and legitimacy in liberal democracies, any forces that undermine the ability of citizens to make independent and rational decisions about matter of common interest are detrimental to the "public interest." As you've certainly realized by now, this body of scholarship is very closely linked to the journalism codes of ethics discussed earlier in this chapter.

According to communication theorist Jürgen Habermas (1991), the "public sphere" is a space—literal or metaphoric—that exists independent both of the government and of private interests such as those of corporations or other commercial forces. It is, ideally, a space where all citizens can deliberate on equal terms about issues of shared importance to arrive at a collaborative agreement on these issues. Once we move beyond small communities that can actually congregate at the same time and allow everyone's voice to be heard, the public sphere must, of necessity, be a *media sphere*. And this is where the difficulties really begin. Journalists and pundits on news outlets ranging from the BBC to *Haaretz* to Buzzfeed can *represent* a range of viewpoints and they can share information, but they cannot act as a space where citizens can actually gather to deliberate.

Scholars such as Edward Herman and Noam Chomsky (1988/2010) and Robert McChesney (1999, 2004) focus their ethical critique of news media on the structures of media ownership in a capitalist society arguing that, as Chomsky and Herman put it, the role of media is to "manufacture consent" rather than encourage democratic deliberation and participation. As long as the profit motive overrides all other ethical concerns, we will continue to see the democratic role of the news media being undermined as alternative opinions are marginalized, delegitimized, or simply excluded. Not only are the media not fulfilling their role as sources of accurate information and spaces of democratic debate and exchange, but they are also failing in their role of holding politicians and powerful business figures

FIGURE B.2   The practice of journalism, space for vigorous public debate, independence of thought, and room for dissenting voices are all necessary for a healthy democracy, Credit: Tupungato.

accountable to the public. Indeed, within a commercial media environment, we are not addresses as citizens but as consumers or as the "audience commodity" since we are counted, packaged into groups by age, gender, income, race, etc. and sold to the advertisers who actually fund commercial media production (Smythe, 2012/1981; Meehan, 1990).

Habermas has been critiqued for ignoring or minimizing how access to the public sphere is limited or difficult for women, racial and ethnic minorities, those whose concerns are simply not seen as worthy of the status of "public interest," or those whose ways of deliberating do not meet the norms for rationality (Fraser, 1990; Chatterjee, 1993; Benhabib, 1992). These critiques are even more relevant today as we see the struggle between different forms of journalism and the emergence of new and powerful, but also often unruly and impolite, voices in the "new media publics" created around Twitter, blogging, YouTube and other social media.

Another way of thinking about how citizens can come to have things in common with one another is Benedict Anderson's (1983) concept of nations as "imagined communities." Shared communicative practices—for example, reading a national newspaper—allow people to imagine a kinship with millions of others that they never have met and never will meet. Media rituals such as national day parades, award shows, or sports events can all produce a sense of community.

Keeping the democratic and community function of the media in mind, the concerns expressed by scholars about the growing customization of our media environments resonates more strongly. As a media consumer or user, you might love the fact that you can choose to follow only those journalists on Twitter whose work you trust and like, and, as a media producer, you might enjoy the greater creative freedom that comes with having to reach only a small like-minded audience. However, as Robert Putnam (2001) and Sherry Turkle (2012) warn us, our increasingly personalized media environments may bring a greater sense of connection with smaller communities of interest, but they also mean the loss of a wider national public.

In addition to the theorists who powerfully remind us that the "public interest" never really included *all* members of the public, the media and democracy paradigm is also challenged by scholars who understand political participation and citizenship more broadly as cultural belonging, literacy, recognition, and participation. Scholars in this tradition do not prioritize the news media and look instead at a range of popular media including soap operas, teen programs, and reality television.

Politics of Representation

The cover of the April 2008 issue of the fashion magazine *Vogue* (U.S. edition) showed the African-American basketball star LeBron James, dressed in sports gear, squarely facing the camera, teeth bared in an aggressive expression, dribbling a basketball with one hand and holding blonde Brazilian supermodel Gisele Bündchen around the waist with the other hand. Taken by famous portrait photographer Annie Leibovitz, the image immediately sparked controversy because of its clear resemblance to the posters for the 1933 film *King Kong*, which shows a giant gorilla holding a terrified white woman in his hand. Was it repeating racist stereotypes of African-American men as dangerous brutes? Or, was it reworking those stereotypes? After all, in the cover image Bündchen is relaxed and smiling, not at all like the terrified Fay Wray in the 1933 movie poster. Should *Vogue* have chosen this image for the cover?

That there were no obvious answers to these questions supports one of the central claims of scholars from the critical media studies paradigm: media representations do not "contain" their own meaning. Instead they *become* meaningful in the encounter between the media text itself and the audience (Hall, 2012; Fiske, 2010). The meaning of a media text is uncontested only to the extent that the creators and audiences share the same cultural and linguistic codes, that is, they speak the same visual "language" and share the same cultural knowledge. Furthermore, media representations do not simply describe the world (denotative meaning), they also activate cultural associations (connotative meanings). Often the most powerful images are the ones that evoke the strongest cultural resonance.

However, these cultural meanings are not universal. Dominant and subordinate cultures struggle over whose interpretation of the world will become "common sense" or the obvious meaning. In this paradigm, media images and stories are actually the very place where social struggle happens and not simply a neutral mirror held up to reflect social processes. Whether or not the *Vogue* cover was interpreted as racist depended on—to list just a few factors—the audience's knowledge of African-American history, of how stereotyping works, of the racial and gender politics of the fashion industry, and of James and Bündchen. The ethical question of whether or not we can say if the cover *was* racist depends on our analysis of whose cultural and linguistic codes are privileged in American society.

Framing theory is another approach, discussed in detail by Annette Danto in Chapter 7, that reminds us that professional media practices and the norms that emerge for the "best" way of telling a story are not ethically neutral. This approach analyzes how our aesthetic and technical choices encode certain perspectives on and beliefs about the world and are thus always political choices (Entman, 1993; Gitlin, 1994; Zelizer, 1992; Gray, 1991).

Who has to explain themselves, and who can assume that their position is the norm? Viewers from dominant cultures have the privilege of assuming that media texts will naturally reflect their interests and pleasures. On the other hand, viewers from marginalized cultures have to work hard to find moments of pleasure in texts that are not designed for them. In her foundational essay on how male pleasure is encoded into the very structure of mainstream Hollywood films of the mid-20th century, feminist film scholar Laura Mulvey (2012/1975) argues that "cinematic codes create a gaze, a world, and an object, thereby producing an illusion cut to the measure of desire" (p. 352). The visual and narrative codes of these films are structured around the desires of the (heterosexual, white) masculine subject. Women exist in this world, she argues, only as objects in relation to the male protagonist and, by extension, the male spectator. Thus, for Mulvey, the ethical move for filmmakers and for viewers is to destroy this kind of pleasure to enable a new form of cinema and spectatorship that does not reproduce patriarchy.

Mulvey's argument has been embraced and challenged in a number of ways, not least by black feminist scholars and postcolonial scholars who point to how Mulvey assumes that heterosexual white women can represent all women, and that the psychoanalytic theories she uses are relevant across all cultural contexts (hooks, 1992; Mohanty, 1988). This may seem like academic in-fighting, but the ethical stakes in this debate are far from insignificant. If we are interested in challenging stereotypes and exclusionary norms in our media practice,

FIGURES B.3 AND B.4 These two images, one of the Iwo Jima Memorial in Washington, D.C., and the other of the Memorial Cenotaph at the Hiroshima Peace Memorial Park in Hiroshima, are both evocative of loss and sacrifice. But, the power of each image depends on the extent to which its content resonates with the cultural experiences of the viewer. Credit: Vacclav/Shutterstock.com and Sean Pavone/Shutterstock respectively.

we cannot forget to be self-reflexive about our own position and privilege. We also cannot ignore that our aesthetic and technical decisions (e.g., deciding to do a slow revealing pan down our lead actress's body) are invariably ethical and political decisions where we either deliberately, or through habit, privilege the perspective and pleasures of some groups over those of others.

Scholarship on stereotypes rejects the notion of "good" and "bad" stereotypes as well as the goal of replacing "negative" representations with "positive" ones. Instead it emphasizes what stereotypes *do*, that is, on the social and cultural function of stereotyping. A stereotype allows us to think we *know* what *all* members of a group are like. It denies any possibility of individuality and instead insists, for example, that women are *naturally* better at nurturing than men. Ella Shohat and Robert Stam (1994), for example, present the idea of the "burden of representation" where each image or narrative of an underrepresented group carries the burden of standing in for an entire race, sexual orientation, or religious ,group. Concerns over racism in the *Vogue* cover came, at least, partially from the fact that James was the first African-American man and one of a small handful of African Americans to ever be featured on the cover during this magazine's century-long history.

Shohat and Stam's discussion of *voice* rather than *image* in relation to stereotyping is also an important intervention. As diversity and multiculturalism moved from being civil rights and social justice issues to sound marketing decisions from the 1980s on, we have actually seen a considerable growth in minority representation in television and film as well as in music and sports. From discussions of equality and inclusion, we now hear that we are living in a "post-feminist" and "post-racial" society where discrimination by gender or race is no longer a significant factor. As our social constructions of race and gender change, the ways in which minority images, voices, and narratives are constructed and circulate have become more complex (Goldberg, 1997; Mukherjee, 2006). We need to look beyond simple numbers or visual diversity to question the ethics of inclusion (Amaya, 2010; Becker, 2006; Fuller, 2010; Smith-Shomade, 2008). Are all these diverse bodies speaking with the same voice? Or, do we see a range of distinctive characters and hear a range of stories that have distinctive histories?

As Fraser (1990) and Benhabib (1992) both note, the ideal "public sphere" prescribes norms of rational communication that are exclusionary. Modes of speech or representation (e.g., legal reasoning) meet these norms while other modes (e.g., autobiographical narratives) can be rejected for being too particular or simply too emotional. As journalists and documentary producers, understanding how these communication norms work and learning about the complexities of representation can be central to a media practice that is ethical and respectful toward marginalized groups. In particular, you might keep in mind questions such as: Who is seen as deserving of the label of an expert? Who or what is seen as the source of the problem and who or what is seen as the solution? Who has to explain what they are doing, and whose position is already familiar?

Finally, a central ethical role of the media is to bear witness. The documentary *Seeing is Believing: Handicams, Human Rights, and the News* (2002), for example, shows how a group of farmers in the Philippines used camcorders provided by Witness, a U.S.-based media activist organization, to document their struggle against a big company and corrupt local officials. This is a literal example of the camera bearing witness, but the underlying principle—that ethical obligations inhere in the act of recording reality—applies to all factual genres.

FIGURE B.5 During the "Arab Spring" of 2013, protestors across the world—from Tahrir Square in Cairo to Times Square in New York—came out in the streets and used the power of networked, mobile media to bear witness to history as well as to forge connections with one another. Credit: lev radin/Shutterstock.com.

News, documentary, and social media producers often have the explicit goal of giving testimony on an issue or acting as a conduit for others' testimony. As we see with examples of citizen video of police violence or livestreaming of protests across the world, or the Iraqi blogger who described the bombing in Baghdad as it was happening, media producers often explicitly speak out to draw our attention to events in a way that reminds us in the audience of our responsibility to those on the other side of the lens or screen.

To witness something is also to situate yourself as *part* of the event rather than as a distant observer. It is to accept that you are implicated in what is happening and to be willing to engage in mutual recognition, dialogue, and interaction. It is, metaphorically speaking, to share the space behind the camera with your subjects and to be willing to step in front of the camera as well. For example, when you post or comment on a YouTube video, or on any form of social media, think about your obligation to make sure that the intentions, uses, and audiences for your media are known to all participants.

New Media and Everyday Life

Although there is debate on what exactly constitutes "new media" and on the label itself, most scholars agree that the internet, digital cinema, social media, video games, and numerous hybrid media forms we see today are part of a qualitative shift in our ideas about what "the media" are and in our media practices. Marshall McLuhan (1964/1994) famously said that the medium is the message. The most significant impact of any new medium (e.g., the internet) is not the content of that medium, but how it reorganizes our life. How are our notions of intimacy, presence, or privacy altered? Furthermore, media are no longer simply a part of our life, they often structure the very environments we live in and are an intrinsic component of our everyday life. Sherry Turkle (2012), for example, asks are we now "alone together" as our technologies offer more of what humans used to offer each other? danah boyd (2014), however, shows in her ethnography of teenagers online that teenagers have a strong desire to be sociable and to be members of a larger public, and have their own understandings of privacy. They simply do all of this online and it is our responsibility as scholars, policy-makers, or parents to recognize and understand these "networked publics" rather than disparaging them or reproducing reductive ideas of alienated and anti-social young people.

The "moral panic" around the damaging effects of social media on teens is simply a recycling of earlier panics about comic books in the 1930s, rock and roll music in the 1960s, rap music and video games in the 1980s, and the internet in the 1990s. Thinking of media as practice, ask yourself, what social function do these outcries of concern and anxiety serve? In periods of social change, "moral panics" become occasions for reaffirming social norms, adapting to changes, and, importantly, to regulate and discipline those at the forefront of these changes to make sure that the change is not too drastic.

New media technologies are often described as "revolutionary" or "disruptive." That is, they are often framed through the idea of "technological determinism," which is the tendency to say that a technology such as television or a social media platform such as Facebook somehow directly causes—or determines—changes in society and in individuals. Such an approach ignores how any technology, such as mobile phones, is actually imagined, developed, and used *within* and as *part of* the very society that it is being said to affect.

One of the most significant aspects of these changes is that the lines between media producers and media audiences have been radically redrawn. Henry Jenkins, Sam Ford, and Joshua Green (2013) describe how "spreadable media," that is, media that are designed to allow audience participation, have become the norm. The goal of media texts ranging from the reality television franchise *The Real Housewives* to BBC News to the crowdsourced documentary *18 Days in Egypt* is to create a space for audience engagement and co-creation.

The very term "social media" draws our attention to how platforms such as Twitter, Instagram or Facebook—but also Yelp, Amazon reviews, and online news sources—are designed as spaces rather than media texts. The content comes from us. While this invitation to interact can be exhilarating and has been described as empowering, Terranova (2000) asks us to consider the "free labor" we provide to the companies who create these platforms. Furthermore, as "remix" culture—remixing songs, editing together clips from various sources, creating gifs and memes, compiling tweets—becomes part of our daily lives, we have to address issues of copyright and intellectual property (Lessig, 2008). As you will see in Chapter 13 by Annette Danto and Tami Gold in this book, recognizing and respecting other's intellectual property becomes a more pressing issue in our current media environment.

A second key aspect of new media is the convergence of computing and media. For the first time, our media behaviors—surfing the web, posting a picture on Instagram, watching a documentary, reading the newspaper—can be tracked and surveilled in ways that are both alarming and impressive because so many of us live our lives through and in relation to new media forms and platforms (Andrejevic, 2006).

COMBINING THEORY AND PRACTICE

Stuart Hall, one of the central figures in the development of cultural studies, famously said, "I am not interested in Theory, I am interested in going on theorizing" (Grossberg, 2006, p. 150). We need to take the time and space to reflect on the implications of our choices and actions. We need to be able to step back from the pressure of making a very specific decision (e.g., who to cast as the lead?) to remember the broader context in which our decision will make a difference.

Theory with a capital 'T' can provide that space for reflection, but it can never be a simple prescription or provide an answer. As we go on theorizing in conversation with others— past and present—who have grappled with similar issues, we grow, change, make different choices, and take different actions. And then we go on theorizing and changing.

Some forms of media, for example, livestreaming a protest, have a simultaneity of production, postproduction, and distribution that does not allow time for detailed ethical pondering. Thus, the ethical demands of such media is the cultivation of an ethical self. Other forms of media (e.g., long form investigative journalism or feature film production) allow the luxury of time to make deliberate choices. Here, established professional ethical codes lay out the parameters of possible choices. In these instances, there is more external ethical guidance available, but the danger is in shifting the burden of ethical reflection onto these guidelines and off our own shoulders. As you read the chapters in this book, keep the following "theoretical" questions in mind:

- How are you thinking about cause-and-effect relationships? We are often asked to think about the "impact" or "effect" of our actions. Although useful everyday language, the question of how exactly our actions have an "impact" is much more complicated than it might initially seem. Did his roommate's actions *cause* Tyler Clementi to kill himself? How exactly did the extensive media coverage of the Arab Spring empower or hinder the activists involved in the protest? Trying to simplify complex relationships into clear causal connections is often a strategy to deny ethical responsibility or to assign it to one clear entity. All theories carry with them *some* sense of the forces that are most significant in any instance and it helps to know what these are. But, we should not assume that there is a simple answer or solution to an ethical dilemma.
- Are you thinking of media production as creating a distinct *media object or text* or are you thinking of media production as an *ongoing practice*? Everyday thinking about complex issues of representation often focuses on the end "product," that is, the video game or television program or Instagram post that is then assumed to have a "positive" or "negative" representation of a particular group or effect. This tendency overlooks how media practice creates and sustains ongoing relationships between people. The growth of social media has made this active process-oriented aspect of media more

apparent because social media creation and participation is so clearly something that we *do*, and not just something we create or consume.

- What is the *scale* of your media creation, commentary, or distribution? Are you dealing with a very specific local context, such as posting pictures from a friend's party, or are you trying to decide how to distribute the app you've designed? As we saw with public sphere theory, ethical norms developed for one context or scale do not necessarily work at a different scale. Keep in mind that your work might circulate outside the context you've imagined for it.

NOTES

1 From *deon*, the Greek word for duty, this approach seeks to identify normative principles for what we should or should not do in light of our duties and obligations to others.
2 Nick Couldry's (2006, 2010) work is an excellent starting point for understanding the influence of philosophy on media ethics from the disciplinary perspective of critical media studies; he also provides a useful review of the scholarly literature on media ethics.
3 Accessed on November 11, 2015 from http://ethics.npr.org/

BIBLIOGRAPHY

Abu-Lughod, L. (1995). The objects of soap opera: Egyptian television and the cultural politics of modernity. In D. Miller (Ed.), *Worlds apart: Modernity through the prism of the local* (pp. 190–210). New York, NY: Routledge.

Amaya, H. (2010). Citizenship, diversity, law and *Ugly Betty*. *Media, Culture & Society, 32*(5), 801–817.

Anderson, B. (1983). *Imagined communities*. London, UK: Verso.

Andrejevic, M. (2006). The discipline of watching: Detection, risk, and lateral surveillance. *Critical Studies in Media Communication, 23*(5), 391–407.

American Anthropological Association. (2012). Principles of professional responsibility [web log post]. Retrieved from http://ethics.aaanet.org/category/statement/

Becker, R. (2006). *Gay TV and straight America*. Newark, NJ: Rutgers University Press.

Benhabib, S. (1992). *Situating the self: Gender, community, and postmodernism in contemporary ethics*. New York, NY: Routledge.

boyd, d. (2014). *It's complicated: The social lives of networked teens*. New Haven, CT: Yale University Press.

Carey, J. W. (1989/2008). *Communication as culture, revised edition: Essays on media and society*. New York, NY: Routledge.

Center for Journalism Ethics. (n.d.). Ethics in a nutshell. Retrieved from https://ethics.journalism.wisc.edu/resources/ethics-in-a-nutshell/

Chatterjee, P. (1993). *The nation and its fragments: Colonial and postcolonial histories* (Vol. 11). Princeton, NJ: Princeton University Press.

Couldry, N. (2006). *Listening beyond the echoes*. Austin, TX: Paradigm Books.

Couldry, N. (2010). *Why voice matters: Culture and politics after neoliberalism*. Thousand Oaks CA: Sage.

D'Acci, J. (1994). *Defining women: Television and the case of Cagney & Lacey*. Chapel Hill, NC: University of North Carolina Press.

Entman, R. M. (1993). Framing: Toward clarification of a fractured paradigm. *Journal of Communication, 43*(4), 51–58.

Fiske, J. (2010). *Understanding popular culture*. New York, NY: Routledge.

Fraser, N. (1990). Rethinking the public sphere: A contribution to the critique of actually existing democracy. *Social text, 25/26*, 56–80.

Fuller, J. (2010). Branding blackness on US cable television. *Media, Culture & Society, 32*(2), 285–305.

Gitlin, T. (1994). *Inside prime time*. Berkeley, CA: University of California Press.

Goldberg, D. T. (1997). *Racial subjects: Writing on race in America*. New York, NY: Routledge.

Gray, H. (1991). Recodings: Possibilities and limitations in commercial television representations of African American culture. *Quarterly Review of Film & Video, 13*(1–3), 117–130.

Grossberg, L. (2006). On postmodernism and articulation: An interview with Stuart Hall. In D. Morley & K. H. Chen (Eds.), *Stuart Hall: Critical dialogues in cultural studies* (pp. 131–150). New York, NY: Routledge.

Habermas, J. (1991) *The structural transformation of the public sphere: An inquiry into a category of bourgeois society*. Cambridge, MA: MIT Press.

Hall, S. (2012). Encoding/decoding. In M. G. Durham & D. Kellner (Eds.), *Media and cultural studies: Keyworks* (2nd ed.) (pp. 137–144). Malden, MA: Wiley-Blackwell.

Herman, E. S., & Chomsky, N. (1988/2010). *Manufacturing consent: The political economy of the mass media*. New York: Random House.

hooks, b. (1992). *Black looks: Race and representation*. Boston, MA: South End Press.

Jenkins, H., Ford, S., & Green, J. (2013). *Spreadable media: Creating value and meaning in a networked culture*. New York, NY: NYU Press.

Lessig, L. (2008). *Remix: Making art and commerce thrive in the hybrid economy*. New York: Penguin Press.

Lippmann, W. (1995/1920). *Liberty and the news*. New Brunswick, NJ: Transaction Publishers.

Mayer, V. (2008). Studying up and f** cking up: Ethnographic interviewing in production studies. *Cinema Journal, 47*(2), 141–148.

Mayer, V. (2003). Living telenovelas/telenovelizing life: Mexican American girls' identities and transnational telenovelas. *Journal of Communication, 53*(3): 479–495.

McChesney, R. W. (1999). *Rich media, poor democracy: Communication politics in dubious times*. Evanston, IL: University of Illinois Press.

McChesney, R. D. (2004). *The problem of the media: US communication politics in the twenty-first century*. New York, NY: NYU Press.

McLuhan, M. (1964/1994). *Understanding media: The extensions of man*. Cambridge, MA: MIT Press.

Meehan, E. (1990). Why we don't count: The commodity audience. In P. Mellencamp (Ed.), *Logics of television: Essays in cultural criticism* (pp. 117–137). Bloomington, IN: Indiana University Press.

Metz, T. (2015). African ethics and journalism ethics: News and opinion in Light of ubuntu. *Journal of Media Ethics, 30*(2), 74–90.

Mohanty, C. T. (1988, Autumn). Under Western eyes: Feminist scholarship and colonial discourses. *Feminist Review, 30*, 61–88.

Mukherjee, R. (2006). *The racial order of things: Cultural imaginaries of the post-soul era*. Minneapolis, MN: University of Minnesota Press.

Mulvey, L. (2012/1975). Visual pleasure and narrative cinema. In M. G. Durham & D. Kellner, (Eds.), *Media and cultural studies: Keyworks* (2nd ed.) (pp. 267–274). Malden, MA: Wiley-Blackwell.

The New York Times (2004, September). Ethical journalism: A handbook of values and practices for the news and editorial departments. Retrieved from: www.nytco.com/wp-content/uploads/NYT_Ethical_Journalism_0904-1.pdf

Nichols, B. (2006, April). What to do about documentary distortion? Toward a code of ethics. *Documentary Magazine*. Retrieved from www.documentary.org/content/what-do-about-documentary-distortion-toward-code-ethics-0

NPR (n.d.). NPR ethics handbook. Retrieved from: http://ethics.npr.org/

Putnam, R. D. (2001). *Bowling alone: The collapse and revival of American community*. New York, NY: Simon and Schuster.

Rao, S., & Johal, N. S. (2006). Ethics and news making in the changing Indian mediascape. *Journal of Mass Media Ethics, 21*(4), 286–303.

Rivero, Y. M. (2003). The performance and reception of televisual "ugliness" in *Yo soy Betty la fea*. *Feminist Media Studies, 3*(1), 65–81.

Shohat, E., & Stam, R. (1994). *Unthinking eurocentrism: Multiculturalism and the Media*. London, U.K., & New York, NY: Routledge.

Silverstone, R. (2007). *Media and morality*. Cambridge, MA: Polity Press.

Smith-Shomade, B. E. (2008). *Pimpin' ain't easy: Selling Black Entertainment Television*. New York, NY: Routledge.

Smythe, D. W. (2012/1981). On the audience commodity and its work. In M. G. Durham & D. Kellner (Eds.), *Media and cultural studies: Keyworks* (2nd ed.) (pp. 230–256). Malden, MA: Wiley-Blackwell.

Society of Professional Journalists. (2014, September 6). SPJ code of ethics. Retrieved from: www.spj.org/ethicscode.asp

Terranova, T. (2000). Free labor: Producing culture for the digital economy. *Social text, 18*(2), 33–58.

Turkle, S. (2012). *Alone together: Why we expect more from technology and less from each other*. New York, NY: Basic Books.

Ward, S. & Wasserman, H. (Eds.). (2008). *Media ethics beyond borders: A global perspective*. Cape Town, SA: Heinemann.

Zelizer, B. (1992). *Covering the body: The Kennedy assassination, the media, and the shaping of collective memory*. Chicago, IL: University of Chicago Press.

Section One   # Think

Introduction to Section One
Think

Annette Danto and Mobina Hashmi

THERE has never been a more exciting time to enter the world of media. Inventive cameras, apps, and software innovation have made it easier than ever to turn dreams and ideas into realities.

No longer do you have to be a passive spectator. With new media it is now possible to engage and interact with others from all over the world. This is indeed an exciting time thanks to extraordinary technological inventiveness

Tools of production today are affordable and easy to access. Distribution is no longer only available to the privileged few. Today, your media can be viewed across the globe through a growing range of distribution options: Vimeo, Netflix, YouTube, iTunes, Amazon.

Although it has become much easier to create media, deciding what you want to create and what you want to say remains, perhaps, the most challenging part of production. Are you drawn to personal stories, emotional situations, problems and challenges of living? Do you want to become an investigative journalist, examining injustice and serious social problems? Or, would you rather design an environment where people can interact, or perhaps a successful lifestyle blog? Answering these questions may point you in the right direction regarding coming up with a story, finding a target audience, potential funders, and suitable collaborators.

Identifying key sources of inspiration can help you craft a stylistic approach. For example, are you drawn to the humanistic filmmaking styles of Indian filmmaker Satyajit Ray,[1] and Iranian filmmaker Abbas Kiarostami?[2] Or do you prefer the quirky, action-adventure movies of Joel and Ethan Coen?[3]

A no less important point to clarify during this early stage is: why do you want to create? If your ultimate goal is to be able to afford a house in Hollywood Hills with a swimming pool, then you need to focus on commercial media creation. For commercially driven media projects it is often important to select a topic that will appeal to a sizeable audience. Selecting media content based on Google Keyword Traffic Estimator, for example, will allow you to

FIGURE S1.1   Although it has become much easier to create media, deciding what you want to say remains a challenge. Credit: Rawpixel.com.

gauge the number of people likely to be interested in a particular topic. Alternatively, if your goal is to communicate an idea that you are strongly passionate about to the public at large regardless of monetary gain, then the size of the audience is of secondary importance. Creating media that enables a conversation between members of a specific group is yet another option you may want to think about.

With all these possibilities it is important to be honest with yourself as you clarify your motivation and goals.

The moment you start talking about an idea for a media project, you are in early preproduction. Preproduction is about coming up with a story concept, making decisions, and setting goals. Reactions to things we see, hear, or experience generate ideas or may inspire us to create or communicate. Asking salient questions as part of this process will guide media-makers along a creative path that is both ethical and principled:

- Am I thinking of the public interest? Or, am I focusing only on my individual creative desires or on what will be profitable?
- Am I aware of my cultural standpoint? How does this influence the conceptual frame of the story and is this reflected in the theme and premise?

- Is it my goal to describe what exists or to advocate for a specific position? Do I have an obligation to promote "virtuous"[4] behavior in my audience?
- Am I ascribing too much or not enough agency to the audience? Do I give the audience what it wants even at the risk of reinforcing problematic attitudes and behaviors?

The time between having a thought and engaging in media creation and distribution may be the split-second it takes to share a social media post, or it may be the months it takes to create an investigative television news story. This is when you need to take the "detour through theory" described in the introduction and need to ask the questions listed above.

MEDIUM-SPECIFIC PREPRODUCTION

The preproduction process is not the same for all media. Below, we briefly describe considerations specific to three of the main types of media creation in our current environment.

Filmmaking: Narrative and Documentary

Preproduction is about writing a treatment, based on careful research. This includes watching other media about the topic. It is about identifying potential funding sources, selecting a target audience and evaluating distribution deals that may offer funding up front. Finding possible collaborators and contacting them is another necessary step to initiate during the preproduction period. Overall, this is the time to figure out how to make your story come alive.

If we had to pick one single ethical consideration to keep in mind at this stage, it would be stereotyping. As you are framing your story, be aware of the perspective you are privileging. That is, who is the "us" and the "them" in your story? Have you considered how your narrative and aesthetic choices support or challenge existing norms and biases?

New Media and Social Media

Diverse forms of media function and progress in dissimilar ways through this early stage. Operating at varied speeds, with contrasting approaches to interactivity, diverse media allot inconsistent amounts of time for conscious thought.

With new media, what we are calling "preproduction" can be almost simultaneous with production and distribution. Furthermore, new media and social media creation can take place in isolation, within the privacy of one's own space. There are fewer gatekeepers. This, along with the time differential, places increased responsibility on the media creator to predict ethical dilemmas intrinsic to the topic or concept being considered. This demands forethought along with greater self-reflection and self-regulation even before preproduction. For example, we might consider the degree to which our choice of social media platform contributes to what Andrejevic (2006) calls "lateral surveillance" when we participate in, and implicitly endorse, a culture of surveillance by spying on what our friends, family, colleagues, or partners are doing online.

Journalism

Preproduction is a time of research and development. It is a time to think carefully about sources, words, visuals, and headlines. It is about what best suits the target audience and goals of the story.

Preproduction presents an opportunity for thoughtful construction of messages, images, characterizations, and stories. Accuracy, transparency, and objectivity are three key news values repeated in professional codes of ethics. But, keeping framing theory in mind, we have to ask how an unreflective adherence to objectivity, for example, can simply reinforce a "consensus narrative" by not acknowledging perspectives that lie outside the dominant news frame.[5] So, we have to ask how the "facts" are established and how "facts" and "the truth" are connected in news narratives. How, for example, does the commercial imperative to be profitable affect how mainstream news media define objectivity and transparency?

ETHICAL CONSIDERATIONS IN PREPRODUCTION

It is important to consider ethics during preproduction. You have to ask if varied media demand alternative strategies when considering ethical process and content.

One important theoretical issue to keep in mind at this stage is whether you are thinking of media as "object" or as "practice." In other words, are you thinking of your film, web series, news story, or blog post as a project that you create and complete, or are you thinking of your media project as a way of participating in diverse ongoing practices of funding, distribution, viewing, and interaction? Your answer to this question will influence your strategy as you consider, for example, which platform is the best choice for distributing your web series, or the extent to which your television commercial reinforces or challenges existing stereotypes.

For narrative and documentary production, a timeline may continue for months or years, allowing media-makers to ponder potential story issues and ethical dilemmas. With social media there is less time to think about ramifications and consequences. Creating or repurposing a social media post can happen very quickly. When working with media where all stages of production are simultaneous, pre-production in effect can mean the cultivation of an ethical self.

Writing

Writing is not an easy or simple process for most of us. Working on a treatment, a script, or a draft of an article can be stressful. Adding a layer of ethical calculation may slow down the process, increasing doubt and hesitation, and exacerbating cases of writer's block.

With social media, the writing process happens almost simultaneously with the self-monitoring process. Instantaneous reflection while writing means carefully weighing the pros and cons, what might be right or wrong, who will benefit and who might be harmed; the answers to these dilemmas are never easy or simple.

Writing in the privacy of your own room, you become your own gatekeeper. When

FIGURE S1.2 Preproduction is the time to cultivate an ethical self. Credit: Jan Faukner.

translating thoughts into text or ideas into images, remember, once you hit the enter key it is all over. The ethical consequences are beyond your control.

Consider the impact of your idea on others, apart from your own circle of friends. Feeding into negative stereotypes can happen unwittingly by ideas or story concepts you think are somehow unusual or unfamiliar. This happens often when coming up with ideas about cultures or rituals different from one's own.

Our aesthetic judgments about what makes for a compelling composition or a moving story are centrally shaped by cultural stereotypes and narrative biases. For example, finding the "human interest" angle in a news story about a workers' strike can stimulate greater interest in readers, but it can also reduce a complex story about institutional structures to a conflict between individuals. Identifying sensitivities must happen well before hitting the enter key, or pressing the record button on a camera.

Context matters

In preproduction it is necessary to consider who the target audience is, and how they will interpret the form and content of the media being developed. For text-based media, the use of headlines, words, and sources provide reference points for an audience by identifying the perspective of the media source. This directly influences how an audience will interpret the material being presented.

Understanding the realities of our pluralist societies means acknowledging diverse points of view. Thoughtful consideration of where and how your media will be screened is an essential first step in determining the ethics of that media.

When the famous Greek satirist Aristophanes wrote *The Frogs* in 405 BCE, there was no such thing as "global distribution." There was no internet. Aristophanes brutally satirized all of Greek society, and it had the kind of impact that the *Charlie Hebdo* political cartoons have recently had. Caricatures of different classes of society—the manners of the Spartans and other non-Athenians, the conceits of public officers, the avidity of news vendors, priests, poets, not to mention astronomers, sausage-sellers, soldiers, informants, and even flute-girls—left audiences with emotions ranging from tears to hysterics. Nothing and no one was sacred.[6]

Like many contemporary filmmakers and media creators, Aristophanes used stories as a general mockery of human nature and of the world as he knew it. What seems new today is the potential for global circulation of media. Along with this is the added possibility that whatever is created and posted might get repurposed and reposted with radically different interpretations from the ones originally intended. Keeping in mind how not only your intended audience, but also a plurality of diverse audiences will interpret the form and content is an essential first step in the creation of ethical media today.

Sometimes government media regulators and censorship boards intervene in the distribution process. During preproduction, media creators need to familiarize themselves with government regulation and censorship laws if it applies to a target audience. Choices made during preproduction are essential determinants regarding whether the media created will reach the intended target audience. If some government media regulators determine your content is inflammatory, biased, or provocative, they can prevent successful distribution from taking place.

Preproduction Collaboration

Apart from social media tweets and posts which can be done solo, most media creation is collaborative, involving crisscrossing functioning of people. The traditional three stages of preproduction, production, and postproduction are all interrelated and intertwined. All have direct and indirect cause/effect relationships.

This means that early story decisions have a domino effect on nearly every aspect of the production, cast, and crew. In terms of media ethics, creative screenplay choices made during preproduction become the blueprint for the production team. A story about failing New York City public schools that only casts black and Latino students in lead roles while ignoring the reality that there are Asian, as well as Jewish students in many public schools, may feed into stereotyping. Any depiction of social and political issues can feed into stereotyping if the media creators are unaware of ethical implications. When planning a verite-style documentary, instruct your cinematographer to learn about and capture the actual diversity of students. This will allow you to present material without profiling or stereotyping.

For documentaries, choices during research and development impact all that follows. Documentaries on victims of domestic violence often require, in addition to legal releases, a decision as to whether or not the victims' identity will be revealed on camera. The impact on the life of the subject is of utmost concern.

Will you recreate painful past histories on screen, or will you present history through archival footage? Decisions about archival material will affect how a story is told and whether any crew will be needed. This directly impacts production costs. Location cinematography may not be needed if a story unfolds through the editing of archival footage.

Successful media creators tolerate differences of opinion. Recognizing the needs and interests of crew, actors, and participants throughout each stage of a project is a very good idea. Beginning in preproduction, all participants behind and in front of the camera should be accorded respect regardless of their status in the project's hierarchy. Whether it is a lowly production assistant, or the executive producer who is forking up all the funding, the equal dignity of all crew is an ethical fundamental.

Media students will be more effective when tackling unanticipated ethical hurdles if they have clear awareness of difference but also empathy for shared human needs.

OVERVIEW OF CHAPTERS

Section One is divided into five chapters:

- Conceptual Framing
- Funding and Competing Agendas
- Convergence of Journalism and Documentary
- F-Stop: Power Differentials
- Identities: Race, Ethnicity, Gender, and Class Privilege

Using case studies, each chapter offers examples of ethical predicaments during preproduction, and puts forth strategies for resolving them.

A list of key take home points is offered at the conclusion of each chapter. These take home points are guideposts for fundamental strategies during the early stage of media research and development.

In the initial chapter, "Conceptual Framing," Annette Danto discusses the early preproduction process of coming up with a story, premise, and theme. Conceptual framing decisions require attention to the interplay of story content and audience consumption. In the chapter, "Funding and Competing Agendas," seasoned activist-documentarian Christine Choy draws upon extensive experience as a documentary filmmaker to tell some harsh truths about funding and competing agendas. In his chapter "Convergence of Journalism and Documentary," Lonnie Isabel discusses how the explosion of online journalism using narrative and documentary techniques may conflict with the cardinal rule of journalism to never bend the truth. Tami Gold's chapter, "F-Stop: Power Differentials," examines ethical dilemmas posed by power differences between media creators' and subjects. How does this influence outcome? How can power differentials be identified and then negotiated effectively and fairly? Gold presents strategies for dealing with some of these ethical challenges, and also addresses best practices for payment and consent. Yoruba Richen's chapter, "Identities: Race, Ethnicity, Gender, and Class Privilege," challenges us to think about racial identity, and the ethical pitfalls of creating media about a racial group other than one's own.

FIGURE S1.3   Preproduction requires complicated choices and important decisions. It is not always possible to predict all the ethical issues that may arise, but it is a good idea to try. Credit: Michael D Brown.

The task of media ethics education is to cultivate technically trained people with the ability to recognize differing interests as well as shared human priorities. Mastering technological skills is only part of the equation. Along with technology, a firm grasp of media ethics ensures balanced and effective practitioners.

It is now time to think.

- Think before pointing the camera at vulnerable people, situations, or circumstances.
- Think about the impact of what you are doing on others before plowing forward with a creative idea, image creation, or designing a remix project.
- Think about whom you are making this for and why.
- Think about your ethical obligations to those you will collaborate with in front of and behind the camera.

NOTES

1   Satyajit Ray's three films about the boyhood, adolescence, and manhood of Apu, *Pather Panchali* (1955), *Aparajito* (1956), and *The World of Apu* (1959)—collectively known as The Apu Trilogy—are established classics of world cinema. The Trilogy was the chief reason for Satyajit Ray's receiving a Hollywood Oscar for

lifetime achievement in 1992, just before his death. For further reading on Ray's life and process creating The Apu Trilogy, see Robinson (2011).

2 Abbas Kiarostami is an Iranian filmmaker whose films are notable for using documentary-style narratives, often involving child protagonists in stories taking place in rural villages. His films set in the northern Iranian village of Koker received critical acclaim: *Where is the Friend's Home?* (1987), *And Life Goes on* (aka *Life and Nothing More*) (1992), and *Through the Olive Trees* (1994).

3 Joel and Ethan Coen, known as the Coen brothers, have written, produced, and directed more than 15 films together including: *Blood Simple* (1984), *Raising Arizona* (1987), *Barton Fink* (1991), *Fargo* (1996), *O Brother, Where Art Thou?* (2000), *No Country for Old Men* (2007), and *Inside Llewyn Davis* (2013).

4 We put the word *virtuous* in quotes because the meaning of the word can be culturally specific.

5 For more on framing, see Entman (2004), Parisi (1997), and Thorburn (1987).

6 For Aristophanes, poetry exists not only to entertain, but also to impart a moral message aimed at instructing listeners to be better citizens and human beings. His poem/play was written during a period of Athens's decline and the play reflects tensions between the "old ways and the new." Throughout the play Aristophanes attacks those who seek to harm Athens. These ethical messages were often communicated by other tragic poets of the time. Euripides claimed to teach people to think rationally and critically. Aeschylus aimed to teach his audiences good values, tactics, and other life lessons.

BIBLIOGRAPHY

Andrejevic, M. (2006). The discipline of watching: Detection, risk, and lateral surveillance. *Critical Studies in Media Communication, 23*(5), 391–407.

Aristophanes. (405 BCE). *The Frogs,* Retrieved from: http://classics.mit.edu/Aristophanes/frogs.html

Atkens, J. B. (2002). *The mission: Journalism, ethics and the world.* Ames, IA: Iowa State University Press.

Berkman, R. I., & Shumway, C. A. (2003). *Digital dilemmas: Ethical issues for online media professionals.* Ames, IA: Iowa State Press.

Berry, D. (2000). *Ethics and media culture: Practices and representations.* Boston, MA: Focal Press.

Boeyink, D. E., & Borden, S. L. (2010). *Making hard choices in journalism ethics: Cases and practice.* New York, NY: Routledge.

Christians, C. G., Rotzoll, K. B., Fowler, M., McKee, K. B., & Robert H. Woods, J. (2005). *Media ethics: Cases and moral reasoning.* Boston, MA, & London, UK: Pearson/Allyn & Bacon.

Entman, R. M. (2004). *Projections of power: Framing news, public opinion, and US foreign policy.* Chicago, IL: University of Chicago Press.

Parisi, P. (1997). Toward a "philosophy of framing": News narratives for public journalism. *Journalism & Mass Communication Quarterly, 74*(4): 673–686.

Patterson, P., & Wilkins, L. (2002). *Media ethics: Issues and cases.* Boston, MA: McGraw Hill.

Piper, T. R., Gentile, M. C., & Parks, S. D. (1993). *Can ethics be taught?* Boston, MA: Harvard Business School.

Richards, I. (2005). *Quagmires and quandaries: Exploring journalism ethics.* Sydney, NSW, Australia: University of New South Wales Press.

Robinson, A. (2011). *The Apu trilogy: Satyajit Ray and the making of an epic.* London, UK: I. B. Tauris.

Thomson, D. (2015). *How to watch a movie.* New York, NY: Alfred A. Knopf.

Thorburn, D. (1987). Television as an aesthetic medium. *Critical studies in media communication, 4*(2): 161–173.

Underwood, D. (2002). *From Yahweh to Yahoo!: The religious roots of the secular press.* Urbana, IL: University of Illinois Press.

Chapter 1

Conceptual Framing

Annette Danto

ABSTRACT

This chapter discusses conceptual framing and the role it plays in creating ethical media. A foundation for any media project, the premise and theme establish parameters for what is being communicated, and why. Conceptual framing steers audience perceptions by providing storylines, characterizations, and style for subsequent visual imagery. The interrelatedness of early conceptual decisions and subsequent technical framing choices is presented through case studies.

Once upon a time, visual storytelling followed conventional screenwriting rules. Today those rules have morphed as the range and forms of media have multiplied. The current media landscape features mini-movies, fragmented storytelling, circular narratives, convergent genres, reality television, and social media platforms. Lines between filmmaker and film, reality and fiction are blurred.

Audiences today watch everything from mini ten-second videos to four-hour movies. New media interactivity has ushered in so much variation in media duration, style, and approach that it is a steep challenge to provide a one-size-fits-all media ethics framework.

In all its variations, media has as its primary mission the challenge of communicating to audiences. Applied media ethics has the potential to *enhance* and *enrich* our shared global communications.

We begin our discussion of media ethics with the conceptual frame.

THE CONCEPTUAL FRAME

Sometimes visible, at other times invisible, the conceptual frame articulates the essential creative and structural building blocks for media creators and consumers. Framing shapes *what* is being communicated and *why*.

FIGURE 1.1   Rural village in the Dindigul District.

FIGURE 1.2   High-rise apartment building in urban Chennai.

FIGURE 1.3   Modern shopping mall in Madurai.

When representing a culture or country, visual choices can have ethical implications. These three images, all of which were taken in the state of Tamil Nadu, present India in different ways. Each uses a different conceptual frame: rural, urban development, and commercial. These visual choices can profoundly shape the messages viewers receive, potentially altering audience impressions of the Indian subcontinent. Courtesy of Ilango Samuel Peter.

Conceptual framing choices lead to what the audience sees and understands about a given story or visual sequence. It establishes the parameters. For example, with a conceptual premise such as "poverty leads to crime," the media creator needs to make certain choices about the visual representation of poverty. Will the images include rural poverty as well as urban poverty? What kind of demographic diversity—for example, of race, ethnicity, family structure, or region—will be included in the representations of the poor? Telling details on these matters advance the storyline, determine visual imagery, and steer audience perceptions and reactions.

Framing manipulates the options being offered. Showing an incident such as a poor, black, male teenager robbing a store creates an association between race, age, and gender. Furthermore, it endows that association with a veracity that has consequences for subsequent assumptions and stereotypes. The media creator has initiated or perpetuated a chain reaction of stereotyping. In this example the audience has been led to conclude that young, poor, black men are more likely than others to commit robberies. One can imagine framing decisions that would lead to different conclusions; for example, representing poor, black men as victims of poverty, or showing that poverty yields virtue.

Students find that they make the best stylistic decisions when they understand the interplay between initial story concepts and subsequent technical framing decisions. It is best to control the fascination with the exotic because this often leads to misrepresentations. Some wish to present the world as it is; others aspire to create change through media advocacy. Clarity of motivation behind selecting an appropriate frame is critical.

By understanding the ethical dimensions of conceptual framing, students can become critical observers, empowered consumers, and effective creators of media programs and digital communication strategies.

THE PREMISE

The first thing a media creator needs to establish is a premise. The premise becomes the frame for all that follows.

In any narrative or visual project, the premise becomes the foundation for the story. This frame maps the narrative structure from beginning to end.

How do ethical considerations relate to the premise? A premise contains assumptions which lead to consequences. Examples of common premises include:

- Hard work leads to success.
- Wealth produces apathy.
- Foreigners create danger.

In each of these examples, the storyline begins with an assumption containing ethical implications. The filmmaker and media creator needs to be mindful of the role of such assumptions in framing each part of the story.

Many stereotypes grow out of the initial story premise.

Translating a story premise into the nuts and bolts of production is a complicated matter. The premise serves as a central determinant for stylistic choices including use of camera, casting, costumes, make-up, art direction, set design, locations, sound design, and the use of music.

In the classic text Aristotle's *Poetics* (1961), the protagonist is a vehicle for the premise.[1] The specifics of the character may vary, but the story consists primarily in the sequence of events. The narrative is propelled by how the character responds to events such as obstacles. The character's response to each escalating obstacle provides the audience with a deeper understanding of the character's personality in addition to advancing the narrative structure.

In Aristotle's *Poetics*, the premise is proven or refuted by whether the protagonist has achieved the desired goal(s). What does the protagonist want? What obstacles prevent the protagonist from getting what he or she wants? Will the protagonist be able to over-come the obstacles? How is the protagonist's struggle resolved? These final questions and answers lead to the specific frame of the narrative structure.

There is extraordinary power in the framing of stories—what is included and what is left out. Stories cross time and space. They depict life through the eyes of characters from diverse cultures, socioeconomic backgrounds, psychological profiles, educational backgrounds, and political perspectives. Stories deal with reality, possibility, and imagination. They act as vehicles for learning about cultures, religions, and civilizations. Conceptual frames establish what exists and what does not.

By opening up new worlds, storytelling has significant impact on global audiences and perceptions. When media creators ignore orientalist and racist frames of reference, they encounter ethical pitfalls. The resulting images often perpetuate storylines that are offensive, disrespectful, and/or divisive.

Historically, Western writers, painters, and filmmakers have taken great liberties in representing the non-Western "other" such as Filipinos. These single-perspective historical

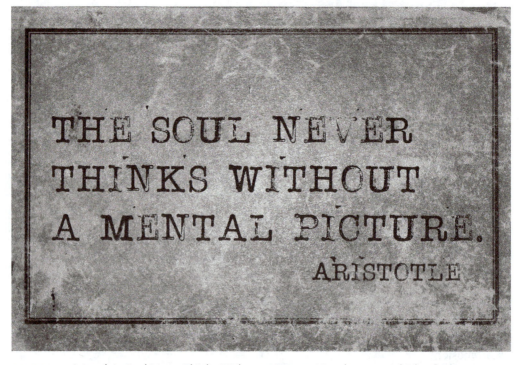

FIGURE 1.4   Aristotle's Soul Never Thinks Without a Picture. Visuals act as vehicles for learning about cultures, religions, and civilizations. They possess enormous power in influencing audience perception. Credit: YuryZap.

BOX 1.1   "THE WHITE MAN'S BURDEN: THE UNITED STATES AND THE PHILIPPINE ISLANDS" BY RUDYARD KIPLING

Kipling's (1899) famous poem, written as a response to the American takeover of the Philippines after the Spanish-American War, begins with the following verse:

> Take up the White Man's burden—
> Send forth the best ye breed—
> Go bind your sons to exile
> To serve your captives' need;
> To wait in heavy harness
> On fluttered folk and wild—
> Your new-caught, sullen peoples,
> Half-devil and half-child.

Historical context is important to keep in mind here: in 1899, the phrase "white man" was used as a term of commendation—meaning straight or decent. Kipling's poem reflects his belief that non-Western peoples were waiting to be developed and improved. This belief was shared by contemporary thinkers who took their lead from Social Darwinism: the "more evolved" nations must guide those which are "less evolved" into a more "civilized" way of running their societies. In our context today, more than a hundred years later, the references are insulting and racist.

BOX 1.2　*THE BIRTH OF A NATION* (1915)

D. W. Griffith produced and directed this classic film which was adapted from Thomas Dixon, Jr.'s controversial 1905 novel, *The Clansman: An Historical Romance of the Ku Klux Klan*. The film tells the story of two white families—one from the North and one from the South—during and right after the Civil War. Nicholas Cull (2003) aptly summarizes Griffith's perspective on race as well as the significance of his film:

> In Griffith's hands black Americans were presented as happy, loyal slaves or deranged rapists desperate for white women. He did much to advance a new stereotype of the "mulatto," mixed-race Americans who were particularly dangerous since they possessed both the superior intelligence of the white race and a desire to better their position . . . Its climax showed a "heroic" charge by the Ku Klux Klan to restore white Southerners to power . . . Griffith's film became a model for combining entertainment and propaganda filmmaking.
>
> (Cull, 2003, p. 40)

narratives defined, reinforced, and perpetuated demeaning negative stereotypes. Whether intended or not, the frame of these narratives conveyed limited meaning, information, and truth.

The Birth of a Nation demonstrated the power of visual storytelling to shape audience perceptions. Employing a narrow conceptual frame, this popular film became a vehicle for perpetuating negative racial stereotypes.

Nearly one hundred years later, *12 Years a Slave* (2013), directed by Steve McQueen, presents a very different portrayal of similar racial issues. In part determined by a different historical perspective and context, *12 Years a Slave* presents the personal portrait of a slave with respect and compassion. Solomon Northup, a free black man from upstate New York who, in 1841, was drugged and sold into slavery in Louisiana, is deeply sympathetic on screen. Chiwetel Ejiofor's performance is rich with emotional subtext, often conveyed on-screen through subtle changes in his facial expressions. An abundance of extreme close-ups of his eyes brings the audience into an empathic relationship with him.

Filmmaking is almost always a matter of selection. *The Birth of a Nation* and *12 Years a Slave* offer a historical comparison. While both deal with the issue of slavery, they do so with very different agendas. The differing conceptual frames make different aspects of reality more salient as a way of promoting a particular point of view and perspective. It is well known that perceptions of factual information can vary depending on the conceptual and technical framing of that information.

PHILOSOPHICAL FRAMING: ETHOS, PATHOS, AND LOGOS

Media creators and filmmakers are most effective when applying Aristotle's classic formulation—a balance of ethos, pathos, and logos.

These fundamental building blocks guide media creators in developing ethically imaginative, profitable, and entertaining media. They enhance the ability to move audiences in myriad ways.

Ethos

Audiences are more inclined to respect material if producers, directors, and the creative team are well regarded in the field. A good reputation seems to carry an ethical veracity that is almost self-justifying. In assessing the reputations of filmmakers and media creators, audiences in a sense "frame" their expectations of the media that is produced. Audience regard for the creative team influences how the media product is received.

In Box 1.3, we consider how drug companies use their established and respected reputations in the medical field to increase their profit margins.

Pathos

Pathos refers to the emotional content of any work of art as seen in terms such as: sympathy, empathy, and in the depiction of pathetic scenes. Characters can be sympathetic and/or empathetic; scenes can involve pathetic moments. Emotional dimensions of content and form, images, and sound grab audience attention. This is especially the case with sound effects and music.

Audience reactions to emotionally loaded material vary. Viewers may feel deadened and desensitized, yet feel a thrill of addiction to violent imagery, for example. Others may feel compassion toward victims in atrocity images. Painful images can also make people angry: inciting and provoking acts of violence and/or activism. Overall, powerful emotional reactions can easily overshadow the cognitive dimension of audience reaction. Do media makers need to consider what happens to viewers after they leave the theater or walk away from their computer screens?

Logos

Every story contains a particular point of view. Many contain a rhetorical argument. Media creators use deductive and inductive reasoning as well as empirical methods—providing

BOX 1.3   DRUG MARKETING

FIGURE 1.5   Naïve consumers are often targeted by drug company advertisements filled with messages promising instant relief from ailments and eternal happiness. Only discerning viewers detect the falsity in many of these claims. Credit: El Nariz.

Drug company advertisements encouraging men and women to use performance-enhancement drugs are ubiquitous during primetime television viewing hours in the United States. Some in the pharmaceutical industry have also employed ethically questionable marketing tactics as a way of increasing profit margins. These include: opulent sets, gimmicky special effects, and manipulative visual storytelling strategies.

By incorporating narrative storytelling and conventional cinematic techniques, including extreme close-ups, elaborate dolly shots, crane shots, and sweeping musical scores, these companies influence consumers to request various medical treatments and drugs from their physicians.

Naïve consumers are targeted with high production value commercials disguised as pseudo-documentaries. Aimed at a general population of viewers, the commercials are filled with messages promising instant relief from ailments and eternal happiness. Only discerning viewers detect the falsity in many of these claims.

documented facts—to make strong arguments. Cognitive reasoning is persuasive in convincing audiences of particular points of view.

Balancing the Elements

A balance of the three elements of ethos, pathos, and logos is central to an impactful media creation. Without ethos and logos, pathos alone can sway an audience in ways both anticipated and unpredictable. Considering what happens to viewers after they leave the theater or walk away from their computer screen leads to questions of long-term ethical responsibility.

Conceptual framing has the capacity to manipulate audience hearts, minds, and behavior. Strategic design of the conceptual frame can directly and indirectly influence the way an audience perceives reality, truth, and the world.

FICTION AND NON-FICTION FRAMING

Conceptual frames and the technical manifestations of those frames are inextricably intertwined. New and innovative storytelling approaches result from the convergence of media forms. Alternative storytelling styles often confuse audiences in terms of what is real or staged, and what is fiction or non-fiction. Audiences traditionally assume that non-fiction presents truth and reality. Fiction as entertainment is allowed to take more license when representing truth and reality. These assumptions are often not valid.

Reality programming has confused the public. With fake competitions and staged sequences involving humiliation and tense interpersonal confrontation, some reality programming taps into the worst aspects of humanity. Scenes of public mockery, embarrassment, and painful emotional circumstances broadcast to millions of viewers has allowed those on-camera to become important, rewarding them with public recognition. This is nothing new. For generations we have known of religious revival meetings where someone stands up and confesses sins in front of a large audience. Such revival meetings allow audience members to gain notoriety within their religious group or community.

Selfies and the obsession with personal display have exploded in all forms of social media. Here again the desire to be noticed is not a new phenomenon, but the perpetual use of social media presents exponentially multiplied opportunities for self-promotion. What to reveal, how much to reveal, and what to include in a frame should be essential ethical questions for anyone looking into the lens of their smart phone. Addiction to heightened visibility leads to distorted perceptions and notions of self.

How much does a media creator need to reveal? How much needs to be explained? How much context should be included? Stylistic choices and patterns of presentation, selection, and emphasis can exert a powerful influence, both consciously and unconsciously, on the viewer.

Starting in the mid-1990s, digital technology became affordable and accessible, opening up creative possibilities for filmmakers. With this democratizing development, people around the world gained the power to tell personal stories. Inexpensive cameras and editing software

FIGURE 1.6   Selfie addiction can lead to distorted perceptions and notions of self. Credit: Zeljkodan.

further paved the way for the creation of documentaries and narrative films about subjects that had never before been explored. Larry Clark's pseudo-documentary *Kids* (1995) comes to mind as an example. *Kids*, produced on a relatively low budget, portrays a day in the life of a group of teenagers in New York City and their unrestrained behavior toward sex and substance abuse during the era of HIV/AIDS in the mid-1990s. The film includes explicit sexual dialogue and depicts scenes of date rape, physical violence, drug dealing, alcohol abuse, theft, and the seduction of young teenagers.

Billions of people around the globe now have the power to come up with a concept, an idea, or notion for media creation. Sometimes this leads to blurred lines and obscures the relationships between subject and object, between filmmaker and film.

An example of this phenomenon is Jonathan Caouette's documentary *Tarnation* (2003) which blurs the lines between artist and creation. Throughout the documentary, the filmmaker is on-camera and narrates his life.

Tarnation presents sequences of edited super-8 home movies interspersed with still images distorted by editing effects such as split screens, prisms, and color manipulation. Disturbing, but powerful footage of the filmmaker as a child, dressed in women's clothing and dramatizing odd behavior on camera, are set to rhythmic music. As a teenager, the filmmaker continues to narrate his life and repeatedly points the camera at various members of his nuclear family—with haunting images of his psychiatrically disturbed mother and grandparents. The voiceover narration emphasizes statements of extreme emotional

BOX 1.4   *TARNATION* (2003): THE DOCUMENTARY AS SELF-EXPLORATION

Using the camera lens as his mirror, Caouette sets up adoring close-ups of himself. He poses. He sasses. He vomits. He flirts. He writhes in agony. When not busy recording young Jonathan's boyfriends or his playacting performance of a junk-TV psychodrama (in dialect yet), the footage is deployed for Grand Guignol shocks about the family's descent into mental illness. Badgering his Alzheimer's-addled grandfather—the one who bought him the camera—he never stops shooting, but the apogee of cruelty comes in his treatment of his grandmother. First aiming for grotesquerie ("I don't have any teeth at all!" she cackles at one point), after the poor woman gets hospitalized with a stroke, he exploits her vulnerability by tossing a fright wig on the protesting old lady as he piles on lurid horror movie effects.

(Reprinted courtesy of Robert Keser (2004) and *Bright Lights Film Journal*)

and physical abuse by the grandparents. Using simple storytelling title boards interspersed throughout, such as "Jonathan Makes Plans," the documentary moves forward in a linear narrative. The impact is disturbing and disorienting, but effective.

Cameras and creative media can become tools for escape and for self-exploration. These devices are able to offer insights into personal traumas and the psychological impact of early childhood experiences. With sensitive and careful analysis, the content of such creative work has the potential to reveal important personal insights and growth. Without sensitive interpretation, such material might seem harsh, disturbing, and sensational. Critics argue that the exploitation of personal trauma for general audience entertainment is macabre.

CULTURAL FRAMING

Filmmakers have the power to create illusions of life and reality. Media creators present innovative perspectives on global issues, especially those of unfamiliar cultures or places. These visual depictions are often viewed by audiences as accurate representations of life.

For students trying to establish a cultural frame, it can be useful to ask the following questions:

- What motivates your project?
- What underlies your desire to explore unfamiliar worlds?
- How faithfully do you want to replicate what you perceive as reality?
- Do you have the desire to use media for advocacy or as a catalyst for change?

A compelling example of cultural framing is *Born into Brothels: Calcutta's Red Light Kids*, a 2004 U.S. documentary about the children of sex workers in Calcutta's (Kolkata's) red light

FIGURE 1.7 Delat, Vietnam.

FIGURE 1.8 Hanoi, Vietnam.

Illustrating conceptual contrasts, these two juxtaposed images present the photographer's perspective: working women on a rural rubber plantation are contrasted with urban office-workers enjoying leisure time while on lunch break. Courtesy of Mary Edith Mardis.

district. The widely acclaimed film won the Sundance Film Festival Audience Award in 2005, and the highly coveted Academy Award for Best Documentary Feature in 2005. Zana Briski, a documentary photographer, went to Calcutta to photograph sex workers. While in India she got to know the sex workers' children and offered to teach them photography. The documentary follows the lives of these children as they learn photography and have their photographs of life in the slums exhibited. The filmmakers recorded their efforts to place the children in boarding schools, away from their sex worker mothers and families. The majority of children did not end up staying very long in the boarding schools they were placed in, and the documentary clearly presents this as a tragic consequence.

In fact, one of the scenes in the documentary features a conversation with one child's grandmother, who is unhappy that her grandchild will be driven to a boarding school on a specific Thursday, which she describes as an "inauspicious day." The grandmother proceeds to tell the filmmakers that the "astrologer informed the grandmother of the inauspicious date, and [she] would like the filmmakers not to take the child to the boarding school on this date." The filmmakers, who are actually visible on-camera in this scene, appear perplexed by the grandmother's reaction. After all, how could she listen to the predictions of an astrologer when here they are offering the grandchild a free boarding school education? What difference does it make if they take the child to the boarding school on a Thursday!

The grandmother's reaction prompted widespread laughter in the New York City Film Forum theater where I saw *Born into Brothels*, and it was clear to me that neither the filmmakers, nor the majority of audience members had any idea of the importance astrology carries in India. Families consult with astrologers prior to moving forward with marriage arrangements, business ventures, medical plans, and career choices. It is a respected and highly honored profession. Clearly the filmmakers didn't realize this and also chose not to clarify this for the mostly Western audience.

The cultural emphasis and importance of the role of the extended family appears minimized by the filmmakers. The children placed in boarding schools did not want to remain there—all wanted to be near their primary family and prioritized family over the educational opportunity presented to them by the filmmakers. Perhaps if the filmmakers had been more aware of these cultural values, they might have attempted to create educational opportunities for the families and children in the vicinity of their homes.

The filmmakers never approached the Durbar Mahila Samanwaya Committee, an organization of 65,000 sex workers in West Bengal and India, and active in Sonagachi—the location of the families depicted in the documentary. Since 1992 this organization has created and maintained schools in West Bengal for the families and children of sex workers. Besides developing formal literacy initiatives, this widespread educational program provides women and children with workshops, classes, and programs within their communities. The committee's primary strategy has been to mainstream the sex workers' children within the local school system rather than sending them away to residential boarding schools. The committee has criticized *Born into Brothels* for presenting the children's parents as abusive and for ignoring sex workers' efforts to provide education programs and career-building activities for their children.

Unfortunately, the documentary presents the children's parents as ignorant, abusive, and ultimately as obstacles to the positive development of their children. No mention is made of the sex workers' efforts to provide education and career-building activities for their children through the Durbar Mahila Samanwaya organization.

In India, *Born into Brothels* was unpopular and widely criticized both for perceived racist stereotyping and for exploiting children. It was seen as Western "Indophobic" propaganda echoing the travesty of orientalism.

A more principled approach to documentary representation is exemplified in the work of pioneering filmmaker George Stoney. In documenting the lives of poor sharecroppers in Georgia, George Stoney confronted ethical dilemmas regarding representing truth.

The sharecroppers worked barefoot in the fields, unable to afford work boots on their subsistence wages. In considering where and how to film, George Stoney and the sharecroppers agreed to allow filming to take place on-location, in the fields. On the day of filming, one

BOX 1.5   *BORN INTO BROTHELS*: THE WHITE WOMAN'S BURDEN?

A scathing review of the documentary in *Frontline*, India's leading national English-language magazine, included the following sentence:

> If *Born into Brothels* were remade as an adventure-thriller in the tradition of Indiana Jones and the Last Crusade, its posters might read: 'New York Filmmaker Zana Briski sails forth among the natives to save souls.'

(Swami, 2005)

sharecropper arrived wearing shoes. He wanted to present himself to audiences as being successful and having some dignity. George Stoney chose to carry out the interview with the sharecropper wearing shoes even though this wasn't the "truth." By prioritizing the dignity of the sharecropper in controlling how he was represented on camera, George Stoney made an ethically principled decision.

Collaboration is an important part of the filmmaking process as the above example illustrates. We collaborate most with the people in front of the camera—why are they there, and what are they getting out of the process? If you've tricked them into participating, that is a violation of documentary ethics (Danto, 2011). Collaboration is also about transparency. Open communication between filmmaker and subject about documentary frame, purpose, distribution plans, and compensation are important components of ethical practice.

ALTERNATIVE FRAMES OF REFERENCE

The psychology of perception reveals pathways to alternative frames of reference. Perceptual and cultural differences influence approaches to storytelling, attitudes toward conflict, views on power structures, sensitivities toward disclosure, and communication styles.

In Gestalt framing, figure, and field are reversible coordinates. Reframing can entail reversals of figure and field—foreground and background—manipulating audience perception through various image emphases. These maneuvers produce shifts in priorities.

Akira Kurosawa's classic *Rashomon* (1950) is known for a plot device which involves various characters providing alternative, self-serving, and contradictory versions of the same incident. *Rashomon* famously illustrates how several people can witness the same story, yet have alternate and contradictory accounts of the same event.

Understanding alternative frames of reference leads to informed creative and structural decisions. Classic mysteries and police investigative dramas such as *Law and Order* (NBC, 1990–2010), show how audience attention is sustained through presenting alternative frames—some deemed to be more ethical than others; for example, the criminal's rationale versus the perspective of the victim.

Noam Chomsky is among those who have raised the following questions regarding ethical relativism (Danto, 2011). Is there a fixed, ethically "absolute" frame that applies to everyone? Debates on moral relativism and moral absolutism are ongoing.

Moral absolutism reflects global concerns about human rights and human rights violations. This entails comparing ethical standards across different nations and cultures, with some practices judged to be ethically unacceptable in all instances. With this perspective, issues such as female genital mutilation, slavery, and torture become absolutely unethical and wrong. This global perspective includes all cultures and all countries under one ethical umbrella.

Moral relativism complicates and sometimes refutes such positions. Context sensitivity has influence over what is deemed to be right and wrong. Contextual ethics, contingency ethics, and situational ethics allow discernment according to designated criteria. Absolutists would consider these criteria to be subjective and, consequently, less valid.

In applying contextual ethics and moral relativism to social media, the ethics of whatever a media creator decides to post on Web 2.0 platforms like Twitter, Facebook, YouTube, and

BOX 1.6   *PORTRAITS OF TWO WOMEN FROM BURKINA FASO (2002)*: CASE STUDY OF FEMALE GENITAL MUTILATION

In 2001, I travelled to Burkina Faso with a three-woman crew to direct a documentary on the topic of female circumcision. In the village of Fada N'Gourma, on the border of Burkina Faso and Niger, Adjaratou Lompo, a 35-year-old Burkina public health worker, spoke of her concerns about female circumcision in her native village. Thousands of young girls had died from complications related to unsanitary surgical practices, including the use of HIV-contaminated razor blades and the spread of tetanus from performing the procedure on dirt floors in ritual huts.

My crew and I were introduced to Adjaratou's extended family on a blisteringly hot afternoon. The family was welcoming, friendly, and gracious. We received permission to interview Adjaratou's father, a devout elderly Muslim with multiple wives and children. During the interview, he emphasized the necessity of "female circumcision" as a way of managing multiple wives and their demands. Without circumcision, it would be too difficult for one man to satisfy so many wives. Female circumcision was seen as a necessary tool for "female management."

By understanding his frame of reference of "female circumcision as a tool for multiple wife management," it became possible for us to open up a dialogue about how best to eradicate the very real health complications to the young girls in the village and his family. We chose not to use the term "female genital mutilation" in our conversation with the elderly patriarch. This would have likely caused discomfort and awkward reactions. Our emphasis wasn't on whether female circumcision was "wrong," but rather on the premature deaths and serious illness caused by unsafe medical practices. Understanding the cultural and religious frame of reference was a necessary way of building a bridge leading to effective communication—which, in turn, was necessary for eradicating a dangerous and lethal practice in the remote village.[2]

Vimeo is permissible and valid. Although social media platforms have policies for removing offensive, illegal, and pirated content, current social media postings suggest flexible ethical standards.

In producing any media, it is essential to understand the issue as thoroughly as possible and from as many perspectives as possible before establishing the premise. Once the premise is established, messages and perspectives can be appropriately framed.

FRAME: FORM AND FUNCTION

In previous discussions of fiction and non-fiction framing we have seen the close connection between what is presented (content) and how it is presented (form). Aristotle famously distinguished form and function in terms of the contrast between *logos* (logical content) and

BOX 1.7   STRATEGIC USES OF CONCEPTUAL FRAMING

Visual media, radio, and text-based media can be extremely powerful tools in promoting violence or peace as witnessed in Rwanda, the former Republic of Yugoslavia, the former Soviet republic of Georgia, and elsewhere. As Jamie Metzl (1997) observes, "mass media reach not only people's homes, but also their minds, shaping their thoughts and sometimes their behavior" (p. 15).

Manipulation of myths, stereotypes, and identities in the media can provide further legitimization of conflict:

> This often occurs through the dehumanization of members of the 'other' group. For example, in Rwanda, frequent [radio broadcast] references to Tutsis as 'cockroaches' in the Rwandan media are an example of this . . . As soon as people in the other group are perceived as 'less than human,' engaging in conflict with them, and killing them, becomes easier to justify.
>
> (Frohardt & Temin, 2003, p. 7)

lexis (the style or form of delivery). To distinguish form and content is not to place one above the other. For media development this means highlighting the interdependence between visual forms and ideas/language/meaning.

A further consideration arises when specific agendas are in play.

John Grierson viewed documentary as a tool for communication, change, and information exchange between governments and people.[3] The power of the documentary to influence and create positive change motivated early documentary filmmakers. Visuals and sound were used as communication tools for social uplift and as ways of addressing political, economic, and social disparities. The style and frame of these documentaries was focused and direct. The objectives of the media were designed to change attitudes through providing information—often one-sided.

What is not included in the frame or sequence is as important as what is included. Choices are made, and media-makers should be held accountable for those choices. Frames select some aspects of reality and make them more salient. This promotes a particular point of view and perspective. Perceptions of factual information will vary based on the "framing" and presentation of the information given.

TAKE HOME POINTS

- When creating a story, remember that the conceptual frame is represented by the premise or theme. This "frame" maps the narrative structure from beginning to end. Choose it with care.
- These three dimensions of conceptual framing—ethos, pathos, and logos—can directly and indirectly influence the way an audience perceives reality, truth, and the world.

- Blurred lines between fiction and non-fiction have created new approaches to communication in our current media environment. Set boundaries and expectations with care in order to avoid confusing the audience.
- Collaboration and transparency are foundations of ethical practice. Remember to include the subjects of your media project in framing discussions.
- Learning about and acknowledging cultural difference is essential for designing material that is effective and respectful of others. This applies not only to global audiences, but also to local and regional ones.
- Alternate frames of reference have an impact on approaches to storytelling, reactions to conflict, power structures, attitudes toward disclosure, and communication styles. Keep this in mind at every step, including concept development, screenwriting, production, postproduction, and distribution.
- Consider your position on moral absolutism and moral relativism. Contextual ethics, contingency ethics, and situational ethics allow discernment according to designated criteria. Absolutists would consider these criteria to be subjective and thus less valid.
- Principled creative decisions come from thorough analysis of multiple perspectives and frames of reference. When designing media for global audiences, nothing is more important.

NOTES

1. This deceptively thin classic has provided the foundation for dramatic narrative construction. It is commonly assigned in all levels of screenwriting and dramatic writing courses/workshops.
2. The segment on Adjaratou Lompo's family is viewable as *If Only They Knew* on YouTube: www.youtube. com/watch?v=xnCK2cO_Rpo.
3. John Grierson, who directed only one film himself, was a most important influence on documentary filmmakers and the institutions that supported them worldwide from 1929 until his death in the early 1980s. He was a persuasive producer, an innovative bureaucrat (he founded the Crown Film Unit in England and created and directed the National Film Board of Canada from 1939 to 1945), and a masterful writer.

BIBLIOGRAPHY

Aitken, I. (1990). *Film and reform: John Grierson and the documentary film movement*. London, UK: Routledge.

Alia, V. (2004). *Media ethics and social change*. New York, NY: Routledge.

Aristotle. (1961). *Poetics*. (S. H. Butcher, & F. Fergusson, Trans.). New York, NY: Hill and Wang.

Aristotle, Hobbes, T., & Buckley, T. A. (1853). *Aristotle's treatise on rhetoric/also, the poetic of Aristotle, literally translated, with a selection of notes, an analysis, and questions, by Theodore Buckley*. London, UK: H. G. Bohn.

Aufderheide, P. (1998, October 23). The camera as conscience: How social issues inspire moving documentaries. *The Chronicle of Higher Education*, B7.

Briski, Z. (Director). (2004). *Born into brothels: Calcutta's red light kids* [Motion Picture]. ThinkFilm.

Clark, L. (Director). (1995). *Kids* [Motion Picture]. Shining Excalibur Films.

Cowgill, L. J. (2005). *Writing short films: Structure and content for screenwriters* (2nd ed.). New York, NY: Watson-Guptil.

Cull, N. J. (2003). *The birth of a nation* (1915). In N. J. Cull, D. H. Culbert, & D. Welch (Eds.), *Propaganda and mass persuasion: A historical encyclopedia, 1500 to the present* (pp. 40–41). Santa Barbara, CA: ABC-CLIO.

Curran, S. (2016). *Documentary storytelling: Creative nonfiction on screen.* Burlington, MA: Focal Press.

Danto, A. (Director). (2001). *Portraits of two women from Burkina Faso* [Documentary]. Ouagadougou, Burkina Faso.

Danto, A. (Director). (2001). *Shea nut gatherers of Burkina Faso* [Documentary]. United States: United Nations Development Fund for Women.

Danto, A. (Director). (2004). *Shanti's story* [Motion Picture]. Belgaum, Karnataka, India: Pathfinder International.

Danto, A. (Director). (2006). *The never ending path* [Documentary]. San Francisco, CA: Forwardintime.com.

Danto, A. (Director). (2011). *Reflections on media ethics* [Documentary]. San Francisco, CA: Forwardintime.com.

Danto, A., & Ilango, S. P. (Directors). (2003). *A daughter's letter* [Music Video]. Madurai, Tamil Nadu: Gandhigram Institute of Rural Health and Family Welfare Trust.

Everson, W. K. (1998). *American silent film.* New York, NY: Da Capo.

Frohardt, A., & Temin, J. (2003, October). Use and abuse of media in vulnerable societies. *United States Institute of Peace Special Report,* 2–16. Retrieved from: www.usip.org/sites/default/files/sr110.pdf

Harris, K. M. (2006). *Boys, boyz, bois: An ethics of black masculinity in film and popular media.* New York, NY: Routledge.

Herman, E. S., & Chomsky, N. (1988). *Manufacturing consent: The political economy of the mass media.* New York, NY: Pantheon Books.

Katz, S. D. (1991). *Film directing shot by shot: Visualizing from concept to screen.* Studio City, CA: Focal Press.

Kerbel, M. R. (2000). *If it bleeds, it leads: An anatomy of television news.* Boulder, CO: Westview Press.

Keser, R. (2004, October 31). Going mental: The travesty of *Tarnation.* (G. Morris, Ed.) *Bright Lights Film Journal.* Retrieved from: http://brightlightsfilm.com/going-mental-the-travesties-of-tarnation/#.Vpbn4JMrJ8c

Kipling, R. (1899). The white man's burden: The United States and the Philippine Islands. *Norton Anthology of English Literature, 8th.* New York, NY: W. W. Norton. Retrieved from: www.wwnorton.com/college/english/nael/victorian/topic_4/kipling.htm

Kohlberg, L. (1981). *The philosophy of moral development: Moral stages and the idea of justice.* San Francisco, CA: Harper & Row.

Kurosawa, A. (Director). (1950). *Rashomon* [Motion Picture]. Daiei Film Co., Ltd.

Malcolm, J. (1990). *The journalist and the murderer.* New York, NY: Knopf.

Metzl, J. (1997). "Information Intervention: when switching channels isn't enough", *Foreign Affairs, 76*(6), 15–20.

Nussbaum, M. C. (1986). *The fragility of goodness: Luck and ethics in Greek tragedy and philosophy.* Cambridge, UK, & New York, NY: Cambridge University Press.

Perebinossoff, P. (2008). *Real-world media ethics: Inside the broadcast and entertainment industries.* Amsterdam, Netherlands, & Boston, MA: Focal Press.

Rabiger, M. (2015). *Directing the documentary* (6th ed.). Burlington, MA: Focal Press.

Spence, E. H. (2011). *Media, markets, and morals.* Malden, MA: Wiley-Blackwell.

Swami, P. (2005, March 12). A missionary enterprise. *Frontline, India's National Magazine, 22*(08). Retrieved from: www.frontline.in/static/html/fl2208/stories/20050422000408100.htm

Treem, S., Levi, H., Reiner, J., Overmyer, E., & Epstein, A. (Producers). (2014). *The affair* [Television Broadcast]. New York, NY: Showtime.

Wolf, D., & Stern, J. (Producers). (1990). *Law & order* [Television Broadcast]. New York, NY: National Broadcasting Company.

Yust, L. (Director). (1969). *The lottery* [Motion Picture]. Encyclopedia Britannica's Short Story Showcase Series.

Chapter 2

Funding and Competing Agendas

Christine Choy

ABSTRACT

Filmmaking, whether fiction or documentary, long or short format, requires funding. This chapter considers approaches to financing media productions as well as the positive and negative consequences of funding agendas. The aim of the chapter is to provide filmmakers with a framework that can lead to ethical fundraising strategies at each stage of the preproduction, production, postproduction, and distribution process.

In the last section of his famous essay, "The Work of Art in the Age of Mechanical Reproduction," Walter Benjamin (2008/1936, p. 228) describes how film uniquely combines a range of creative disciplines such as painting, music, performance, and science. He didn't mention, however, that film production and media creation also significantly embraces commerce. A filmmaker, unlike other artists, must raise a substantial amount of money before commencing production of a film—in other words, before practicing his or her craft.

When one contemplates making a film, conceptual, practical, and creative decisions are often driven by the budget. A filmmaker, especially an independent filmmaker, has to be an entrepreneur and savvy salesperson. Filmmakers need to be able to pitch an idea to television stations or production companies, write a juicy proposal to funding agencies, or, as is today's popular way of raising money, know how to launch and manage a crowdfunding campaign.

These budget and funding considerations shape not only the films you make but also the type of filmmaker you will become.

Unless working as a "one-man band,"[1] most filmmakers have to hire a production team—for example, a camera person, sound recordist, a gaffer or lighting person, and an editor. The crew for a moderately budgeted narrative film may consist of as many as 50 people. For a documentary, the production team will normally be four to six people. For a concert documentary, the crew can range between 20 and 40 people because multiple camera angles need to be covered: individual performers, musicians, front and back stage action, and audience reactions. These production choices will drive up the budget. Today, documentaries intended for theatrical release have budgets that resemble those of major concert documentaries, often in excess of $1 million.

Often a first-time producer or director will ask for favors, paying crew a minimum salary. This pro bono situation can be exercised only once because filmmaking deals with human beings, who if not inherently greedy, are loath to be exploited. Though filmmaking is a collaborative venture, egos often get in the way—especially when it comes down to dollars and cents.

Negotiating salaries for crew includes using credits as selling points. In general, if a particular film is not successful in getting accepted to major film festivals, no filmmaker will complain about credits. However, when it's the other way around, everyone suddenly wants a better credit than previously agreed upon. Everyone wants to be a co-producer or co-director. A better credit on a noteworthy film means potential for better work in the future and thus more money. Credits can become so contentious that I have often seen filmmakers taking the battle over a credit to court. Many times a film is already in the can (and if we're dealing

BOX 2.1   TEN TIPS FOR PROPOSAL WRITING

1. Be specific about the length, genre, and amount of money that you are requesting. This should be at the top of your proposal. Indicate the urgency or timeliness of the project, if relevant.
2. List your objectives and the goals.
3. Provide historical background, if pertinent.
4. Discuss your visual style. What will give your film a distinctive look? How will you use any of the following: animation, re-enactment, archival footage, interviews, graphics, cinema-verite, or multiple cameras?
5. Lay out your production schedule or timeline, including preproduction, production, postproduction, and distribution. Which film festivals will you submit to and why?
6. Introduce your team. Provide the names and backgrounds of the filmmakers including brief biographies. Do not submit résumés.
7. Indicate how you will measure the qualitative and quantitative impact of your documentary. Define your target audience, which can be tricky. Will you do any outreach through social media to target a different audience?
8. Provide a total budget. Include in-kind contributions, deferred payments, and the amount already raised. Always add a 10% contingency to cover unanticipated expenses.
9. Prepare a strong sample reel, trailer, and/or selects. Also send in a previously finished film, if the funder requests one.
10. Give careful thought to your fundraising strategy. Consider community outreach, social media, and reaching out to your target audience for funding and support.

with an actual film print, changes are very time-consuming and expensive) and one of my colleagues will try sweetly to convince me to change his or her credit. Almost always there is no justification for the change and I must refuse. However, on certain occasions when I have gotten stuck in terms of a film's structure, there have been editors who have helped me reshape the film, and I will often offer them a co-director credit in those cases because they have made a large aesthetic contribution. The budget of my films does not always allow me to offer the editor more money, but many times a credit can be worth just as much.

CONFLICTING AGENDAS: IMPLICATIONS FOR FUNDING

Demands of funding agencies sometimes conflict with a filmmaker's approach to a topic. These differing agendas can sometimes interfere with truthful presentation of a topic.

I have often faced the issue where "money people" have tried to influence my films so that they fit with the sponsor's agenda. I have been urged to cut out parts that do not present the message they are interested in propagating. This is not only true of commercial and industrial films, but also of films made for the educational or broader documentary market. Imagine the repercussions of money men influencing the creative storytelling process! I encourage young filmmakers to do their best not to acquiesce to these pressures, and to present the truth of the subject.

What about the ethics of funding transparency? Raising funds for sensitive media projects can present filmmakers with significant ethical questions. How does a filmmaker propose a project about a sensitive story, when the subject's life may be at risk if their identity is revealed to anyone including the funding source? Should you always reveal your funding sources to the subjects of your documentary? How does a filmmaker straddle the demands of pitching or selling a project when larger issues of individual safety are at stake? What about the nature of the project itself?

BOX 2.2   ADVICE TO STUDENTS ON FUNDING ETHICS

I often ask my students whether the information one provides or withholds when gaining access to funding violates any of the following:

- One's own moral standards.
- The well-being of the subjects in your proposed story.
- The truthful objectives of the documentary.
- The concept of documentary work itself.
- The professional standards of your colleagues.

These are important ethical guideposts for production students to think about as they seek funding sources.

Filmmakers must sometimes work in secret to tell their stories. The 2010 Oscar-winning feature documentary, *The Cove*, about dolphin killing in Japan, was filmed with hidden cameras; the 2010 Oscar-nominated short documentary, *China's Unnatural Disaster: The Tears of Sichuan Provin*ce, about children killed when their schools collapsed after an earthquake, was shot without a permit; and the 2007 Oscar-winning documentary short, *The Blood of Yingzhou District*, about AIDS in China, had to be shot secretively.

In situations such as these, it is necessary for filmmakers to consider carefully that the subjects who cooperate with filmmakers might be put in jeopardy.

On June 4, 1989, the Tiananmen Square protests in China began. Out of the blue, I was asked to interview the first protesters who escaped China to asylum in the United States. The documentary interviews were being financed by Citibank. I was more than happy to film these dissidents, beginning in Chicago, then New York City, and finally Long Island. Fifty rolls of 16mm color film made me trigger-happy. Once we completed the 16mm work print, Citibank stopped the financing because they became concerned about possible retaliation from the Chinese government. We were unable to complete the film once the finances were withdrawn.

It's also increasingly hard to hide identities whether of funders, filmmakers, or subjects— a downside of life in the internet era. People can gather information about everyone; and they can see your work and check out your background, so transparency goes both ways. Once someone learns about a filmmaker's political or social profile, funding might be withdrawn.

THE INFLUENCE OF FUNDING SOURCES ON THE FILMMAKER'S CREATIVE PERSPECTIVE

Of most concern is that filmmakers, instead of making films they truly want to make, will tend to cater instead to what will make films more attractive to funders. Filmmakers' output becomes more segregated and compartmentalized because of the mandate of funding agencies. The gay community makes films about their own community. Black people make films about their history. But white people, on the other hand, can make films about black people, Asians, Latinos, and even Native Americans. This pattern reflects our society itself. Compartmentalized fundraising is a new but unsurprising outcome of the digital era and the proliferation of niche media.

More than ever, the commercial world needs young visionaries, educated in film and well versed in media vocabulary. Yet, once a filmmaker steps into the advertising world, where so much money is available, very few are able to return to non-commercial work.

Today, more than ever, commerce drives our celebrity-obsessed society. Ultimately, what is the filmmaker's position in this world of commercials? Aside from creating a lucrative visual spectacle, does she make final content and conceptual choices? Unlike the feature narrative or documentary, commercials seldom lose money because they are not selling tickets—they are selling a ready-made product. This is very different from film production, where high risk is a given. The advantage of commercials is that they are everywhere: in taxicabs, on the exterior of buses, on cell phones, and on your computer screen when you're

BOX 2.3 FILMMAKER OBJECTIVITY

I was born in Shanghai, People's Republic of China, which is a socialist/communist society. When I was age nine, we moved to Hong Kong, which had a colonial system under British control; then we moved to South Korea, where 45,000 U.S. troops had their bases, a semi-neo-colonial set-up. When I was 13, I went to Japan for high school, a country that had been a monarchy since its inception.

By the time I came to the United States, the land of advanced capitalism, I began to realize that if one wants to be a writer, a filmmaker, or an artist, one must be objective. In other words, one must open one's outlook—almost like a Zen Buddhist.

Interviewees often say what they think you want to hear and at times avoid giving honest answers. I have been successful interviewing people for my films because I make sure that I treat them and their answers with respect.

FIGURE 2.1 Christine Choy, Washington Square Park, New York, 2003. Courtesy of Christine Choy.

searching or playing solitaire. Is making commercials creative? Yes. But producers of commercials are 100% motivated by business interests, unlike filmmakers who are usually less so.

Why are we talking about producers of commercials? It is not very much different from what we call a hired director. You come up with a conceptual idea. You organize the crew and you execute the production under the finances of the funder. But ultimately you do not control the content, and you do not own any rights to your creative work. The income is good, but where is your integrity? It is not for me to judge since financial needs vary.

My advice to young filmmakers is to make small films and build a body of work. This will give you a great opportunity to be a teacher for the younger generation because your experience is *your* experience. Whether your films meet with failure or success, your own experience is the best guide.

I am not one to endorse the commercial world uncritically, but I do know many film-makers who are able to finance dream projects by making commercials and industrials. This strategy works as long as one has strong discipline and does not become totally seduced by the income potential of commercial work. Murray Lerner is a case in point.[2] He did many industrials for Exxon while simultaneously filming some of the most important concerts at the Newport Folk Festival from 1963 to 1966 and the Isle of Wight Festival in the summer of 1970, from which he produced several films. Lerner's work in music documentaries eventually led to his Oscar win in 1980 for his documentary *From Mao to Mozart: Isaac Stern in China.*

NON-PROFIT PUBLIC MEDIA: FUNDING STRATEGIES

Since the inception of the Corporation for Public Broadcasting (CPB) under the mandate of Congress and the Public Broadcasting Act of 1967, part of our tax money is earmarked to be distributed as production funds to the 350 public broadcasting stations around the country.[3] However, there is no mechanism for taxpayers to have any decision-making power regarding the content or aesthetics of programs selected for funding.

In its attempt to meet legal requirements for fair representation, funded programs with multiple viewpoints must be balanced: that is, a Palestinian point of view must be countered with an Israeli point of view. For journalistic documentaries, this insistence on "objectivity" has restricted a filmmaker's ability to tell a story and present conclusions arrived at fairly; the result is a loss of emotional impact. In fearing controversy, the Public Broadcasting Service (PBS) became bland and rapidly lost viewership. Not only has the PBS audience grown smaller and older, but also hundreds of other outlets targeted to different demographics and age groups have sprung up in the past 20 years. Independent filmmakers began to exhibit their work through much more daring channels such as HBO, Sundance Channel, IFC, and MTV. On-demand viewing has changed the way many Americans watch programs. Binge-watching on Netflix and Amazon is the latest way.

After establishing PBS in 1969, the Corporation for Public Broadcasting limited support to PBS stations. This angered many thousands of independent filmmakers. The Association for Independent Video and Filmmakers (AIVF) was established in 1982 and lobbied Congress to divert funds from CPB to finance independent filmmakers. The Independent Television Service (ITVS) was created through these efforts; however, minority communities raised objections about establishing one entity for all independent media-makers.[4]

Activists lobbied for separate organizations and, in response, the CPB created minority consortia beginning 35 years ago in 1980. The National Black Programming Consortium, Latino Public Broadcasting, Vision Maker Media (for Native Americans), the Center for Asian American Media, and Pacific Islanders in Communication provide public seed money for minority productions. A few years later, in 1988, a large corporation was formed to serve the independent filmmaker—ITVS, or Independent Television Service. To acquire funding from ITVS, one must write an extensive proposal. Should the filmmaker succeed in getting

FIGURE 2.2 J.T. Takagi (sound recordist), Christine Choy (producer/cinematographer), and John Esaki (assistant camera) in North Korea, 1999, working on *Homes Apart: Two Koreas* (1999), a 60-minute documentary on the lives of families separated by the geographical border between North and South Korea. Funded by the National Endowment for the Humanities, New York Council on the Humanities, and the New York State Council of the Arts. Courtesy of Christine Choy.

funding, the contract between the filmmaker and ITVS runs 50 pages with a three-stage review. For a newcomer, this process is daunting and presents innumerable bureaucratic obstacles.

Other public funding is available on the state level—for example, through the New York State Council on the Arts (NYSCA). But this state funding is contingent upon Congressional funding for the National Endowment for the Arts and the National Endowment for the Humanities. To receive such funding, the filmmaker must partner with a non-profit media organization, which will collect proposals from the independents and submit them to the government agency. Not only must you have a creative idea, but you must also be savvy with a budget and learn the art of proposal writing. The most horrific question the funder will ask you is: who is your audience? Your personal target audience may actually be very small. That is not going to fly with your funders, especially if you make an experimental film. It is interesting to note that famous and influential experimental films found their audiences over time—for example, Luis Buñuel's *Un Chien Andalou* (1929), Maya Deren's *Meshes of the Afternoon* (1943), and Nam June Paik's *Global Groove* (1973). History has proven that they are among the most creative works of art, but their makers weren't asked to estimate or characterize their audiences in order to get funding. These days if you say to funders, "I don't know the size or gender of my audience," your film will not be funded.

Major foundations sometimes form subsidiaries for funding controversial projects. CreativeTime, funded by the Rockefeller Foundation, is one example; Newsreel, funded through trust funds, is another. Newsreel, the oldest alternative media organization in the history of the United States, was born and incorporated as a non-profit 501(3)(c) in 1967. This non-profit status also applies to religious and educational institutions, such as New York University or Harvard University. Newsreel, created by a group of independent filmmakers, opposed the Vietnam War and continued to address discrimination against minorities and working-class women.[5] The trust fund babies' parents got tax write-offs for donations to the non-profit organization. Newsreel funds were then used to make agitprop films critiquing the American media, Hollywood, and the suppression of people of color. Controversial subject matter included films about the Black Panther party, the Young Lords party, Wounded Knee, and women in prisons. These topics were important but would never have been accepted by mainstream funders at that time. The funders themselves believed such topics were anti-capitalism, anti-corporation, anti-imperialism, and anti-United States. But because financing came from an independent source, the filmmakers did not have to submit to the dictatorship of a funding agency. Forty years later, productions from Newsreel have become an important archive, preserving historical movements of that time. The films were not slick, but had energy and truthfulness.

To become familiar with current practice, I advise students to begin by noting down the foundations listed in credits of films. The Foundation Library on Fifth Avenue in New York is a great resource for doing research on different foundations and the types of projects they are interested in.

COMMERCIAL FEATURE DOCUMENTARIES: FUNDING STRATEGIES

Documentaries are hot commodities. Theatrical and broadcast audiences have renewed enthusiasm for this challenging factual genre. Access to resources needed to make them have become increasingly affordable. Inexpensive, highly versatile digital cameras and sophisticated home editing systems have revolutionized and democratized the production process for first-time filmmakers.

Festivals touting international documentaries have bubbled up around the world. (I just returned from one in Accra, Ghana.) It is amazing that almost each week a new, creative, YouTube-like website surprises us with a bold avenue for distribution. The future has never looked more exciting for cinema independents. You don't need a huge bank account or a large crew to make a documentary. But you do need a story that will involve and challenge your audience, blocks of time to work on it (a year or two), the guts to ignore friends who tell you this is a crazy idea, and willingness to launch yourself into a prolonged adventure that transforms your idea into a film.

Feature documentaries have become a good investment because they don't cost millions of dollars. On average, feature documentaries run between $350,000 and $750,000. Broadcasters and film festivals find them easier to program than short films. With short films, programmers have to look for thematically similar stories to fill screening slots of 1.5 to 2 hours. Some stories are very difficult to match. Take, for example, *Long Story Short* (2008), my 56-minute documentary about Larry and Trudie Leung's nightclub act popular in the 1940s and 1950s on the so-called San Francisco–New York "Chop Suey Circuit." The San Francisco International Film Festival paired it with a documentary film about Anna May Wong, the first Chinese American movie star. Though both films feature Chinese American characters, it is rather ridiculous to pair a Hollywood movie star with variety performers!

What further shocks me is that major film studios like Sony Classics, the Weinstein Company, Samuel Goldwyn, Focus Features, MGM—and new entrants like Netflix, Amazon and CNN—are producing more and more documentary features. New technology enables the industry to make a quick financial gain. Consumers can receive multiple choices of documentary features instantly with just a small charge on their credit card.

I am not against making money but I don't believe it should be the first priority of filmmakers or the people who fund them. Bill and Melinda Gates, Just Film, and Chicken and Egg are, I think, examples of foundations that make clear in their mission statement that profits are secondary, if important at all.

On the surface, globalization and new technology have resulted in great communication tools, but I believe that in terms of depth and substance, learning has become much more generalized and vague. With massive incoming information from the internet, young people have shortened attention spans. When they watch a movie, they are no longer critically analyzing it. Subsequently the film loses the primary objective of the filmmaker to raise the consciousness of the viewer. For example, the subtext of *The Bicycle Thief* (1948) is that even though they are in extreme poverty and forced to break the law, the characters still have a sense of right and wrong. One can learn a great deal about humanity from the film, but today's viewer might have difficulty sitting through a slower-paced black and white film. I don't blame the viewers for this problem. Each generation is different than the one that preceded it, but what concerns me is that some filmmakers purposely design their film with quick pacing, useless computer-generated imagery, and surround sound because this style will sell. Is this when cinema art ceases and cinema becomes a commodity?

I see this problem a lot with music videos. There are excellent musicians, there are mediocre ones, and there are very bad ones. It's not only hypocritical to hype the bad musician's work, but it doesn't contribute anything to the historiography of visual language. Many of the biggest music videos cost over seven figures. Meanwhile our society is divided more and more between the haves and the have-nots. This is not something that will be accepted by everyone, but for me being part of a society with a social conscience is a must for me to enjoy my work. I do not enjoy propaganda or very didactic political outcry. But, if a filmmaker wants to be self-serving, regardless of how much money he makes, his films are not likely to make history. On the other hand, there are great filmmakers who possess a social conscience and are discovered only after they die, never getting to enjoy the glory of widespread acclaim. However, their films, if they are important, will become a part of history.

CROWDFUNDING

Kickstarter, Indiegogo, and other crowdfunding platforms are the current rage for independent filmmakers seeking funding. Some filmmakers embrace crowdfunding now because they believe it is expected more than because it is effective. One usually has to reach more than one's own contacts to raise money to fund a certain project within a certain timeframe by paying a fee to the platform. It helps greatly if the subject of your documentary has a "fan base" or is a social issue that will excite donors. More than one filmmaker has described the experience of running a crowdfunding campaign as "exhausting"—several people work 14-hour days for a month to post updates about the progress of raising money. Is it really

FIGURE 2.3 Crowdfunding is based on three things: the project initiator who proposes the idea and/or project to be funded; individuals or groups who support the idea; and a moderating organization (the "platform") that brings the parties together to launch the idea. It has emerged as a popular form of fundraising in recent years. Credit: Mattz90.

about the perks or rewards that donors can get? Can you have a successful campaign without repeatedly annoying friends and colleagues?

One of my biggest concerns is: how do you know that the email address you have supplied is secure? We say we are concerned about our privacy, and at least some of our private information has been recorded by the National Security Administration (NSA). I ask this question based on my personal experience regarding purchasing "mailing lists" before the advent of the internet. In order to reach a large constituency in the 1980s and 1990s, one needed a solid database of people's mailing addresses. It was a big business and one that I found to be unethical because people often did not agree to have their personal information sold. Furthermore, I have read articles about crowdfunding projects and their true nature, which sometimes diverges widely from what they describe or promise: "an important cause," "great monetary return," or the alluring jargon about "tax write-offs."

Personally, I have never done a crowdfunding campaign because I think it is rather impersonal and the messages are often exaggerated just to get money from your old pal. We live in a society that is already impersonal, so to participate in this alienated world by crowdfunding is not what I choose to do.

CABLE TELEVISION

After receiving my Oscar nomination, I received a phone call from HBO. Since I had never had a TV, I didn't know what HBO was and mistook them for H&R Block (a tax preparation company). After overcoming the confusion, HBO commissioned me for a film called *Best Hotel on Skid Row* (1990). With HBO, there was no discussion about money, which I found to be very refreshing. However, I was naive. I didn't realize the entire copyright of the film belonged to HBO.

Television has an entirely different financial arrangement with independent filmmakers. They are always seeking fresh ideas. They need skills and the production budget is often very high. Since my first experience with HBO, I have worked for Lifetime and the Sundance Channel. I was hired by Lifetime to make a film called *Jennifer's in Jail* (1992) about female gangs in America. The structure of such television shows is highly formulaic and segmented. In spite of being unable to retain the copyright and knowing that my work must fit into a rigid formulaic structure, I enjoyed working in cable television. The pay was better than anything else. This brings up a question of media ethics I've already touched upon—giving up your artistic aesthetics for financial satisfaction.

CORPORATE FILM AND HIDDEN AGENDAS

Several times during my career I have taken on work commissioned by corporations to promote their products, services, or overall agenda. For instance, I was once hired by the satellite communications corporation Hughes Communication to promote their education department, Galaxy Classroom, which was all about finding a new way to teach children and making the classroom a fun place to learn.

Another film I made was commissioned by the Greater Blouse, Skirt and Undergarment Association (GBSUA), a garment workers' union, to make a film highlighting the migration of garment manufacturing from Seventh Avenue in Manhattan to Third World nations.

With both the Galaxy Classroom and GBSUA films, it was interesting to discover that these companies already had a definite agenda for what the project would look like, but they didn't share this with the filmmaking team. Instead during meetings, they gave the impression of complete artistic freedom. However, there was a hidden agenda imbued in every corporate logo. Coverage of race, gender, or any other controversial issue was absolutely off limits. I did not realize until the final screening with the executives of the companies that my message was too critical and had to be altered. In this situation, if you are a young filmmaker, I would advise you to swallow your artistic pride and give the companies what they hired you for.

I set aside the money I made from these and other commissioned works as seed money in my company for personal projects which I am passionate about.

PRODUCT PLACEMENT

New and emerging media platforms are born global. All of the platforms are fueled by the internet and they are reshaping the media landscape in pursuit of a borderless communication experience. According to *The New York Times*, the tastes and habits of the baby-boomer generation—those born between 1946 and 1964—have largely defined marketing strategies for decades. But new media targets consumers and spenders of the next generation: the millennials. Born between 1982 and 2000, they comprise 83 million youths or 26% of the U.S. population (Stout, 2015, p. A1).

Apart from more traditional advertisements, marketers use subtler strategies, including product placement. Our society seems to be creating endless products for this millennial generation to consume in more ways than ever. Product placement in films is not as obvious today as when it began during the baby-boomer generation's youth in the 1960s. In that time period, feature films frequently included scenes of drinking whiskey, smoking Marlboro cigarettes, or air travel. Today's product placements are indirect and often subliminal. Personally, I am not against people who have particular hobbies or enjoy habits such as luxury goods, cigarettes, alcohol, or exotic travel, but I do find it difficult to accept these subliminal images in mass media. On December 6, 2014, *The New York Times Magazine* featured a young woman in a beaded dress by Chanel. The price tag was $75,700 before tax. Though not a product placement in film, this ad has a subliminal message: you have to be young and wealthy. Many feature films—for example, *The Great Gatsby*, *Out of Africa*, and *Annie Hall*—have similar stylistic subtexts. In doing so, the films become vehicles for mass marketing.

In recent years, as a member of the Academy of Motion Picture Arts and Sciences, I discovered that more journalists are engaging in the creation of visual media. Journalists, especially war journalists who have first-hand knowledge, capture reality on video. This I believe is an act of courage with enormous risks. On the other hand, other journalists exploit their access to stories. For instance, an established female journalist who could not bear children decided to adopt a child from a remote village in China. During the process of adoption, she wrote a book. When her child became a teenager, she decided to make a documentary film of the child's return to China to visit her orphanage. On the surface, the child's life is much better in the United States than in the poor countryside of her birth. However, the documentary will be also used for an e-book, and the child has no say in any of this. To me, this is a kind of human product placement.

The point is that filmmakers need to be aware of the current environment of pervasive commodification as they make personal and creative decisions. Just as it impacts our daily lives, the presence of consumerism in a film impacts how it will be received by audiences.

WHO KILLED VINCENT CHIN? (1987)

None of my earliest works garnered me the type of acclaim that deep down I craved. As a person of color, as a woman, and as an immigrant, I felt as though I still had something to prove. I decided to go for a big bang and try to win an Oscar nomination, and thus *Who Killed Vincent Chin?* was conceived as a true murder case involving race, sex, economics, and politics. An Asian autoworker was beaten to death in Detroit by two white autoworkers.

FIGURE 2.4 Production Still from the documentary *Who Killed Vincent Chin* (1987). Directed by Christine Choy and Renee Tajima. Edited by Holly Fisher. In the photo, Jesse Jackson and Lilly Chin are at a rally demanding justice for Vincent Chin in Oakland, California, 1984. Courtesy of Christine Choy.

The white men believed that the man, Vincent Chin, was Japanese; however, in reality he was of Chinese descent.

I wrote the proposal and attached a sizzle reel. I applied to the Corporation for Public Broadcasting. The budget was over $250,000. Because of the size and scope of the project, there were certain concessions I was forced to make along the way. The catch with trying to obtain financing was not that I didn't have a track record—I was an experienced director and cinematographer. However, I had never done a murder case. CPB asked me three questions during my pitch: Who are your constituencies? Since you don't have experience in journalism, how will you be able to approach the subject? Since you are Asian, how can you be objective?

I was able to resolve the first two by having a local PBS station in Detroit as co-producer which would guarantee me viewership in Detroit and Toronto and by collaborating with Juanita Anderson who has not one but two journalism degrees. To address the CPB's third concern, I had to swallow my pride and attach a white, male story editor to the project. The story editor and I did not see eye to eye from the start. Motown is my favorite music and Detroit is the birthplace of Motown music, and so I was very excited to have the opportunity to use the music I love in one of my films, but the story editor didn't like music. After finishing principal photography, the story editor and I got into a big argument. We could no longer collaborate. The story editor left the editing room, and the CPB grant went along with him.

I was determined to finish the film after dedicating five years of my life to it. I thus invented an alternative fundraising strategy: Party! With all the food and drinks donated by local vendors, along with one DJ, I put on one event after another, asking for donations. Eventually I raised enough money and was able to complete the film. Involving the local community is a different kind of strategy, a sort of early form of crowdfunding.

In closing, when it comes to finding funding for your films—whether it be dealing with financiers or finding a way to raise the money yourself—you have to be just as creative as when you're shooting or editing.

TAKE HOME POINTS

- Budget and funding considerations can not only shape the films you make, but also the type of filmmaker you will become.
- Most times it is easier to acquire funding if you have an original story and exclusive access to that story. How you pursue finding an original story can have ethical implications.
- Being transparent about your funding decisions is not always an easy decision.
- Raising funds for sensitive media projects, including stories that can put the subject's life at risk, require careful consideration of consequences.
- Before seeking funding, be sure you have thoroughly researched your topic. For feature-length documentaries, two to three years of research and development is considered "thorough."
- Contemporary funding sources often involve a privacy trade-off. Are you willing to make the privacy trade-off when using Crowdfunding and other internet sources?

NOTES

1   "One man band": with digital production, media makers are able to direct, operate a camera, record sound, and edit their own media projects. This one-person production team approach can be highly effective for investigative documentaries or personal diaries. Ross McElwee's *Sherman's March* (1986) is a fine example of this.

2   Personal communication with Murray Lerner, January 21 and 22, 2015 at The Film Center, 630 9th Avenue, New York. He showed Christine Choy the Exxon commercial and she viewed all his Isle of Wight films. Also present: Eliot Kissileff (Murray Lerner's assistant), Cody Power, Wei Hie Lim (cinematographer), and Lillian Run (sound). www.murraylerner.com/Site/Films.html.

3   The number of Public Broadcasting Service member stations in 2015 according to www.pbs.org/about/about-pbs/stations/.

4   The "Statement of Values" on the ITVS website lists six core values: "a) freedom of expression is a human right; b) a free press and public access to information are foundations of democracy; c) an open society allows unpopular and minority views to be publicly aired; d) a civilized society seeks economic and social justice; e) a just society seeks participation by those without power, prominence or wealth; f) a free nation allows all citizens forums in which to tell their stories and express their opinions" (Retrieved from http://itvs.org/about).

5   The New York chapter became Third World Newsreel in the early 1970s.

BIBLIOGRAPHY

Alpert, J., & O'Neill, M. (Directors). (2009). *China's unnatural disaster: Tears of Sichuan province* [Documentary]. United States: HBO Films.

Amato, G. (Producer), & Sica, V. D. (Director). (1948). *The bicycle thief* [Motion Picture]. Italy: Ente Nazionale Industrie Cinematografiche.

Benjamin, W. (2008). *The work of art in the age of mechanical reproduction*. (J. A. Underwood, Trans.) London, UK: Penguin. (Original work published 1936.)

Benjamin, W. (2009). *One-way street and other writings*. (J. A. Underwood, Trans.) London, UK: Penguin.

Bernstein, P. (2014, December 14). *How do you make a living as an independent filmmaker? It's not easy.* Retrieved from Indiewire: www.indiewire.com/article/how-do-you-make-a-living-as-an-independent-filmmaker-its-not-easy-20141216

Buñuel, L., Braunberger, P. (Producers), & Buñuel, L. (Director). (1929). *Un chien Andalou* [Motion Picture]. France: Les Grands Films Classiques.

Choy, C. (Director). (1989). *Who killed Vincent Chin?* [Documentary]. United States: Corporation for Public Broadcasting and WTVS.

Choy, C. (Director). (1990). *Best hotel on Skid Row* [Documentary]. United States: HBO.

Choy, C. (Director). (1991). *Homes apart: Two Koreas* [Documentary]. United States: National Endowment for the Humanities, New York Council on the Humanities and New York State Council on the Arts.

Choy, C. (Director). (1992). *Jennifer's in jail* [Documentary]. United States: Lifetime Network.

Davies, A. P., & Wistreich, N. (2007). *Film finance handbook: How to fund your film* (digital edition, 2011). Glasgow, UK: Netribution.

Deren, M. (Producer), Deren, M., & Hammid, A. (Directors). (1943). *Meshes of the afternoon* [Motion Picture]. United States: Mystic Fire Video.

Godfrey, J., & Paik, N. J. (Directors). (1973). *Global groove* [Motion Picture]. United States: Electronic Arts Intermix.

Guay, R. (2015, February 7). Why we need diversity incentives for film and television. Retrieved from *Indiewire:* www.indiewire.com/article/why-we-need-diversity-incentives-for-film-and-television-20150207

Hjort, M., & Petrie, D. J. (Eds.). (2007). *The cinema of small nations.* Edinburgh, UK: Edinburgh University Press.

Joffe, C. H. (Producer), & Allen, W. (Director). (1977). *Annie Hall* [Motion Picture]. United States: United Artists.

Kang, C., Thompson, K., & Harwell, D. (2014, December 23). Hollywood's race problem: An insular industry struggles to change. *The Washington Post.* Retrieved from www.washingtonpost.com/business/economy/hollywoods-race-problem-an-insular-industry-struggles-to-change/2014/12/19/d870df04-8625-11e4-9534-f79a23c40e6c_story.html

Lerner, M. (Director). (1979). *From Mao to Mozart: Isaac Stern in China* [Documentary]. United States: Docurama.

Liu, S. (2014, November 11). *Three tips for diverse filmmakers seeking documentary funding.* Retrieved from PBS: POV's Documentary Blog: www.pbs.org/pov/blog/news/2014/11/three-tips-for-diverse-filmmakers-seeking-documentary-funding/

Merrick, D. (Producer), & Clayton, J. (Director). (1974). *The great Gatsby* [Motion Picture]. United States: Paramount Pictures.

Pollack, S., Jorgensen, K. (Producers), & Pollack, S. (Director). (1985). *Out of Africa* [Motion Picture]. United States: Universal Pictures.

Psihoyos, L. (Director). (2009). *The cove,* [Documentary] United States: Participant Media.

Stout, H. (2015, June 21). Oh, to be young, millennial, and so wanted by marketers. *The New York Times,* Retrieved from page A1. www.nytimes.com/2015/06/21/business/media/marketers-fixation-on-the-millennial-generation.html?_r=0

Young, R. (Director). (2006). *The blood of Yingzhou district* [Documentary]. Smiley Film Sales.

Chapter 3

Convergence of Journalism and Documentary

Lonnie Isabel

ABSTRACT

Journalism and documentary have always been linked, and with the migration of news online, documentary journalism has seen a big resurgence. This chapter describes the key features of this productive nexus of journalism and documentary, the challenges it poses for traditional codes of ethics, and the evolving response by professional organizations to the use of visual storytelling as part of online journalism.

The legendary television journalist Edward R. Murrow's last great project at CBS was a classic documentary that is sometimes credited with the extraordinary marriage of journalism and documentary filmmaking. *Harvest of Shame* aired on Thanksgiving night, 1960. It was a brilliant stroke of scheduling since the film was about the shabby treatment of East Coast migrant farm workers, whose misery and poverty must have framed the plates of celebrants gouging on feasts of Brussels sprouts, cranberries, and green beans like a sour ring of guilt. Murrow's biographer, A. M. Sperber (1998), wrote: "'Harvest of Shame' burst upon the public, an updated *Grapes of Wrath*, a black-and-white document of protest ushering in the sixties on TV" (p. 610).

Murrow was a pioneering giant of audiovisual news. The success of *Harvest of Shame* launched three decades of network and local television documentaries. News organizations giddy with the creative and financial possibilities of the rapidly developing medium of television employed their own film crews. This trend faded, mostly because of cost and the success of television news magazines like *60 Minutes*. Documentaries began to disappear from broadcast TV, except for PBS. By the late 1990s, the marriage was heading toward a final separation.

Then came cable television and ultimately the digital revolution. Since then, journalism has been scrambling to re-embrace documentary. Journalism schools with documentary programs are growing each year. At Columbia's Graduate School of Journalism, the number of documentary students has doubled, and other schools are scrambling to add enough courses to satisfy students of multimedia storytelling, most including training in the techniques of documentary filmmaking explored in this book.

Traditional newsrooms, like *The New York Times*, *Washington Post*, Associated Press (AP), and Reuters, have added video units. Documentaries produced by journalists, like *Restrepo* (2010) and *Citizenfour* (2014), have scored festival awards and box office success, sometimes to the frustration of traditional documentary producers. And conversely, documentaries have taken on some of the subjects that news organizations have given scant attention to, like the role of women in ending the Liberian Civil war, as told wondrously in Abigail Disney's *Pray the Devil Back to Hell* (2008), where the voices and actions of the women dressed in white carry the narrative of the final chapter of one of the most horrific conflicts in memory.

What happened? News organizations have migrated online, where the demand and appeal of visual storytelling were obvious to even the most print-centric journalist. And technology cut the costs precipitously since digital cameras and audio equipment didn't require a huge crew, and editing software adapts facilely to the demands of deadline. Since the docs, often ten minutes or less, are shown almost always online, the work is distributed with little cost and at maximum speed; prime necessities of journalism. This is particularly true now in a time of scarcity for media organizations that are seeking ever-elusive target audiences that increasingly get their news in ways never imagined in the time of *Harvest of Shame*.

And of course, the target audience is changing almost daily—not the people themselves, but how they want to access news. A 2014 Pew Research report on the state of the news industry found that more than 60 percent of U.S. adults watch videos online and 36 percent of those adults watch news videos. "This is roughly the same percentage of Americans who now get news from Facebook or watch cable news channels regularly," the report stated (Olmstead et al., 2014).

Journalists may frame their approach to target audiences in a way that is different from advertising, the entertainment industry, and documentary media-makers. Journalists have an obligation to the public. And thus, a journalist tries for maximum inclusion and that requires creating media that is useful to most consumers. Media organizations want users to come back habitually; once it was a daily dose of news, now it's continual. The online news audience is voracious for video that stands alone or is matched with graphics, photo slideshows, and text. And the advent of multimedia journalism has given reporters, editors, and producers many more creative options, most often with video in the form of mini-docs, narrative stories that are often done with the words of a primary source or character; but also in longer form documentaries that Murrow would likely be proud of.

This has breathed life into a media sector that is struggling mightily both to maintain target audiences and to find new streams of incoming cash to stay afloat, or at least to increase fading profits. News organizations don't generally separate digital video advertising revenue figures from overall revenue, but digital advertising has been increasing sharply each year. According to eMarketeer, revenues grew 44 percent to an estimated $4.15 billion from 2012 to 2013 (Olmstead et al., 2014). That's a sizable infusion into cash-strapped traditional media and into start-ups, like MediaStorm, that have developed their own style of visual storytelling

FIGURE 3.1   Reporter in Nottingham, England readies camera for street scene. Credit: Lucian Milasan/ Shutterstock.com.

that uses the techniques of documentary. HBO, Showtime, ESPN, and even Netflix now produce their own documentaries.

News organizations have traditionally targeted audiences based on geography (local television), point of view (Fox News), or specialty (Politico, ESPN). The internet has blown up this scheme. News websites, like everyone else, are looking for hits—for computer and smartphone users to click on the icon that leads to their content. Advertising rates are based on this, and every advertiser knows that video is a proven effective eye-catcher. So video has become an essential draw on media websites, and digital journalism, including video, has been an area of significant job growth in an industry that has been losing jobs for several years in the United States.

The Pew Research Center (Olmstead et al., 2014) found in a survey that 468 digital news organizations have produced nearly 5,000 new full-time jobs while more traditional jobs have been in a steady decline. Many organizations also upload video news and docs on popular sites like YouTube in hopes of bringing more eyes to their websites. Some major news websites like ABCnews.com have had a screen in the newsroom that displays the metrics of whose looking at what in real time.

Additionally, broadband has cleared the way for more and longer video online. Now an estimated 60 percent of long form traditional documentaries have been viewed only online, and websites abound that offer unlimited viewing of docs.

FIGURE 3.2   Broadcast television reporters gather on a rooftop at the Turkish-Syrian border in 2011. Credit: Thomas Koch/Shutterstock.com

This all seems ideal for journalism as it migrates online, but it has come with some growing pains and some navel gazing. Despite sometimes far-reaching efforts at sustaining audiences, the truth is that professional journalists occupy a smaller and smaller portion of the total media audience. Advocacy groups, citizen journalists, and almost anyone else with an image and text recording device and an internet connection can commit an act of journalism.

Who is a journalist? Who is a documentarian? Are the multimedia stories on news websites documentaries? Do the same rules apply to both documentary and journalism?

LINES OF DEMARCATION?

These questions are still working their way toward answers, or perhaps there are no definite answers. The lines are blurry. Practitioners are wearing several hats—reporter, document-arian, photographer, and editor. Journalists are making documentaries. And interestingly, documentary producers are creating breakaway work in journalism, covering stories that reporters have missed or given small attention to. For example, Abigail Disney's *Pray the Devil Back to Hell* (2008), where the voices and actions of women dressed in white carry the narrative of how they goaded and embarrassed the two sides of the intensely brutal 12-year-old Liberian Civil War to peace negotiations.

In interviews with *Documentary*, the magazine of the International Documentary Association, a number of journalists discussed becoming documentarians. They told author Jeff Swimmer that the transition, though not seamless, was a natural one. Sam Green, co-director of Oscar-nominated *The Weather Underground* (2002), about radical activists of the 1960s, said his journalism training at UC-Berkeley was essential to his work as a documentarian: "Journalism taught me to develop a thick skin and go out and talk to strangers. I'm grateful for the skills I learned in J-school: tracking people down, gaining their confidence" (Swimmer, 2004).

Kay Hwangbo, a former *Los Angeles Times* reporter who has directed a documentary about K. W. Lee, one of the U.S.'s first Asian-American journalists, told the magazine: "As a daily reporter, you need good people skills. You have to persuade, beg, cajole, flirt, cry—whatever it takes. You have to bond with people quickly and show that you're not some fruitcake" (Swimmer, 2004).

This blending of roles has led to some confusion and tension. A panel at the 2015 Sundance festival discussed this. When asked if she were a documentary filmmaker or a journalist, Laura Poitras, director of *Citizenfour*, the story of Edward Snowden, insisted there is no real boundary. She called her work "journalism plus" (Das, 2015). Other panelists insisted there has always been a facet of journalism in documentary, since both are about truth telling. *3 and 1/2 Minutes* (2015) is a documentary about the death of Jordan Davis who was shot after an argument over loud music. Its director, Marc Silver, told the audience he didn't consider himself a journalist, but found himself providing a courtroom feed to live TV during the trial of the man who shot Davis (Das, 2015). Was Silver a journalist then? In the rapidly shifting environment and an era of citizen journalism, almost anyone can commit an act of journalism, with the right equipment and an internet connection. Should it matter what the practitioner is called—documentarian or journalist?

In another article for *Documentary* magazine, writer Elisabeth Greenbaum Kasson seeks answers to the question of whether a line exists between journalism and documentary:

> What is the place of documentary journalism within the relentless crush of the 24-hour news cycle? Are there differences in methodology between the filmmaker and the journalist? Does the medium matter (print versus broadcast vs. the Internet versus film)? Are there clear lines of demarcation, or does one leave off where the other begins?
>
> (Kasson, 2010)

The similarities are obvious. Reporters document. Documentarians report. And both have a commitment to truth telling. But the differences may lie in what journalism has been, the place journalism holds in a democratic society, and the strict ethical codes that journalists have tried to follow.

ETHICS: GORILLA IN THE NEW NEWSROOMS?

Ethics is, perhaps, the most significant area of challenge in the new media environment. Journalists have been a prickly lot about ethics, and breaches are punished often with loss of

BOX 3.1   EXCELLENT DOCUMENTARIES BY JOURNALISTS

Restrepo (2010)
Sebastian Junger and Tim Hetherington's documentary that followed a U.S. Army platoon fighting in Afghanistan. Grand Jury Prize for best documentary at 2010 Sundance Festival.

Citizenfour (2014)
Laura Poitras directed this 2014 documentary on National Security whistleblower and wanted man Edward Snowden. Winner of an Academy Award for Best Documentary Feature.

No Fire Zone: In the Killing Fields of Sri Lanka (2013)
Director Callum Macrae's documentary reports extensive evidence of war crimes in the government's push to end a decades long civil war.

The New Black (2013)
Director Yoruba Richen tells the story of the African-American community grappling with the issue of gay marriage.

Section 60: Arlington National Cemetery (2008)
Jon Alpert and Matthew O'Neill directed this gripping look at visitors to a section of the national cemetery, where soldiers killed in Iraq were buried.

job or career. In a highly competitive industry, ethical mistakes lead to loss of readers and viewers. Ethics and truthful representation are the cornerstones of the news media sector's survival. As polls show eroding confidence in reporting, the concept of fairness has a particularly significant weight.

Some see an ethical crisis as journalists venture into techniques that documentarians use for greater narrative impact and drama. These include adding music in editing, restaging events, directing sources on what to say or do, juxtaposing video clips in a misleading way, and interfering with an event as it is unfolding. For journalism these have almost always been taboo; although there's less resistance to music.

Prof. Stephen J. A. Ward, an internationally known media ethicist who was also a war correspondent in Bosnia and Northern Ireland, writes that "media ethics, like media is in turmoil" (Ward, 2013). Ward has called for a radical change in media ethics to reflect the new media environment, including visual storytelling: "Rather than stress fidelity to past principles, we construct editorial guidelines for journalists in new "media ecologies"—such as integrated newsrooms" (Ward, 2013).

Ward and others see a clash between the applied ethics of journalism that have evolved over time and what journalism is becoming online, primarily because the professional values of ethics require that each story is accurate and verified before it is published.

Newsrooms have had an editorial process that vets all stories and possible breaches of ethics are discussed. The new media environment values instant posting of information even when uncertainty exists.

How does this fit into documentary craft? For full-length features, it may not affect the process as much as for shorter, more time-sensitive documentary-style pieces that are common on news media websites.

As this is written, the industry is establishing new ethical codes for visual storytelling and documentary news. But what will those principles be and what will newsrooms look like? With the disruption of the industry that has led to the creation of thousands of smaller media organizations and even more freelance practitioners, what challenges await both journalism and documentary? Several journalism organizations have taken up this topic head on. As you can see in the excerpt in Box 3.2, the Radio, Television, Digital News Association's code of ethics specifically singles out the techniques of some documentarians as banned for the visual journalist.

Most ethics codes leave some room for exceptions. Documentarians haven't had a specific code. A comprehensive 2009 study of filmmaker ethics by the Center for Media and Social Impact found that documentarians resist establishing an ethics code and revealed that "profound ethical conflicts" were evident. Most operate independently and make decisions

BOX 3.2   EXCERPTS FROM JOURNALISM ETHICS CODES

Radio Television Digital News Association

Journalism's obligation is to the public. Journalism places the public's interests ahead of commercial, political and personal interests. Journalism empowers viewers, listeners and readers to make more informed decisions for themselves; it does not tell people what to believe or how to feel.

Ethical decision-making should occur at every step of the journalistic process, including story selection, news gathering, production, presentation and delivery. Practitioners of ethical journalism seek diverse and even opposing opinions in order to reach better conclusions that can be clearly explained and effectively defended or, when appropriate, revisited and revised.

Journalism accepts responsibility, articulates its reasons and opens its processes to public scrutiny.

Deception in news gathering, including surreptitious recording, conflicts with journalism's commitment to truth. Similarly, anonymity of sources deprives the audience of important, relevant information. Staging, dramatization and other alterations – even when labeled as such – can confuse or fool viewers, listeners and readers. These tactics are justified only when stories of great significance cannot be adequately told without distortion, and when any creative liberties taken are clearly explained.

(RTDNA, 2015)

National Press Photographers Association

Visual journalists operate as trustees of the public. Our primary role is to report visually on the significant events and varied viewpoints in our common world. Our primary goal is the faithful and comprehensive depiction of the subject at hand. As visual journalists, we have the responsibility to document society and to preserve its history through images.

Visual journalists and those who manage visual news productions are accountable for upholding the following standards in their daily work:

1. Be accurate and comprehensive in the representation of subjects.
2. Resist being manipulated by staged photo opportunities.
3. Be complete and provide context when photographing or recording subjects. Avoid stereotyping individuals and groups. Recognize and work to avoid presenting one's own biases in the work.
4. Treat all subjects with respect and dignity. Give special consideration to vulnerable subjects and compassion to victims of crime or tragedy. Intrude on private moments of grief only when the public has an overriding and justifiable need to see.
5. While photographing subjects do not intentionally contribute to, alter, or seek to alter or influence events.
6. Editing should maintain the integrity of the photographic images' content and context. Do not manipulate images or add or alter sound in any way that can mislead viewers or misrepresent subjects.
7. Do not pay sources or subjects or reward them materially for information or participation.
8. Do not accept gifts, favors, or compensation from those who might seek to influence coverage.
9. Do not intentionally sabotage the efforts of other journalists.

(NPPA, n.d.)

based on the moment. The report found much evidence of conflict with journalism. Here's an example:

Singled out for notice was the attention at some television networks—even when not in the news division—to factual accuracy. One filmmaker, for instance, created archival material to use in her documentary and was asked to take it out by the broadcaster when they found out it wasn't real. "We loved the texture of the campaign commercials for various candidates. [Our subject] had one for radio; we used the audio and made a commercial [to go with the audio]. [Our broadcaster] asked if it was real. And it wasn't, so we had to take it out. It's too misleading to the audience." They also respected broadcasters' fact-checking departments, and some found that people in those departments were willing to push back against network pressures to fudge facts or artificially enhance drama.

(Aufderheide, Jaszi, & Chandra, 2009).

The Online News Association (ONA), the primary organization for digital journalists, recognizes the new ethical challenges and acknowledges the need for more flexibility. It has devised a tool that allows individual practitioners and organizations to build their own codes of ethics. The effort grew out of a discussion in 2013 among multimedia journalists who saw as Prof. Ward proclaimed a need to establish a code for a new media environment. The project was made into a "build your own application" because ONA "recognizes that no single ethics code can reflect the needs of everyone in our widely varied profession" (Kent, n.d.).

Creating something even marginally false for dramatic effect is absolutely banned in journalism overall. But digital manipulation and restaging are the primary journalism sins in video and visual images. In 2015, the World Press Photo's awards committee initiated even stricter prohibitions against altering images after ten (about 8 percent) of the 2014 finalists were disqualified for digital manipulation (Estrin, 2014).

And RTDNA's code of ethics forbids this emphatically in moving images: "Professional electronic journalists should not manipulate images or sounds in any way that is misleading." The Code also says journalists should not "present images or sounds that are reenacted without informing the public" (RTDNA, 2015).

That apparently doesn't apply universally to music. Journalism has lowered its guard on using a musical soundtrack despite previous prohibitions against it as a possible pollutant of the truth. Retired DePauw University Prof. Bob Steele, a guru of video ethics with the Poynter Institute, a journalism think tank and training organization, agrees that music can be a reasonable addition to other elements. But he and other media ethicists won't budge on permitting anything that doesn't include journalism's ironclad ethics codes that proclaim authenticity and accuracy as unassailable. Some have called for more ethics training of video journalists and more controls in newsrooms, similar to the example of the network not allowing documentarians to make up political ads.

But newsrooms have been trimming their editing staffs while some have added video storytellers. This has become part of the new language of newsrooms to refer to the flourishing genre of doc-like news videos that focus tightly on individual stories told often in the voice of the primary source. Journalists now refer to those sources as characters, another addition to the journalists' lexicon and something Murrow and other pioneers likely would have objected to. Rarely is there a narrator with a microphone standing at the scene. Increasingly these stories spend less actual screen time with background information and alternative perspectives that slow the narrative and rob the videos of narrative flow and drama, essential to the documentary craft.

DOCUMENTARY AS JOURNALISM: CHALLENGES OF AUTHENTICITY

As with *Harvest of Shame*, the rejuvenated documentary branch of journalism is producing some remarkable and controversial works that have fulfilled the journalism objectives of

BOX 3.3   ETHICAL CHECKLIST FOR VIDEO JOURNALISTS/ DOCUMENTARIANS

FIGURE 3.3   Documentarians Sophie Ibbotson and Bryn Kewley shoot in Nechem, Afghanistan, where villagers had never seen a video camera. Credit: Tracing Tea/ Shutterstock.com.

- Ask, what is my objective as a journalist?
- Treat sources as you would want to be treated.
- A news story or documentary should represent the truth.
- Staging, overdubbing an interview, adding sound, using video archives in a way that distorts truth is forbidden.
- Journalism is the first draft of history. Respect that.
- Music should not editorialize or add disproportionate emotion.

exposing of hidden truths and wrongdoing of the powerful. Here's one example of how the canons of journalism and documentary collided in the mind of the practitioner. Journalist and documentarian Callum Macrae directed *No Fire Zone: In the Killing Fields of Sri Lanka*, a piercing, graphic account of war crimes in that country when the military pushed north in a major offensive to defeat the Tamil Tigers in 2006. It ended a civil war that began in 1983 when the Tamil ethnic group sought to secede from the Sinhalese majority after decades of grievances. It was a war of almost unspeakable violence that included about 400 suicide bombings. Much of the offensive to end the war was uncovered because the government didn't allow in foreign war correspondents. Macrae employed video taken by soldiers, refugees and others to document the military's march north, and a bloody march it was.

At a screening in New York in 2014, representatives from the Sri Lankan consulate sat stoically in the audience until Macrae tried to get their reaction.

Macrae recognized that the documentary represented more than a compelling story. In a video he made for a funder, the Pulitzer Center on Crisis Reporting, Macrae said he had to make hours of horrible footage into a narrative that would engage viewers. But he also recognized that:

> This is a film of record. This is evidence of war crimes and that presents us with two issues in a sense. The first is that we couldn't knock around with this footage. . . . If it happened on a certain day we had to make absolutely sure that we said it happened on that day and that we didn't transpose it from somewhere else. It meant that we couldn't use footage really as wallpaper as you would often use in a documentary—generic footage which kind of illustrates the things which people are talking about.
>
> (Pulitzer Center, 2013)

The other issue, he said was taste, showing people dying without medicine, horribly disfigured bodies: "Justice requires truth telling."

In essence these are the added burdens of authenticity and public service that journalists bring to documentary.

This was true for Edward R. Murrow in 1960 and still prevails today.

TAKE HOME POINTS

- Journalism and documentary have always been closely linked. As journalism migrates to the internet more video storytelling has emerged that is akin to documentary.
- Ethics is at the heart of journalism and strict codes have been developed that ensure accuracy, fairness, and transparency. The amalgamation of journalism and documentary has placed new challenges upon journalist who make documentaries and documentarians who are increasingly practicing journalism.
- Much of the ethical discussion is still ongoing, ever-evolving and unsettled.
- Documentarians and journalists are trying to resolve conflicts over staging events, adding sound, and digital manipulation—all taboo to journalists.

BIBLIOGRAPHY

Aufderheide, P., Jaszi, P. & Chandra, M. (2009). Honest truths: Documentary filmmakers on ethical challenges in their work. Retrieved from Center for Media & Social Impact: www.cmsimpact.org/sites/default/files/ Honest_Truths_—_Documentary_Filmmakers_on_Ethical_Challenges_in_Their_Work.pdf

Das, A. (2015, February 1). Sundance 2015: Documentary or journalism? Retrieved from Center for Media & Social Impact: www.cmsimpact.org/blog.media-impact/sundance-2015-documentary-or-journalism

Estrin, J. (2014, February 16). The world's best (unaltered) photos. *The New York Times*. Retrieved from: http://lens.blogs.nytimes.com/2014/02/14/the-worlds-best-unaltered-photos/?_r=0

Kasson, E. G. (2010). The message is the medium: The difference between documentarians and journalists. Retrieved from International Documentary Association: www.documentary.org/magazine/message-medium-difference-between-documentarians-and-journalists

Kent, T. (n.d.) A customized ethics code for every organization. Retrieved from http://ethics.journalists.org/about/

Macrae, C. (Director). (2013). *No fire zone: The killing field of Sri Lanka* [documentary]. Israel: Cinephil.

NPPA. (n.d.). NPPA code of ethics. Retrieved from https://nppa.org/code_of_ethics

Olmstead, K., Mitchell, A., Holcomb, J., & Vogt, N. (2014, March 26). News video on the web: A growing, if uncertain part of news. *Pew Research Center: State of the News Media*. Retrieved from: www.journalism.corg/2014/03/26/news-video-on-the-web/

Pulitzer Center. (2013, May 28). Meet Callum Macrae: No fire zone: In the killing fields of Sri Lanka. Retrieved from: www.youtube.com/watch?v=jWp55KEEF3A

RTDNA. (2015). RTDNA code of ethics. Retrieved from www.rtdna.org/content/rtdna_code_of_ethics

Sperber, A. M. (1998). *Murrow, his life and times*. New York: Fordham University Press.

Swimmer, J. (2004, September/October). Exchanging the pen for the camera: When journalists make the jump into documentaries. *International Documentary Association*. Retrieved from: www.documentary.org/magazine/echanging-pen-camera-when-journalists-make-jump-documentaries

Ward, S. J. A. (2013, August 19). Why we need a radical change for media ethics, not a return to basics. *MediaShift*. Retrieved from: www.mediashift.org/2013/08/why-we-need-radical-change-for-media-ethics-not-a-return-to-basics

Chapter 4

F-Stop: Power Differentials

Tami Gold

ABSTRACT

Power differentials can significantly impact all forms of media creation: fiction, documentary, journalism, and social media. This chapter explores power differentials in the relationship between the filmmaker and the people portrayed in documentaries. It looks at the principles of personal presentation, agency, equality, and power. I am using my experiences as a filmmaker to look at the ethics of consent, working with teenagers, screening rough-cuts, and the economic relationship between the filmmaker and the people in the films.

LOOKING FOR LOVE (1982)

I first met Audrey when she was 11 years old. Her mother, Gloria, worked with my husband at the U.S. Postal Service Bulk Center in Secaucus, New Jersey. On July 21, 1978, hundreds of postal workers went on a wildcat strike demanding an end to mandatory overtime, forced speedups, and hazardous working conditions. My film partners and I followed the strike as it unfolded for the documentary *Signed, Sealed and Delivered: Labor Struggle in the Post Office* (1980). We were in the thick of the action with a borrowed Sony camera, half-inch video deck, a handheld microphone and a lot of cables. Audrey was often on the picket line, too, with her mother, sister, and two brothers.

Over three years of filming, Audrey and I became close though we came from very different worlds. I was a white Jewish mother in my mid-20s who had just left a job at Public Service Electric & Gas as a pipefitter to return to my passion—documentary filmmaking. Audrey was a young African-American child from East Orange, NJ, about to enter high school. By the time we completed *Signed, Sealed and Delivered* she had become a beautiful 14-year-old young woman.

One day Gloria called to tell me Audrey was pregnant. Recognizing the bond we had, she asked if I would be comfortable encouraging Audrey to have an abortion. Though this was a difficult request, I reached out to Audrey and we talked about the pros and cons (mostly the cons) of having a child and becoming a mother at 15. Audrey made her own decision and eight months later she gave birth to a baby girl.

During this time, Newark, NJ was launching its first cable TV channel and I was invited by a cable consortium to propose ideas for documentaries that would speak to the different communities in the city. Understanding the need for a public discussion about teenage parenting, I proposed a documentary about what it means to be a teenage mother and that is when the film *Looking for Love* began. I asked Audrey to be one of the teenagers featured in the film, and, with all of her 15-year-old enthusiasm, she jumped at the idea.

More than anything, Audrey wanted adult approval about her decision to become a mother.

The first time I planned to film with Audrey, she didn't show up. The second time, Audrey decided to go skating after school while I waited at her home for hours. The third time, Audrey came home from school late and was angry that her one-year-old daughter would not stop crying. She threw her schoolbooks down and stormed into the living room. This was the first time I had worked with teenagers and learned quickly how unpredictable filming would be. What was most important: I learned to be flexible and non-judgmental.

When I began to interview Audrey, I realized she would respond as though the camera wasn't present, never fully understanding what it would mean to share her story in a documentary with the world. She was an open book and I was someone she trusted.

I spent months entering and leaving Audrey's complicated, and at times, painful life with a camera on my shoulder. But I held more than the camera—I held the power in this fragile relationship (see also Cipriani, 2014).

It wasn't until I asked Audrey to sign a Personal Release Form that I began to understand what it means to document the lives of teenagers.

Audrey could not sign because she was underage. She could give birth to a child at 15 but had to have a parent or guardian sign the Personal Release Form to grant me permission to use her story in the documentary.

As I explained this, Audrey burst into tears. She was demoralized that everyone in her life treated her like a child without any agency, and she believed she should be treated as an adult.

At this moment, my priority was to get the Personal Release Form signed. I was concerned that Audrey would decide that she did not want to be part of the film if her mother was the one to sign the release form, so I minimized the whole thing, never taking the time to explain what a release form was. I didn't use this moment to talk about the implications of sharing her story with the public and that she would always be labeled, as a result of being in this film, a teenage mother. I don't think I understood this myself. What does it mean to have your life forever imprinted into a non-fiction film?

Over the next months, I began filming other teenage mothers and found myself needing to protect them from saying too much and exposing things that could come back to hurt them. They would tell me stories that they had never shared with anyone and their need to be loved was woven into everything they expressed. While I was interviewing Diana, a 16-year-old mother, she told me how jealous she was of her daughter and that she had had thoughts of hurting her. She went on to explain that all she really wanted was to be listened to, understood, seen, and loved.

BOX 4.1   HOW TO ASK PEOPLE TO SIGN A PERSONAL RELEASE FORM

I often return to these questions when asking people to sign a Personal Release Form:

- How do I explain why I need it?
- How do I navigate what signing it really means?
- Should I explain that they are giving up significant power to me; that they are agreeing that I can edit the interview, the footage, and the visuals the way I want without any guarantee that they can change the film?
- Do I discuss how much input they can have, but that I would have ultimate control of the final edit?
- How do I explain that the Personal Release Form is a contract like any other binding legal agreement and that they should read it carefully before signing?

As the filmmaker, and also as their elder, I had authority and power, and by deeply listening to them, I became a transference figure as they told me the innermost secrets that they could never tell their mothers.

In recent studies of the brain, researchers have found that the frontal lobe does not fully develop until around 25 years of age. The logic and reasoning functions of the brain are located in the frontal lobe, enabling people to understand cause and effect and to use good judgment. This ability balances our impulsive and emotional reactions with rational thinking. Because their frontal lobes are still developing, teenagers are more vulnerable to their emotions and often act without thinking about the consequences of their actions (NIMH, 2011).[1] This was not something I knew when I was producing *Looking for Love*. I thought I was a great interviewer and this was why Audrey, Diana, and the other teenagers opened up with such spontaneity and candor. I never questioned the psychological or physiological interactions at play.

In 2014, I produced a documentary with David Pavlosky about a violent hate crime in a gay bar perpetrated by an 18-year-old white male. The film, *Puzzles: When Hate Came to Town*, includes interviews with the protagonist's friends who were between 14 and 24 years old. Equipped with a deeper understanding of teenagers and development, we made different choices than we might have made in the past. We were concerned with not dehumanizing the young people though we strongly disagreed with much of their thinking. We also were careful not to include impulsive statements understanding the impact this could have on them in their adult lives. Omitting some of their hate speech may have changed the overall film, but this is an important ethical consideration that documentary filmmakers must weigh.

Documentary filmmakers often tell stories of trauma or personal and political struggle. Under these conditions we enter into someone's life during stressful moments or times of crisis or change, and above all, we listen. To our subjects, we can become a confidante, counselor, minister, or therapist—people who represent, or in fact have, powerful positions.

A difficult—and often unacknowledged—issue is the racial power dynamic that occurs when the filmmaker is white and the people in the film are African American and Latino. In *Looking for Love*, Audrey and Diana were young women of color and I was white. How they were represented meant that they had to have a voice and also veto power during the editing stage. The edit room was five minutes from Audrey's high school and a bus ride from Diana's home and they had ongoing input about editing decisions and how they were portrayed. It was important that I did not, even unintentionally, cause them to be voiceless. They screened many rough-cuts and the completed documentary before its premiere at the Newark Museum.

Audrey's mother, Gloria, however, was very busy with work and the demands of her life and was never able to see a rough-cut or the final edit of the film. The end result was painful. She was not prepared to hear her daughter say difficult things about their relationship in a public venue. She had to process her feelings on the spot. Since this experience, I make a great effort to screen rough-cuts and the final film for all of the main interviewees before ever releasing a film.

Looking for Love was broadcast on the local PBS station, followed by a 30-minute live call-in show. Teenagers from across New Jersey and New York called in to ask questions and talk openly about teenage parenthood. It was clear the film had reached an important audience. The show was a success and the station's programmers decided to rebroadcast the documentary.

After four years of rebroadcasting, Audrey was in her early twenties. She had earned a high school diploma, was entering the workforce and planning her wedding. Audrey was embracing adulthood and having *Looking for Love* televised became a point of conflict. She was no longer a teenage mother and the film and its exposure froze her in time. She asked that the film not be televised any more. I deeply respected her wishes, however, by this time I had entered into a legal agreement with a cable consortium to distribute the film. In doing so I had signed over control of broadcasting. It would be their decision—not mine, not Audrey's—to discontinue the repeat broadcasts. I did not realize that I would have no input into what would happen with the film though I was the producer, director, camerawoman, and editor. I had not considered the long-term consequences of the film's continued broadcasts on Audrey's life. The film, however, had become dated. This fact, coupled with my persistent argument about our responsibility to honor the requests of the women portrayed in *Looking for Love*, convinced the local PBS programmer and cable consortium. The last rebroadcast occurred just months before Audrey's wedding.

JUGGLING GENDER (1992)

In the early 1990s, I met Jennifer Miller who openly and unabashedly lives her life with a full beard and strongly identifies as a lesbian feminist. I asked Jennifer if I could interview her for a film about the meaning of feminism. I understood that facial hair occupies a gender-defining position in our culture and wanted to explore how having a full beard had an impact on her lesbian feminist identity.

Like the teenagers in *Looking for Love*, Jennifer was comfortable, relaxed, and, at times, did not seem to notice my filming. However, having learned so much about the need for open discussion while producing *Looking for Love*, I chose to discuss the Personal Release Form, the importance of screening rough-cuts, and how we would work together on the final cut, with the objective of equalizing the power relationship between the subject, in this case Jennifer, and myself.

Jennifer Miller crosses the gender binary between male and female, and because of this, she has had many experiences in public with people staring at her uncomfortably. However, the act of filming with Jennifer on the street unintentionally gave people permission to look at the "other" without becoming self-conscious or thinking they had broken the cultural taboo of staring and pointing. The presence of the camera became an instrument of power. As in my previous experiences, I had the camera—the power—and Jennifer did not.

The camera empowered bystanders as well. Once, while Jennifer and I were shooting in the East Village, a man stood nearby watching. Then, out of nowhere, he walked into the frame and asked Jennifer, "Is the beard real? Can I touch it?" Without waiting for a response, he leaned in and rubbed his face against her beard. No one had ever before approached Jennifer in public to ask if they could feel her beard, let alone violate her personal space and her body. It was the very presence of the camera and of someone filming that became a catalyst, giving a stranger permission to gawk, to touch, and to break every social code.

FIGURE 4.1 Jennifer Miller. From *Juggling Gender: Politics, Sex and Identity*. Courtesy of Tami Gold.

These experiences raised difficult questions about my role as the filmmaker. When does the camera and the presence of a filmmaker and crew unintentionally encourage aggressive behavior? How does the film crew impact social behavior? Was the act of my looking at Jennifer through a camera interpreted as voyeurism, giving strangers permission to do the same?

As a result of these kinds of experiences while shooting, I made the conscious decision to begin the film with my voiceover in order to create a context explaining why I made the film. My hope was that the voiceover would serve as a surrogate to encourage informed looking and responsibility on the part of the audience—the very opposite of voyeurism.

Juggling Gender includes a scene of Jennifer in the bathtub with frontal nudity, female breasts, and the beard. The decision to shoot her in the bathtub was not premeditated. I was filming in her Brooklyn loft on a frigid day and there was no heat. Jennifer decided a hot bath would take the chill out of her body. I asked if I could film as she bathed and she was flattered. I followed her with the camera.

Jennifer is a performance artist and *Juggling Gender* is structured around her performances—fire eating, juggling, lying on beds of nails, and acrobatics. I include a scene of Jennifer performing at the Coney Island Side Show as the Bearded Lady. When I first learned that she was performing in a side show, I was surprised and judgmental. Off-screen we talked about why she would choose to work there, and if by doing this, she was "selling out" and contributing to a negative discourse about what it means to be the "other," the "outsider," the "freak." I included some of her responses from our discussions in the final edit:

This summer, I worked as a bearded lady in the Side Show. It was a little bit heavy and it was something I thought I would never do. With doing the fire, the nails, I'm doing some sideshow acts. So what does fire eating have to do with gender stuff? It is just that it gives you a context in which to look at how the bearded lady was contextualized as a performer . . . it just talks about the atmosphere of the freak show. That's all it really does. But that's something. That's important.

(from *Juggling Gender*)

Jennifer gradually became a proud Coney Island Side Show performer and used the venue to push an unsuspecting audience. In her unapologetic style, she tells the crowd:

The world is full of women who have beards or at least they have the potential to have a beard if only they would reach out and live up to this potential as I myself have done. Instead of spending the time, the money, the energy on the waxing, on shaving! The electrolysis! The plucking! I mean, we all know someone, don't we, who is out there every day with a little bit pluck pluck pluck. I'm talking about my mother, my grandmother! Pluck Pluck Pluck Pluck Pluck Pluck as if they were chickens.

(from *Juggling Gender*)

Through her performance, Jennifer tells the thousands of people who have seen her show that she is not a "chicken." She is not a victim. She has agency. She is the victor. Her script turns the audience into the "chickens" and the conformists. Jennifer's performance becomes a celebration of female agency and feminism.

Having made a legal agreement with Jennifer stating that she would have final edit approval was liberating. If I crossed an ethical line, she was there with veto power. For me this was an imperative. In addition, Jennifer is a performer and uses performance to challenge the rigid constructs of gender; and in doing so often pushed against cultural conventions, using non-traditional venues such as the Coney Island Side Show: "Historically hair has been a symbol of power. That's why the men don't want the women having too much of it in too many places. You get it? Well, forget it" (from *Juggling Gender*).

Since its release in 1992, *Juggling Gender* has had a long and successful life. However, there have been strong reactions from different viewing communities, and though many people loved the film, I also came face to face with strong criticism, particularly around including Jennifer naked in the bathtub and the side show.

For one, the lesbian and gay community was not ready to embrace issues of gender non-conformity. The film was rejected from many lesbian and gay film festivals throughout the country. With pressure, the New York Lesbian and Gay Film Festival agreed to program *Juggling Gender* only if it was screened at the same time as the closing party. A member of the festival advisory board later told me that the festival programmers thought it necessary to "hide the film."

In addition, many mainstream film reviews, including one in *The New York Times*, accused me of voyeurism while simultaneously insinuating that Jennifer Miller was a "freak." When screened at museums, some audiences were openly disgusted and hostile during the Q&A.

My mentor—the father of public-access and community television, George Stoney—left the theater before the film ended when it screened at the New York Film Festival-Video Showcase. Later, he explained that my voiceover at the beginning of the documentary did not provide the context that was needed for a general audience. He also did not agree with me that Jennifer's performance in the Coney Island Side Show was about her agency and power. In fact, he saw it as "selling out."

I questioned if I sufficiently investigated my own politics and the larger meaning of the side show within a corporate capitalist culture that markets our souls at the same time it shuns difference and the "other." Did I need to set up the film more carefully for a general audience?

Now, years later, when I reflect on those discussions, I am not certain that, had I built a stronger framework, those reactions would have been different. Homophobia,[2] transphobia,[3] and the gender binary[4] construct run deep and *Juggling Gender* challenges all these.

IS IT ETHICAL TO PAY SOMEONE TO BE IN YOUR DOCUMENTARY?

Should filmmakers broach the subject of money with the people in our films? Should subjects be paid for their time, information, contacts, and their talent? The issue of money is always present, whether voiced or silent.

Schools of journalism and documentary filmmaking teach that it is unethical to pay subjects to participate. The principle is that payment will impact the testimony and taint the content of a film; that it will compromise intentions and lead people to believe they have to deliver for the dollar. Others argue that documentary filmmakers make money from their films. They are praised as artists and journalists for their storytelling, for their camerawork, or for finding great "characters," while, most of the time, the characters in the films do not get to share in the glory. I understand this argument; however, paying people to be in a documentary is a slippery slope that can lead to a film's content being challenged. What I attempt to do is to pay the main people in my films through royalties once a film is in distribution.

But paying subjects to be in a documentary is not always the major ethical concern. How race and class are represented often go beyond any economic exchange. In a documentary class that I was teaching at New York University, a student presented his final production which included a group of homeless men on the streets. The student filmed while the men danced and mouthed the words to a song blasting from the student's boom box. He explained that the men were drunk, that he had told them how he wanted them to dance, and that he had agreed to pay them before filming. The student was a young white man and the men who danced were African American.

Would it have been any more ethical had the student asked the men to dance and sing, but not offered to pay them? How filmmakers approach the content and the subjects of their films can be equally unethical and exploitative—even without the issue of financial compensation. The student asked a group of homeless men to dance while they were drunk, and this was unethical on many levels regardless of whether he paid them or not.

MAKING A KILLING (1999)

In 1999, Kelly Anderson and I were hired by Corporate Accountability International to produce a documentary about Philip Morris's newly found markets in the former Soviet Union and throughout South East Asia.

While filming in Vietnam, we were told by a public health activist that Philip Morris was illegally marketing cigarettes by hiring young women to work as "Marlboro Girls." Groups of young women dressed in skimpy white blouses, red mini-skirts, and high heels would go from bar to bar seductively handing out free cigarettes to men.

The public health activist suggested we film this marketing tactic as evidence that Philip Morris was, in fact, breaking the law. With her help, we found the bars and coffee shops where free sampling was common, filmed the women on the motor scooters emblazoned with the Marlboro logo, and followed them handing out free cigarettes. It was uncomfortable filming these scenes because we knew we were making the young women nervous. However, we also understood that, in the spirit of investigative reporting, this was the right thing to do. The public had a right to know Philip Morris was breaking the law. "Free sampling" is not harmless. It is one of the main problems identified by health organizations working throughout the world.

When we interviewed Vietnam's director of public health we told her we had filmed the "Marlboro Girls." She had not known that this illegal marketing tactic continued and contacted Philip Morris. The corporation was forced to stop "free sampling" in Vietnam.

Although Kelly and I knew this footage was critical for the film, we were also aware that by enforcing an end to this illegal marketing tactic the young women would likely lose these jobs.

The reality is that we cannot always reconcile all of the ethical dimensions of our work. In fact, the process of documentary filmmaking often replicates power relationships, and if we tried as filmmakers never to compromise anybody, we would not have been able to make a film with the impact of *Making a Killing*.

Ultimately, this scene stands out as the strongest illustration of the illegal practices of one of the largest tobacco companies in the world. I am glad that we captured that material; it helped to pass the first ever International Framework Convention on Tobacco Control.

EVERY MOTHER'S SON (2004)

In 1999, Kelly and I began filming *Every Mother's Son*. The documentary tells the story of three mothers whose sons were unjustly killed by law enforcement.

FIGURE 4.2   Iris Baez, Kadiatou Diallo, and Doris Busch Boskey. Courtesy of Anna Curtis and Tami Gold.

FIGURE 4.3 The Baez family. Courtesy of Kirk Condyles.

At first we followed a group of ten women who had experienced the death of a child at the hands of the police. We filmed them at demonstrations crossing the Brooklyn Bridge, rallies in Harlem, conferences in Chicago, and national mobilizations in Washington D.C.

After one year of filming, we decided to focus on four of the mothers—Iris Baez, Milta Calderon, Kadiato Diallo, and Doris Busch Boskey—and we continued filming with each woman for a few years as their stories unfolded. They told us of their uphill struggles to bring their cases to court and their determination to never stop fighting on behalf of their sons.

Iris Baez, Milta Calderon, Kadiato Diallo, and Doris Busch Boskey are powerful, dynamic, and vulnerable—always vulnerable. At times we became their confidantes and friends, and in turn, we had the responsibility to share their stories with the world. Though we explained that it could take a couple of years to complete the film and that we hoped *Every Mother's Son* would have a PBS broadcast, we never discussed the fact that we could not guarantee that all of their stories would be included in the final film.

While editing, Kelly and I struggled with how to tell the story. We went back and forth between third-person narration versus a more character-driven approach. In addition, *Every Mother's Son* received financial support from ITVS and the contract stipulated that we needed to deliver a one-hour film. Though we requested a longer running time, we were unable to change the agreement.

As directors, we knew the individual stories were complicated and needed time to play out. It was also critical to establish the political climate under newly elected Mayor Rudi

Giuliani. We understood the need to document the growing numbers of stop-and-frisks throughout communities of color, the new aggressive policing tactics, and the growing collective anger in black and Latino communities. All of this needed screen time.

After many attempts to include all four stories, Kelly and I came to the difficult conclusion that we would need to drop one. In the midst of filming, writing proposals, and researching, it had never crossed our minds that this might happen. How could we tell one of the mothers that her story, her experience of loss and pain, would end up on the cutting room floor?

The documentary offered a chance for the mothers to be seen and heard, but it also offered some hope of receiving justice for their child. In the end, documentary filmmakers strive to produce powerful films with the hope of having significant impact. Subsequently, we decided not to use Milta Calderon's story. I remember the conversation we had with Milta and her dignified response; nonetheless, Milta did not hide her sense of rejection.

The Personal Release Form states that there is no guarantee the interviews and footage will be made into a film or included in the final production. Most documentary filmmakers try to maximize the chances that people will sign the Personal Release Forms. In that moment we are concerned about the film. It is almost always a tense moment no matter how we try to spin it.

Should we have risked not getting the release form signed and explained this to all the mothers before we began filming? Would doing so have even made a difference in this situation?

This dilemma had come up before when Kelly and I produced *Out at Work: Lesbians and Gay Men on the Job*. Following the completion of that film in 1997, HBO wanted to acquire it for its renowned series *America Undercover*, with the caveat that we change one of our stories. HBO wanted the film to focus exclusively on the Civil Rights Act of 1964 which does not include sexual orientation as a protected class. In 1997, this meant that gay men and lesbians could be fired in 47 states without any legal recourse because of their sexual orientation.

With this new focus, we would have to omit Nat Keitt, one of the featured characters in the original *Out at Work*. Nat was part of the struggle in New York City to win recognition of domestic partnership for same-sex couples. His story was not about being fired.

Ultimately we decided that the visibility of the issues raised would best be served to have the film included in HBO's documentary series.

The original *Out at Work*, which includes Nat Keitt's story, continues to have great distribution. Nat was invited to speak with the film at major events, so the sting of this decision was less difficult than the experience we later had with *Every Mother's Son*.

As hard as documentary filmmakers try, there are no guarantees that all the people filmed and interviewed will end up in the film.

When we make documentaries we are walking in and out of the lives of real people, and by definition, we have a lot power. Many times, we have more money, more ability to navigate in the world, and ultimately the final decision-making power.

While this chapter is specifically about power differentials and the collaborative process in documentary filmmaking, it raises issues that are also relevant in a variety of media approaches—for example docudrama, reality shows, news, and fiction.

FIGURE 4.4 Nat Keitt from *Out at Work*. Courtesy of Andrea Ades Vasquez and Tami Gold.

In the end, the commitment to full transparency and honesty is the responsibly of the filmmaker. The moral principles that govern my life and my behavior must be in sync with how I approach filmmaking.

TAKE HOME POINTS

- Collaboration and transparency are the foundations of ethical practice.
- Take the time to explain what it means to be the subject of a documentary film. Many people are eager and excited to tell their story, but do not understand that the film will be seen for many years by diverse and potentially expansive audiences.
- Demonstrate your understanding that you are an outsider and that you welcome their opinions and input.
- Be considerate and compassionate. The people in your documentaries are real people and subject to comments and criticism when the film is released. Remember this throughout the editing process.
- Paying someone to be in a documentary can appear to—or can actually result in—the interviewee saying what they think you want them to say since they are being paid. It is best and ethical to not pay the people who are in your documentary.

- The Personal Release Form is a legally binding contract. When interviewing people, take the time to explain why filmmakers need a signed release in order to use them in the film. Consider adjusting the Personal Release Form if someone requests his or her concerns to be added to the contract.
- Clearly explain the editing process and how the final edit will be determined. Be forthright about who has control and "final say" over the final cut of the movie. Discuss the importance of screening rough-cuts together and the final documentary before public viewings.
- All creative decisions have political implications. Remember "art is political."

NOTES

1 The research has turned up some surprises, among them the discovery that striking changes take place during the teen years. These findings have altered long-held assumptions about the timing of brain maturation. In key ways, the brain doesn't look like that of an adult until the early twenties.
2 Homophobia encompasses a range of negative attitudes and feelings toward homosexuality or toward people who are identified or perceived as being lesbian, gay, bisexual, or transgender. It can be expressed as antipathy, contempt, prejudice, aversion, or hatred; may be based on irrational fear; and is sometimes related to religious beliefs.
3 Transphobia is a range of antagonistic attitudes and feelings against transsexuality and transsexual or transgender people, based on the expression of their internal gender identity.
4 The gender binary is the classification of sex and gender into two distinct, opposite, and disconnected forms of masculine and feminine. It is one general type of a gender system.

BIBLIOGRAPHY

Anderson, K., & Gold, T. (Directors). (1997). *Out at work* [Documentary]. United States: New Day Films and AndersonGold Films, Inc.

Anderson, K., & Gold, T. (Directors). (1999). *Making a killing: Philip Morris, Kraft and global tobacco addiction* [Documentary], Corporate Accountability International Distributors.

Anderson, K., & Gold, T. (Directors). (2004). *Every mother's son* [Documentary]. United States: New Day Films.

Cipriani, C. (2014, October 17). The ethics of documentary filmmaking. *Indiewire*. Retrieved from: www.indiewire.com/article/the-ethics-of-documentary-filmmaking-20141017

Gold, T. (Director). (1982). *Looking for love: Teenage mothers* [Documentary]. United States, AndersonGold Films, Inc.

Gold, T. (Director). (1992). *Juggling gender: Politics, sex and identity* [Documentary]. United States: AndersonGold Films, Inc.

Gold, T., Gordon, D., & Lewis, E. (Directors). (1980). *Signed, sealed and delivered: Labor struggle in the post office* [Documentary]. United States: AndersonGold Films, Inc.

National Institute of Mental Health issuing body. (2011). *The teen brain: Still under construction.* (NIMH publication; no. 11-4929).

Pavlosky, D., & Gold, T. (Directors). (2014). *Puzzles: When hate came to town* [Documentary]. United States: New Day Films and AndersonGoldfilms, Inc.

Chapter 5

Identities

Race, Ethnicity, Gender, and Class Privilege

Yoruba Richen

ABSTRACT

The purpose of this chapter is to investigate how race, gender, and class privilege shape and complicate media-making practice. Topics covered include industry diversity, the politics of representation, and insider/outsider voices. The chapter presents effective strategies film-makers use to showcase authentic voices and to tell stories by and about communities that have been marginalized and traditionally underrepresented in the media.

There has been a growing chorus of voices calling out the film industry for its continued lack of diversity in front of and behind the camera. The American Civil Liberties Union (ACLU) recently launched an investigation into the hiring practices of Hollywood studios alleging gender discrimination, which is a civil rights violation (Khatchatourian, 2015).

The documentary and news industry also suffers from some of the same diversity and representation concerns. Stories about people of color are legion (we do not suffer from a dearth of "roles" in the way that you find in fiction film). However, there are still too few filmmakers and media producers of color telling and reporting on stories about their own communities.

The point of view of the media producer is rarely examined. According to documentarians Joe Brewster and Michèle Stephenson (2015):

> [T]oo rarely is the position of whiteness and middle-classness questioned as a position or point of view with a specificity that pertains to the lived experience of a particular racial group . . . Often, their unconscious perspectives precariously reinforce a point-of-view that perpetuate stereotypes of black and brown people that in turn encourage a national and international pattern of perception. We have to work on changing that gaze with a conversation that begins locally, with our white friends about our complicated black and brown lives.

BOX 5.1   GENDER INEQUALITY IN THE FILM AND TELEVISION INDUSTRIES

A University of Southern California study . . . found just 1.9 percent of the top-grossing 100 films from the last two years [2013 and 2014] were directed by women. Meanwhile, a Directors Guild of America analysis revealed that a mere 14 percent of 220 television shows broadcast in 2013 and 2014 were helmed by women. Almost one-third of the shows, or 31 percent, had no women directing any of the episodes during the 2013–14 season.

Another USC study found in 2013 that the percentage of female characters speaking on screen dipped to a five-year low of 28.4 percent in 2012.

(Khatchatourian, 2015)

This lack of analysis about the position/gaze from which media is produced often results in the reinforcement of racial power positions, in addition to perpetuating stereotypical portrayals.[1]

Traditional news coverage has long been cited as trafficking in stereotypes, offering only surface coverage of issues facing communities of color. A recent study by the civil rights organization Color of Change calls out the media bias of news organizations by analyzing the overrepresentation of African Americans as criminals in news coverage (Color of Change, 2015). According to the Radio Television Digital News Association (RTDNA), this is not surprising since television newsrooms are about 80 percent white (Papper, 2014).

The good news is that the democratization of media has allowed more voices to shape and question the dominant narrative. One can look at the #BlackLivesMatter movement to see how the issue of police brutality—which has been an ongoing issue in black communities for, well, ever—has become a real subject that is being talked about and debated in a way that it never has been before. Social media has been crucial in getting out the message that police killings in cities like Ferguson, MI, Cincinnati, OH, Staten Island, NY, and Baltimore, MA were systemic and not isolated incidents.[2] Young people tweeted and posted from the streets during protests that took place in the aftermath of these killings. Pictures of a militarized police force went viral. Citizen journalists using social media reported on these police killings and the militarized response to protests—issues that had been virtually ignored by mainstream media. In effect, a new civil rights movement was born.

The issue of police brutality is still being hotly debated. Real policy changes have resulted including the use of body cameras on police officers in certain cities. Recently, the Obama administration issued a directive prohibiting federal agencies from providing local police forces with certain kinds of military equipment. This would not have happened without the proliferation of social media coverage of these racially charged events.

The film *Selma* (2014) directed by Ava DuVernay came under heavy fire for shifting the traditional narrative. *Selma* is a rare feat on many fronts: it is a historical fiction film about one of the most important chapters of the civil rights movement told from a black perspective,

FIGURE 5.1 #Black Lives Matter Demonstration. The issue of police brutality is being hotly debated in the United States. Widespread public protests have been fueled by a proliferation of social media coverage of these racially charged events. Credit: a katz/Shutterstock.com.

directed by a black female, and backed by a studio. It is the antithesis of the white-male-directed *The Help* (2013) which tells the story of racism in Mississippi mainly through its white protagonist's voice. DuVernay's perspective is unusual to see in a mainstream film and she has been criticized for certain choices that upset the accepted version of history. DuVernay portrayed President Lyndon B. Johnson not as an ally, but as an obstructionist to Martin Luther King Jr.'s efforts to get the Voting Rights bill passed. In an interview with *Rolling Stone*, DuVernay explained, "I wasn't interested in making a white-savior movie; I was interested in making a movie centered on the people of Selma" (Edwards, 2015).

Though this highly regarded film was nominated for an Oscar in the best picture category, many felt DuVernay was snubbed by the Academy when she didn't receive a best director nomination. It was thought by many that her portrayal of LBJ as an obstructionist to the Voting Rights Bill was the major reason she was left out.

DOCUMENTARY

We are experiencing the golden age of documentary. More documentaries are being produced, broadcast, and released in all different mediums—from traditional broadcast television, cable television, DVD, video-on-demand, and streaming.

BOX 5.2   RACIAL INEQUALITY IN THE FILM AND TELEVISION INDUSTRIES

A 2012 investigation by *The Los Angeles Times* revealed that Academy members are 94 percent white, 77 percent male, and only 14 percent are under the age of 50 (Horn, Sperling & Smith, 2012). This includes the documentary branch—though there were no specific numbers for each branch. But this is not just a problem with the Academy—anecdotally, we know that documentary filmmakers of color are underrepresented in the industry. Even though many stories are about people of color, they are not being told by people of color. How does it affect the storytelling process when a white filmmaker is telling a story about a community of color?

Ironically, given the social consciousness generally associated with the documentary format, there has been very little racial and gender analysis of the documentary industry. A recent Sundance study revealed that there are more women directors and producers in the documentary field than in fiction but there is no analysis of the representation of people of color in the report (Silverstein, 2013). If we look at the Academy of Motion Picture Arts and Sciences as the ultimate industry gatekeeper (choosing Oscar awardees), we see that it is overwhelmingly white and male.

THE SEARCH FOR THE AUTHENTIC STORY

How do we make films that are "authentic" in their representation and shed light on a new story, or tell a familiar story in a new way? What are the ethics we need to consider in both the story content and the filmmaking process when we are an outsider to the community we are documenting?

I began conceiving of *The New Black* in November, 2008.[3] It was the night of the presidential election, and I was in California. The months leading up to the election were intensely emotional for many Americans—especially African Americans. The idea of a black president was one we had routinely dismissed as something that would not happen in our lifetime.

At the same time, marriage equality was on the ballot in California, and as the night progressed, it became clear that the right for same-sex couples to marry—which had recently been granted by the California courts—was going to be taken away.

The euphoria about Barack Obama's election was countered by spontaneous protests and visible outrage at the loss of marriage equality. The day after the election, exit polls showed that African Americans voted for Proposition 8—the ballot measure that California would recognize only marriage between a man and a woman as valid—by 70 percent. That these polls later proved incorrect was not enough to counter the narrative that African Americans were to blame for loss of marriage equality, while gays had helped elect Obama.

FIGURE 5.2 Protestors gathered outside the Los Angeles City Hall on November 15, 2008 to protest the passage of Proposition 8. Credit: Gerry Boughan/Shutterstock.com.

Many of us who were members of both communities watched horrified as latent resentments, outright racism, and homophobia bubbled to the top of the national political scene. In addition, the media narrative that took hold was extremely reductive—pitting African Americans against gays while black LGBT voices were virtually erased from the conversation.

As a black lesbian filmmaker, I felt not only a responsibility to try to get the story right and to go deeper than the coverage I was seeing in mainstream media, but also that I could have access and insight into the complicated nature of the issues and the people who were working to bridge the gap between these two communities. I also had the sense that, now that gay marriage had made its way to the top of the political agenda, this story was going to continue to unfold through election cycles and thus was something I could follow over time. On a personal level, I knew making this film might ruffle some feathers—for too long, some in the black community have been reluctant to discuss issues of sexuality. But, I knew on a visceral level that I had to make this documentary, and because of the way the national politics were aligning, this was the time to make it. It doesn't mean that I didn't get criticism from some in my community, but that is sometimes the price you pay for telling a story that hasn't been told before. Making a documentary is often a risky adventure and can open you up to criticism from your subjects, your community, your family—or random people online. But, it is the risk you take in order to fulfill your vision for your film.

FIGURE 5.3 Still image from *The New Black*: Karess Taylor Hughes canvasing for marriage equality in Maryland. Courtesy of Yoruba Richen.

The fact that I was part of the community whom the film was about, made me even more passionate about getting the film finished and sending it out into the world. And, passion is important in making documentaries—it will get you through those times when you have no funding, or are getting rejections from broadcasters, or are slogging away in the edit room trying to figure out how you are going to cut down your 100 hours of footage to a reasonable length.

The final film, *The New Black*, tells the story of the African-American community grappling with gay rights in light of the gay marriage movement and the fight over civil rights. The film documents activists, families, and clergy on both sides of the campaign to legalize gay marriage in Maryland and charts the evolution of this divisive issue within the black community.

THE DIFFERENT RESULTS OF DISTINCT STORYTELLING APPROACHES

The New Black (2013)

I knew from early on that I wanted to include a diversity of voices. So often, African-American viewpoints and experiences are reduced and flattened out to fit a preconceived narrative—for example, that black people are homophobic. I wanted to tell this story in an authentic way—which, for me, meant revealing complexity and nuance about our feelings on LGBT rights in a way that hadn't been seen before.

But, I also did not want to be seen as speaking for all black people. As cultural critic Kobena Mercer writes:

> Although it is always necessary to document and validate the authority of experience ('who feels it, knows it'), the selection of *who* is given the right to speak may also exclude others . . . Not only does this reduce the diversity of black opinion and experiences to a single perspective assumed to be 'typical,' it may reinforce the tokenistic idea that a single film can be regarded as 'representative of every black person's perception of reality.'
>
> (as cited in Klotman & Cutler, 1999, p. xxi)

Though my main characters are activists working to pass the Maryland ballot initiative,[4] one of the other major characters is a black minister leading the charge against the initiative. I worked very hard to include him and others who were against the marriage initiative. I wanted the documentary to present diverse viewpoints with sensitivity and respect.[5]

I do think that my being African American was helpful in getting my subjects—who were mostly African American—to open up to me, no matter which side they were on. But I wouldn't say that were I not black, they would not have shared their stories with me. And, because I made it clear that I was telling both sides of the story, I don't think how I felt about the issues was relevant to them.

I made a choice early on not to be in *The New Black*. Even though it was about communities that I was a part of, it just didn't feel like this was my own personal journey. However, if the filmmaker does choose to be a part of the film, they need to be aware of the implications.

The search for authenticity is also central to Korean American filmmaker Grace Lee's documentary, *The Grace Lee Project* (2005).

The Grace Lee Project (2005)

When Lee was growing up in the Midwest, she was the only Grace Lee she knew. Once she left the Midwest however, everyone she met seemed to know "another Grace Lee." And they all had the same stereotypes about them: all Grace Lees were reserved, dutiful, piano-playing overachievers—common stereotypes of Asian-American women.

In *The Grace Lee Project*, the filmmaker plunges into a funny investigation of those who share her name and those Grace Lees who defy the stereotype—from a fiery social activist to a rebel who tried to burn down her high school. I interviewed Lee about why she chose to make a film about her name. Lee responded:

> I didn't want to make a film about my name—I don't really care about that. I care about this image and stereotype connected to these people talking about the Grace Lee's that they knew. Because the way people would talk about Grace Lee was the way people seem to talk about Asian Americans. So this is larger than just me. It's about anybody who feels pigeonholed.[6]

Lee's search for the authentic "Grace Lee" actually upends the media portrayals of the "authentic" Asian-American female. Lee documents the stories of Asian-American women who are rebels, misfits, and iconoclasts—categories that she identifies with herself, and she re-positions these Grace Lees as authentic as well. Lee calls these "stories that are beneath the surface," and in fact, part of the pleasure in watching the film is that we are seeing complex portrayals of Asian-American females on screen—something we rarely get to see.

Both Grace Lee and I are telling stories that are within our own racial groups. What challenges around authenticity does the filmmaker face when she is telling a story about a community she is not from? How does her position of race and class privilege help or hinder her efforts to get to the "true" story?

March Point (2008)

Directed by Annie Silverstein, *March Point* follows three teenage boys—Travis, Nick, and Cody—from the Swinomish Indian reservation outside Seattle, Washington. The film came about in a unique way. Silverstein was running a youth program called Native Lens in partnership with the tribe. The program worked with teens to teach them media literacy, visual storytelling, and technical skills they could use in order to create their own media. The three boys had gotten in trouble with drugs and alcohol, and Silverstein struck a deal with their counselor for them to participate in the Native Lens program.

The boys end up making a documentary investigating the impact of two oil refineries on their tribal community. Silverstein, who is white, filmed the boys as they make their own documentary; so *March Point* is essentially a film within a film.

As you watch the film, you can see that Silverstein has built trust with the boys who feel free to reveal themselves on screen. This may be the unique nature of her relationship with them—she was a youth worker with the program, helped the boys through some of the challenges that they were facing, and then started making the film with them. Also, the film came about in an organic way with community input. Silverstein and the boys first made a 20-minute short and screened it for the tribe. The tribe had received a grant from the Environmental Protection Agency to support working with youth to investigate environmental threats to the community. Seeing how important the story was, the tribe encouraged the boys to go further and make a feature film.

Though the circumstances that led to *March Point* are unique, their process shows the importance of community buy-in when making social issue documentaries. And when your subjects, or the community who the film is about, become "collaborators" in some sense; they feel invested in the project and may give you access that you otherwise may not get. Finding collaborators comes from building trust, listening carefully, and—where possible—incorporating storylines and scenes suggested by your collaborators. Even if you may not be able to use these stories in the final film—there may be other ways to use them, such as on your website, as part of your education and engagement campaign, or as DVD extras.

March Point is an example of participatory filmmaking. Silverstein explained to me:

> Travis, Nick, and Cody were part of deciding who we talk to, what questions we ask, where we should go next. They were involved in the decision-making process, which

ultimately determines how people are represented and the story being told. The kind of more traditional power dynamic of a filmmaker, especially a white filmmaker, going into a different community and collecting footage that nobody [in the community] sees or knows what the filmmaker's agenda is, what it is that they are even doing—is a totally different dynamic than what we were doing.[7]

March Point really feels not only like the boys' story of their investigation into their tribe's current environmental challenges, but also like their voice is shaping *how* the story is being told. According to Silverstein:

> It was important to make the film accessible to youth. Our narrators were young people. We worked with them on narration, spoken in their own words. We also used the humor and playfulness that they had in their relationships with each other. We tried to work that into the film wherever we could. Since they were the storytellers, it was important to include the personal struggles that they were going through around family or addiction or whatever they were dealing with. In a different film that would never be included. But it felt totally important to include it because this was also a story about the boys becoming leaders, investigators, and storytellers for their people.

In addition, Silverstein is in the film herself, and so what you see is the transparency of the process which subverts the traditional filmmaker/subject power dynamic. Silverstein says this was especially important for her to do as a white filmmaker making a film about a Native tribe: "There was something about showing your hand as a filmmaker, which opens the channels for more dialogue and thought about representation. It wasn't this super seamless narrative where you don't see the spine."

When a filmmaker is of a different racial, ethnic, gender, or class than their subjects, it is especially important to be transparent, participatory, and collaborative with those in front of the camera. Analyzing how the position of the filmmaker affects the storytelling process is an essential step in developing ethical practice.

NAVIGATING INSIDER AND OUTSIDER POSITIONS

As documentarians, we often navigate insider/outsider positions in some way. Often we are documenting communities other than our own. In these situations, we can encounter challenges in both how we make the film and how it is sent out into the world.

March Point (2008)

So how can we avoid exploitation and appropriation when making a documentary about a community other than our own? Silverstein offers one answer in the following comment about her outsider status making *March Point*:

> I was really, really aware that I was non-native. There was no way I couldn't think about my whiteness and privilege. Often white people have a choice about how conscious they

BOX 5.3   CONCERNS OVER CULTURAL APPROPRIATION: THE CASE OF *PARIS IS BURNING* (1990)

The ongoing controversy around the classic documentary *Paris is Burning* is a prime example of how important it is for outsiders to take an ethical stance. *Paris is Burning* documents Harlem's voguing and ball culture—which was created and performed by LGBT people of color. The film was directed by white lesbian filmmaker Jennie Livingston, and it introduced the world to this subculture that had been around for decades.

When the film was released in theaters, it received major accolades. It was also widely criticized by both its subjects and film critics. Some characters in the film felt they deserved payment when the film received financial and critical success (Livingston eventually paid about $55,000 out to performers in the film). The more pervasive feeling at the time was that Livingston had exploited the characters and culture for mainstream (mainly white) consumption and had given nothing back to the community. This feeling was especially strong because many in the ball community lived in poverty and subsequently died from health issues and the dangers of living in the streets.

The controversy recently bubbled up again when an event planned around the 25th anniversary screening of the film in Brooklyn's Prospect Park did not include anybody from the ball community—only Livingston and another white lesbian DJ. The backlash was swift, and the same critiques about the film surfaced—this time on Facebook. Ball community member Elizabeth Marie Rivera summed it up:

> [W]hen someone from outside comes in and takes something from our culture and makes it theirs, that's appropriation. People were wondering, where is the money that [Livingston] made? How is she giving back to the community? It's like, she just came in and made this documentary and she left.
>
> (as cited in O'Hara, 2015)

Both Livingston and the organizers of the event heard the pain and anger of the community—the event was re-organized to feature members of the ball community. Livingston wrote a statement on the event's Facebook page which included the following:

> I'm grateful the conversations here encouraged me to deeply consider my relationships, both to surviving members of the *Paris is Burning* cast and to the TQPOC (Trans/Queer People of Color) community at large. As we move forward towards the 25th anniversary of the film, I need to keep talking with the cast members themselves about how they feel about the film and its continued distribution. And if they're interested, how can the cast and I work together to benefit the community?
>
> (cited in Juzwiak, 2015).

Once again, social media provided a space for people to speak out and change the narrative.

want to be about it especially when it makes them uncomfortable. In the context of filmmaking, you also have a choice about how much you want to think about it. I decided to think about it a lot, and I decided it was ok if I was uncomfortable all the time and that it was important to recognize that and let that be ok if I was going to be working in this cross-cultural environment.

Silverstein's advice to filmmakers is:

> If you are going to be in a position of representing communities other than your own, it is important to allow yourself to say I really don't know anything. Develop your skills as an active listener, find out what is important to the community. Ask questions. Listen some more. Think about what is being said. Reflect on it. Reflect on your own role and some of the assumptions you brought to the table. Reflect on the historical context and how they might be talking differently to you then their neighbors. Always be as sensitive to that as possible.[8]

The Grace Lee Project (2005)

Sometimes we *look* the same as our subjects, but can still be outsiders in other ways. Differences in geography, religion, age, sexuality, and education can make us outsiders to our own racial or ethnic communities. In *The Grace Lee Project*, Lee is an outsider to some of the stories she is documenting. Lee profiles two Korean-American women who are steeped in the Christian church. She shares their name—in addition to their race and gender—but their experience as religious believers is alien to her. Lee lets the viewer know that she is uncomfortable with religious believers and then goes on to sensitively tell the stories of these two women. Though they are not the rebels that Lee is drawn to, they are also authentic Grace Lees. Lee says, "I was very upfront with the audience about how I may be different from these characters I am documenting. There is no monolithic experience of being Asian American. That's just ridiculous."

The New Black (2013)

In *The New Black*, it was also important for me to show that the black community is not monolithic. The role of the black church is a major part of the story, and I did not grow up in the church, nor do I identify as Christian.

How transparent are we in situations involving identity that is not readily apparent? How important is it for us, as documentary storytellers, to analyze how the position of the filmmaker affects the storytelling process and the story itself? I needed access to this community in order to tell the story. I did a number of things to make sure that the church was represented accurately and respectfully.

First, I did my research and watched films and read books about the black church.

Second, I did my best to make sure I was grounded in both the spiritual and the political importance of the church in the black community. I spoke to an array of people who were either currently involved in the church or had grown up in it. I didn't necessarily interview

FIGURE 5.4   Still image from *The New Black*. Sharon Lettman Hicks and her husband Alvin Hicks on election day. Courtesy of Yoruba Richen.

them for the film—but talking to them gave me a sense of the different experiences people had within the church. These experiences were based on many different things including their own sexual identity, the geographical region where they came from, and the denomination they belonged to.

Third, I added a consultant to my production team: a black church scholar who looked at various cuts of the film and gave me feedback about my representation of the church. I still made the creative decisions about all aspects of the story, and all of my decisions were in service to telling a good story. However, it was very important to have another pair of eyes that were more steeped in this aspect of the culture than I was. The consultant was able to point out inconsistencies in scriptural interpretation and check historical accuracy—things I may not have picked up on without her.

Both Lee's experience and mine shows how we filmmakers may share identity character-istics with our subjects, but we also differ from them in ways that complicate our insider status.

TONE, GENRE, AND APPROACH

Grace Lee takes a humorous approach as she films herself going on her journey to document the "real" Grace Lee. In *The Grace Lee Project*, Lee explains that she is in the film because she had to show why she chose this topic and made this journey:

Though on the surface it was about my name, it really was about my search for Asian-American identity. And there is a way to talk about identity—there are a lot of painful things about identity—but there's also a lot of absurdity around identity that is funny. I had come up in that world of documentaries about identity and history and I thought there is another way—maybe my angle into this is different because it's funny and ridiculous but there's something deeper there. It was about trying to tell something personal that reflected who I was—but was also universal.[9]

In *The New Black*, I chose a more journalistic approach than Lee did for *The Grace Lee Project*. This allowed me to incorporate different viewpoints and follow an unfolding political event. I found that even when you are part of the group that the story is about, other challenges arise. Because we are used to seeing racially stereotyped portrayals, we can be reluctant to show things that are not flattering or that seemingly play into these stereotypes. It put me in a funny bind: part of my motivation for making the film was to counter the narrative that black people are more homophobic then other racial groups because of the influence of the black church; but in order to complicate that narrative, I had to acknowledge that homophobia in the church was indeed a real thing.

FIGURE 5.5 At a demonstration on November 22, 2008 in Sacramento, California against the passage of Proposition 8, a protestor holds up a sign that evokes religious rhetoric. Credit: Karin Hildebrand Lau/Shutterstock.com.

The trick was to go deeper—I needed to show where this homophobia might be coming from. Why has the church been so influential in African-American lives, both historically and today? How and why had the church been politicized on the LGBT issue in the last few years? What work was being done in different congregations to address this? I explored all these issues in the film—looking at how the black family had been regulated since the time of slavery, how that complicated our feelings about gay marriage, how the black church was at the center of the civil rights movement, and how the Christian right had created a political strategy starting in the 1990s to work with conservative black church leaders to speak against LGBT rights.[10]

I also found that the issue was even more complicated than I had thought. Though homophobia was—and still is—a fact in black churches, there was also an evolution that was happening around the issue. *The New Black* shows how this conversation is happening not only politically but also within black communities, churches, and families.

CREWING UP

Do production choices and crew selection impact content?

In *March Point*, the primary crew were the boys and Silverstein. The fact that the boys were the interviewers allowed them to access their interviewees in a different way. Silverstein explains:

> People would speak differently to me than they would speak to the boys. It's interesting as a white, non-native person to be working on a project in collaboration with people from the tribe because that becomes so much more apparent than if I had a white crew and myself and we were just doing the interviewing ourselves.

The fact that the crew was the boys from that tribe shaped how the story was told: not only because of race, but also because they were interviewing their neighbors, friends, and family members. As Silverstein says, "They had insight, connections and trust from the community—how could it not affect what we were getting on camera?"

Though *The New Black* is not an example of participatory filmmaking, I did take elements from that approach because I thought it would garner some interesting results. There is a scene where one of my main characters—Sharon Lettman Hicks—hosts a family barbeque. Sharon ends up talking to various family members about how they feel about the work she is doing around LGBT rights. The scene works well because Sharon is able to elicit emotion, humor, conflict, and honesty from her family members in a way that I don't think I could have if I was asking the questions.

Early on, it became apparent to me that I needed to gain access to spaces that were sacred (the church) and were personal. I needed to speak with my subjects about sensitive issues of race, sexuality, and politics. These hot-button topics can make people uncomfortable. I thought one way to mitigate this was to make sure my crew (camera person and sound person) were also people of color. I knew this was the right choice when I went to film a scene where one of my subjects—Karess Taylor Hughes—came out to her foster mother. Karess was very nervous about doing this, but she felt her mom would feel more comfortable being on camera since both the cinematographer and the director were women of color.

Other larger factors also informed who I hired as part of my crew. I believe that if we are going to make films about a community, then we should put in a good faith effort to have representatives of that community be part of the filmmaking process—especially when the filmmaker is in a position of race, class, or gender privilege.

One of my larger goals is to increase the numbers of us—people of color—telling our own stories. When I do get the opportunity to direct, I feel it is my responsibility to try to find other crew of color so that we get the experience, training, and credit to be able to make more films. Of course that is not the only factor in my hiring—I want my crew to be professional, creative, and good team players—but it is certainly a factor.

DOCUMENTARY AS A TOOL FOR SOCIAL CHANGE

Over the last few years, social issue documentary has been increasingly used as part of movement-building and educational campaigns. From the inception, I knew that I wanted to use *The New Black* as an educational and engagement tool. I knew the film could help advance dialogue around the intersection of LGBT and racial justice, that it could build bridges across communities who support LGBT rights in general and communities who support black LGBT rights in particular.

This meant that I had to start thinking about this use of the film as I was making the film—that it would, in fact, inform the film I was making. It would also affect the roll-out of the film. I shot from 2010 through the election in November 2012. The film was finished in June 2013. My team and I began developing our engagement strategy in early 2013—while we were still editing. The main thing we did was screen clips from the film to a racially diverse group of grassroots LGBT activists. I knew that they would be the people most equipped to incorporate the film into the work they were already doing. We gave them a questionnaire asking how they could see using the film in their own work, what questions it raised for them, and what they wanted to see more of in the finished film. And, although this did not dictate my artistic choices, I did take this feedback into consideration as I finished making the film. More importantly, I began early relationships with the activists who were now anticipating the release of the film and were primed to use it in their organizations, schools, and churches.

The film premiered at the Los Angeles Film Festival in June 2013. It was released theatrically in February 2014 and broadcast on PBS's *Independent Lens* in June 2014. In August 2013, we held two brain trusts—in New York City at the Ford Foundation, and in Washington, D.C., at the Human Rights Campaign headquarters. These meetings convened key stakeholders in LGBT and African-American civil rights and social justice issues. Attendees included the NAACP, Fellowship of Affirming Ministries, and the U.S. Department of Justice. They participated in highly structured conversations about campaign goals and objectives. My team took the information from these meetings and created an engagement campaign entitled "Empowering Equality."

BOX 5.4   "EMPOWERING EQUALITY": THE EDUCATION AND ENGAGEMENT CAMPAIGN FOR *THE NEW BLACK*

We focused on three key areas as part of an overarching education and engagement effort:

1. *Faith-based Initiatives* where we are working with individuals, pastors, and congregations in promoting dialogue and policies that will support their organizations in becoming welcoming and affirming churches and institutions.
2. *Institutional and Organizational Development* where we support the development of diversity and inclusion practices within universities, corporations, and non-profit organizations that want to create and sustain diverse, inclusive environments.
3. *Grassroots Organizing* which entails providing support to grassroots organizations employing the film in their efforts toward LGBT acceptance and inclusion at the local and community level.

We launched a series of activities around this strategy. What has been most amazing about this process is that the outreach campaign is still going strong two years after the film's release. We have also seen some real impact. One of our engagement highlights is our Historically Black Colleges and Universities (HBCU) initiative. Historically, the mission of HBCUs has included social justice, but these campus cultures remain relatively conservative and have been slow to extend this mission to the promotion of LGBT rights. Through our groundbreaking initiative, we have worked with seven HBCUs to screen the film, engage in post-screening dialogues, and support the launch of LGBT diversity and inclusiveness work on campuses.

Education and engagement was also central to the goals of the *March Point* filmmakers. Indeed, the film came out of an organic process reflecting what the Swimonesh tribe felt was important.

The intention of *March Point* was to educate and inform the public about environmental threats to native land. Silverstein says:

The film was used in tribal nation schools and universities across the country. We often held post-screening discussions with the youth. We developed curriculum with our funder enabling communities to screen the material and have discussions. The film contributed to re-opening the legal case between the tribe and the refineries. I think it had a real impact. One of the really important consequences of the film is that young, native people watching it are encouraged to tell their stories too.

Finally, there is no one way to ethically make films that take into consideration issues of race, gender, and class privilege. It is important to continually interrogate your own process and to know that these ethical challenges are usually ongoing and can come up in all stages of production.

TAKE HOME POINTS

- Race/Gender/Class: your race, gender, or class position will influence how subjects/actors/interviewees respond to you. Being aware of your own position can also provide you with unique perspectives on certain issues.
- Stereotypes: when conceiving a media project, be aware of how easy it can be to fall back on stereotypes. Make sure the subjects/actors in your project are complex. Be sure to contextualize: where and how someone lives, as well as cultural variables can provide viewers with greater understanding of story content and meanings.
- Crewing Up: be deliberate with crew selection. Pay careful attention to the racial and gender composition of the crew. This can make those in front of your camera more or less at ease. Consider selecting crew from the community your film is about. This can help establish greater trust and ease of communication.
- Process: if appropriate to your story, make sure your film reflects what the community wants or needs. Making movies, whether documentary or fiction, involves collaboration. Keep in mind that you are collaborating most with those in front of your camera. This includes individuals as well as communities.
- Audience: identify your audience and how you will get them to see your film. Think about what you want your audience to do after watching the film. This can include: grassroots activism, further discussion with others about issues raised, and opportunities to share their own stories.
- Outreach and Engagement: your involvement with the media project doesn't end when the last scene is filmed. It is important to continue to remain connected with the subject. Arranging film festival screenings, as well as educational events and speaking engagements can insure that the issues raised in the film are brought to a wider audience.

NOTES

1 In cinema studies, "the gaze" means a particular way of looking at things. For example, the "male gaze" is about looking and framing from a masculine perspective. See also, Mulvey (1975).
2 See Kang's (2015) widely circulated article in *The New York Times Magazine* about racial violence stirred by police killings of black males.
3 The trailer for *The New Black* is available on the companion website: www.newblackfilm.com/
4 The ballot measure—Proposition 6—was called the Civil Marriage Protection Act and it allowed gay and lesbian couples to get a civil marriage license in Maryland, while allowing clergy and religious institutions the freedom to choose the type of marriage they were willing to recognize.
5 You can watch this clip from *The New Black* at https://vimeo.com/68252396. The password is "press clips."
6 Unless otherwise noted, all the quotes by Grace Lee in this chapter are from an interview I conducted with her on April 7, 2015.
7 Unless otherwise noted, all the quotes by Annie Silverstein in this chapter are from an interview I conducted with her on April 10, 2015.
8 You can watch this clip from *March Point* at: https://vimeo.com/28959731.
9 You can watch this clip from *The Grace Lee Project* at http://gracelee.net/GraceLee.m4v. The clip is at 12:15–14:34.
10 You can watch clip 2 from *The New Black* at https://vimeo.com/68250960. The password is "press clips."

BIBLIOGRAPHY

Bernard, S. C. (2011). *Documentary storytelling* (3rd ed.). Burlington, MA: Focal Press.

Brewster, J., & Stephenson, M. (2015, April 25). Hollywood: The power of the white gaze. *The Huffington Post*. Retrieved from: www.huffingtonpost.com/joe-brewster/hollywood-the-power-of-th_b_6738578.html

Buckley, C. (2015, May 12). ACLU, citing bias against women, wants inquiry into Hollywood's hiring practices. *The New York Times*. Retrieved from www.nytimes.com/2015/05/13/movies/aclu-citing-bias-against-women-wants-inquiry-into-hollywoods-hiring-practices.html

Color of Change. (2015, March). Not to be trusted: Dangerous levels of inaccuracy in TV crime reporting in NYC. Retrieved from https://s3.amazonaws.com/s3.colorofchange.org/images/ColorOfChangeNewsAccuracyReportCardNYC.pdf

DuVernay, A. (Director). (2014). *Selma* [Motion Picture]. Paramount Pictures.

Edwards, G. (2015, January 5). We shall overcome: Ava DuVernay on making *Selma*. *Rolling Stone*. Retrieved from: www.rollingstone.com/movies/features/ava-duvernay-on-making-selma-20150105

Horn, J., Sperling, N., & Smith, D. (2012). Unmasking the Academy: Oscar voters overwhelmingly white, male. *The Los Angeles Times*. Retrieved from: www.latimes.com/entertainment/envelope/oscars/la-et-unmasking-oscar-academy-project-20120219-story.html#page=1

Juzwiak, R. (2015, May 14). *Paris is Burning* screening sparks furor, calls for boycott. *Defamer*. Retrieved from: http://defamer.gawker.com/paris-is-burning-screening-sparks-furor-calls-for-boyc-1704488524

Kang, J. C. (2015, May 4). "Our demand is simple: Stop killing us." How a group of black social media activists built the nation's first 21st-century civil rights movement. *The New York Times Magazine*. Retrieved from: www.nytimes.com/2015/05/10/magazine/our-demand-is-simple-stop-killing-us.html?_r=0

Khatchatourian, M. (2015, May 12). Hollywood's "biased" hiring practices against women subject of ACLU inquiry. *Variety*. Retrieved from: variety.com/2015/biz/news/hollywoods-biased-hiring-practices-against-women-subject-of-a-c-l-u-inquiry-1201493101/

Klotman, P. R., & Cutler, J. K. (Eds.). (1999). *Struggles for representation: African American documentary film and video*. Bloomington, IN: Indiana University Press.

Lee, G. (Director). (2005). *The Grace Lee Project* [Documentary]. Women Make Movies.

Mercer, K. (1994). Black is . . . Black ain't. *Sight and Sound* 4(8): 22–23.

Mulvey, L. (1975). Visual pleasure and narrative cinema. *Screen* 16(3): 6–18.

O'Hara, M. E. (2015, May 13). Why are LGBT people of color protesting the screening of this cult film classic? *The Daily Dot*. Retrieved from: www.dailydot.com/lifestyle/paris-is-burning-facebook-lgbtq-controversy/

Papper, B. (2014, July 28). Women, minorities make newsroom gains. *The Radio Television Digital News Association*. Retrieved from: www.rtdna.org/article/women_minorities_make_newsroom_gains#.VXx4BlVVikp

Rabiger, M. (2009). *Directing the documentary* (6th ed.). Burlington, MA: Focal Press.

Richen, Y. (Director). (2013). *The new black* [Documentary]. United States: Promised Land Film Distribution.

Richen, Y. (2015, January 20). #OscarSoWhite includes the documentary category, too. *Women and Hollywood*. Retrieved from: http://blogs.indiewire.com/womenandhollywood/guest-post-oscarsowhite-includes-the-documentary-category-too-20150120

Riggs, M. (Director). (1994). *Black is . . . black ain't* [Motion Picture]. Newsreel.

Silverstein, A., & Rector, T. (Directors). (2008). *March Point* [Documentary]. Long House Media/Independent Lens.

Silverstein, M. (2013, January 21). Sundance Institute and Women in Film release unprecedented study on women directors. *Women and Hollywood.* Retrieved from: http://blogs.indiewire.com/womenandhollywood/sundance-institute-and-women-in-film-release-unprecedented-study-on-women-directors

Taylor, T. (Director). (2011). *The help* [Motion Picture]. Walt Disney Studios Motion Pictures.

Wildermuth, J. (n.d.). Black support for prop. 8 called exaggeration. *SF Gate.com.* Retrieved from: www.sfgate.com/politics/article/Black-support-for-Prop-8-called-exaggeration-3177138.php

Section Two # Point and Shoot

Introduction to Section Two
Point and Shoot

Annette Danto and Mobina Hashmi

LOOKING through a camera and bringing things to life in new ways is empowering and magical. No longer do you need to be a passive spectator. Media creation and participation has never been more accessible.

Coming up with a concept or idea for a story is thrilling. But then, taking that idea and turning it into the nuts and bolts of production, a digital news story, or a new media presentation is another matter. Production, with its myriad demands, is generally nerve-wracking and often unpredictable.

Narrative feature film production is stressful, especially when it comes to day-to-day directing, cinematography, and coordination of actors and crew. Uncontrollable aspects such as weather, health of cast and crew, or unpredictable location mishaps can call for sudden changes. Resolving unanticipated situations demands immediate focus.[1]

BOX 1 ON THE SET OF *CLOSE ENCOUNTERS OF THE THIRD KIND* (1977)

The spaceship sinks slowly to the ground, billowing dust from its mammoth landing gear. The bottom slides open. A blinding light streams out of the ship, enveloping the awe struck engineers and astronauts.

A large ramp appears in the sulphorous fog, a small spindly extraterrestrial figure slowly glides and rolls down the ramp . . . A creature comes forward haltingly. Then breaks into a disco Hustle. "Cut" yells Steven Spielberg to the rubber-suited children. "Stop fooling around!"

(Balaban, 1978, pp. 105–106)

FIGURE S2.1   Production still from *Out of My Hand* (2014), a feature film directed by Takeshi Fukunaga, cinematography by the late Ryo Murakami. A story of a Liberian rubber plantation worker with dreams of migrating to the United States. Courtesy of Donari Braxton and Takeshi Fukunaga.

Few other forms of media production have the same scale and complexity of coordination as narrative feature film production. Regardless of medium or genre, you can find yourself in unpredictable circumstances that have ethical dimensions, requiring quick but careful decision-making.

MEDIUM-SPECIFIC PRODUCTION

Production duration varies widely. Documentary or narrative film production can go on for months or years. With new media production, speed and duration is compressed and expedited. There is less time to ponder if a blog post or tweet might have negative ramifications.

Often done in privacy, new media has few gatekeepers. Even if there are gatekeepers such as editors or executive producers, writing news stories on deadline, or making television programs on a tight schedule requires juggling what writers, network executives, and advertisers want to achieve. This can create circumstances where decisions about ethical content require speedy and sometimes instantaneous self-regulation from the media creator.

Asking important questions during the production process will help identify potentially unethical actions and consequences.

- Are you looking for content that depicts pain, suffering, and humiliation? Why?
- What is the person in front of your camera getting out of being a part of your media project?
- Remember that your choices and selections can represent "truth" and "reality" for your audience. Whose truth are you presenting and are your technical framing choices ignoring some realities?
- How do you know the information you are receiving from your sources is accurate?

ETHICAL CONSIDERATIONS IN PRODUCTION

Cheap Thrills or Emotional Connection?

Great documentaries and fictions films often tell stories involving human pain and suffering. Many questions arise when weighing how best to cover a tragic story. How does one visually capture human tragedy respectfully and without sensationalism?

Our high tolerance for visual violence, destruction, and cruelty is showcased regularly on the internet, in films and television programs and most dramatically in computer games. Even 30 years ago this level of media violence would not have been tolerated. Today, 24-hour disaster news coverage, often in real-time, simulates an action movie. Mayhem is entertainment.Has the excessive amount of media violence created emotional detachment for media-makers and audiences? Is it possible to provide entertainment that stirs audience emotion without desensitizing viewers to human degradation?

Historically, the camera has acted as witness, documenting evidence of unfathomable episodes of human barbarism. In these situations, the graphic nature of visual footage serves an important purpose—to represent as much as possible the full horror of the atrocities. .Important questions to ask include: How will these images be used? Who is the target audience? Will revealing the identities of the people on-camera harm them in any way? What will happen to them after being part of this story?

The ethical principle of sincerity, that is, honestly saying what you really believe rather than what you think will achieve your ends, is a good one to keep in mind. Drawing on the work of moral philosopher Bernard Williams (2002), Nick Couldry (2006) explains that "sincerity requires the speaker, or the writer, to pay attention to what the recipient is likely to believe as a result of what she says or writes" (p. 128). Keeping this principle at the forefront reminds you of your ethical obligations to the others who are part of the conversation and with whom your media practice forges a relationship.

Complex decisions need to be made; sometimes instantly, and at other times, with less urgency. Regardless of the time factor, technical framing decisions when covering stories about human suffering are never easy or straightforward. There is no simple or clear-cut

FIGURE S2.2 *Shanti's Story* (2004), directed by Annette Danto for Pathfinder International. An eclectic production team of doctors, epidemiologists, nurses, and media-makers from India, Asia, and the United States collaborated on this narrative film, designed to combat unsafe abortion practices in rural regions. A variety of languages and rural dialects were spoken on the set, adding to the diverse and multilayered production experience. Courtesy of: Ilango Samuel Peter.

ethical approach. Media-makers must always weigh and calculate what to present and how best to present it.[2]

Is Seeing Still Believing?

Have new technologies eroded the public's trust in what they see on screen? For visual media production, since the mid-1990s, inexpensive, portable cameras and editing software have blurred lines and created complex relationships between director and actor, subject and object, filmmaker and film.

Docudrama, reality productions, and surveillance-style techniques present dilemmas for media-makers concerned about truth, representation, and the trusting relationship between filmmaker and audience. Silverstone (2007) argues that "[t]he media are becoming environmental . . . [in the] sense of the media as tightly and dialectically intertwined with the everyday. We have become dependent on the media for the conduct of everyday life" (p. 5).

One consequence of this pervasive media environment is that technical framing approaches that were once predictable and associated with a certain genre of media are now appropriated, quoted, parodied, and altered so that they no longer function as a reliable signifier of "reality." The public has become confused about what is real and what is staged. This confusion is only magnified by the fact that, for many of us, thanks to mobile media, the boundaries between our virtual and physical worlds is blurred. For example, as numerous popular anecdotes about online dating suggest, what might be acceptable identity play online can be seen as unacceptable distortion of truth in our material lives. The novel dilemma here is deciding when and in what contexts performing realism is an ethical aesthetic or creative choice, and when representing reality is the correct decision.

Transparency as an Ethical Value

What role does the filmmaker play in influencing what is happening in front of the camera, and how much of this influence is actually disclosed to the viewer? For documentary audiences in particular, transparency is important. Audiences need to believe they can trust the actions of the filmmaker and media team. Audiences believe that the filmmaker is making selections and choices that represent "truth" and reality.[3]

One factor that scholars interested in the role of media in sustaining democracy worry about is the growing commercialization of all our media. If a news story or a documentary is produced with the expectation that it will be commercially profitable, how can audiences know that they are being presented with the unvarnished truth and not a crowd-pleasing version of it?

These concerns are made more urgent, in part, by affordable production gear such as lightweight compact cameras and sound devices that have paved the way for an abundance of media content dealing with self-exploration. Productions about personal traumas are increasingly common. Without a sensitive approach to the production of such material the production process can be disturbing, harsh and destructive to those in front of and behind the camera. For example, as Douglas Rushkoff explores in the documentary *Generation Like* (2014), some young people who are successful YouTube stars are tempted to play out more and more of their lives for an audience in the search for higher view counts, "likes," and advertising revenue or even production contracts.

There continues to be controversy surrounding production strategies when it comes to directing and cinematography. In fiction filmmaking there are approaches to directing actors/actresses that are ethically questionable. Are there lines that should never be crossed when working with actors? Do questionable means ever justify the potential good that will come from a story?

Production Collaboration

Documentary and fiction production nearly always requires collaboration with others, often under stressful circumstances. Participating in new media or social media can be done in relative isolation.

When working with a group of people, conflict is inevitable. Both a cast and crew of hundreds and a cast and crew of three must always balance the creative and practical demands of production. Clear communication skills and diplomacy are essential when navigating

FIGURE S2.3   Lightweight, compact cameras have paved the way for an abundance of media content. Courtesy of Ilango Samuel Peter.

conflict. If you don't agree with a decision being made, but are not in a position to alter that decision, it is important to recognize that being a member of a crew or team sometimes means tolerating differences of opinion.

If you are in a position where you have the power to make hiring or casting decisions, you might make a conscious effort to create a diverse team. Or, you might be the one (or one of a few) who is the "diversity" in the team. Shohat and Stam (1994) point out that in such instances, members of minority communities are often forced to carry the "burden of representation" where they are expected to stand in for or speak on behalf of their entire group (pp. 182–188). If you are a member of the majority group, the ethical burden falls on you to be self-reflexive about your own biases and not expect, for example, the only woman on the sports news beat to represent all women (Genovese, 2015).

As we strive for more inclusive and collaborative production environments, it is also important to remember that diversity cannot be simply the inclusion of more minority bodies and faces. It crucially also involves the much more difficult task of reworking majority perspectives to acknowledge and address privilege, a process that often involves being open to challenges to existing power hierarchies from diverse voices and perspectives. For example, the recognition that the economic and cultural power of U.S. film and television styles and narratives often create the norm to which media producers from other parts of the world have to adapt, poses a very real ethical challenge to U.S media producers (Mendelson, 2015). Ethical production decisions therefore include openness to diverse aesthetic choices and genuinely listening to crew and cast voices.

The director and cinematographer generally establish the tone on a production. How are people encouraged to get things accomplished? Are orders barked from above, or are people treated respectfully? The attitude of key crew members not only sets the mood on the set, but can also actively discourage more vulnerable crew members from speaking up. Sensitive collaboration means understanding what it might be like to be in another person's place, whether a vulnerable interview subject, an actor or a crew member.

OVERVIEW OF CHAPTERS

Section Two is divided into five chapters:

- Ethical Challenges for the Cinematographer
- Technical Framing
- To Zoom or Not to Zoom?
- Hidden Camera: A Conversation on Surveillance
- The Ethics of Sound

In the initial chapter, "Ethical Challenges for the Cinematographer," Scott Sinkler discusses the power of the camera lens: who and what do we choose to include in our frames? What conscious and unconscious choices do we make each and every time we point a camera. Do we always let people know we are including them in our frame? In her chapter, "Technical Framing," Annette Danto explores the potentially misleading nature of composition choices. Technical framing decisions form an audience's field of view by directing what the viewer sees and how. When working with graphic and sensationalized material, media-makers have a range of creative and technical options. Determining major goals of the project is a first step. The relative importance of sparking or provoking an audience, desensitizing or deadening the audience, instilling compassion and humanity in an audience—all are possibilities and need to be clearly thought through and linked to technical framing selections. Jon Alpert's chapter, "To Zoom or Not to Zoom?" explores ethical cinematic approaches to documenting pain and suffering. Should you use a telephoto lens, or go hand-held? Choices relating to camera position, shot size, composition, and eye line always need to be made. These are always subjective choices. In "Hidden Camera: A Conversation on Surveillance," philosopher and computer scientist Samir Chopra unpacks assumptions about privacy and accountability that inform contemporary concerns about surveillance. Is surveillance ever ethically justifiable? The power differentials between those doing the surveillance and those being surveilled require us to ask how the images or information gained through surveillance are used. Chopra explains that instead of the focus on privacy, a more productive line of thinking centers on asking what kinds of lives are enabled or made impossible by surveillance. In his chapter, "The Ethics of Sound," John Gurrin analyzes the links between technical choices, story content, and the ethical treatment of actors and subjects. What is the emotional impact of sound design on the audience? What role does sound authenticity serve when recreating a world for the viewer?

Each chapter provides detailed case studies of ethical predicaments that can occur during production. Suggested approaches and best practices are presented. The list of key take home points at the conclusion of each chapter offer guidance in navigating ethical dilemmas likely to occur during production.

When you point and shoot, keep these ethical fundamentals in mind:

- Everyone should be treated fairly. There should be no double standards.
- Collaboration requires being open to differences of opinion. Refrain from automatically labeling opposite choices as immoral.
- Be accountable for your decisions.
- Do not shy away from ethical challenges. Ignoring difficult questions will not make them go away.

NOTES

1 Murphy's Law is a well-known saying typically stated as, "Anything that can go wrong, will go wrong." The law's name apparently grew out of attempts to use new measurement devices developed by the eponymous Edward Murphy. The phrase was coined in reaction to something Murphy said when his devices failed to perform. To learn more about its origin, see *A History of Murphy's Law* by Nick T. Spark (2006).
2 It is often best to use a long lens at a distance when filming people in pain. This is less intrusive than pointing cameras directly in the faces of crime victims or the suffering.
3 Very much about some of the ethical complexities of documentary media-making, a *New York Times* article by journalist Ben Konigsberg highlights interviews with documentarians concerned about manipulation in the documentary production process (June 26, 2015, "Documentary filmmakers talk about manipulation in their work")

BIBLIOGRAPHY

Anderson, K., Lucas, M., & Hurbis-Cherrier, M. (2016). *Documentary voice & vision: A creative approach to non-fiction media production*. New York, NY: Routledge.

Balaban, B. (1978). *Close Encounters of the Third Kind diary*. New York, NY: Paradise Press.

Bugeja, M. J. (2008). *Living ethics: Across media platforms*. New York, NY: Oxford University Press.

Couldry, N. (2006). *Listening beyond the echoes: Media, ethics and agency in an uncertain world*. Boulder, CO: Paradigm.

Craig, D. (2006). *The ethics of the story: Using narrative techniques responsibly in journalism*. Lanham, MD: Rowman & Littlefield.

Danto, A. (Director). (2004). *Shanti's Story*. [Motion Picture]. Belgaum, Karnataka, India: Pathfinder International.

DeKoven, L. (2006). *Changing direction: A practical approach to directing actors in film and theatre*. Boston, MA: Focal Press.

Genovese, J. (2015). Sports television reporters and the negotiation of fragmented professional identities. *Communication, Culture & Critique, 8*(1): 55–72.

Holben, J. (2016). *Behind the lens: Dispatches from the cinematographic trenches.* New York, NY: Focal Press.

Hurbis-Cherrier, M. (2012). *Voice & vision: A creative approach to narrative film and DV production.* Burlington, MA: Focal Press.

Koughan, F. (Writer), & Rushkoff, D. (Writer). (2014). *Frontline: Generation like* [Television series episode]. Public Broadcasting Service.

Mendelson, S. (2015, November 27). Lionsgate responds to *Gods of Egypt* whitewashing controversy. *Forbes.* Retrieved from: www.forbes.com/sites/scottmendelson/2015/11/27/exclusive-lionsgate-responds-to-gods-of-egypt-whitewashing-controversy/

Ramey, K. (2016). *Experimental filmmaking: Break the machine.* Burlington, MA: Focal Press.

Rea, P. W., & Irving, D. K. (2015). *Producing and directing the short and film video.* Burlington, MA: Focal Press.

Rizzo, M. (2015). *The art direction handbook for film & television* (2nd ed.). New York, NY, & London, UK: Focal Press.

Rooney, B., & Belli, M. L. (2016). *Directors tell the story: Master the craft of television and film directing* (2nd ed.). Waltham, MA: Focal Press.

Shohat, E., & Stam, R. (1994). *Unthinking eurocentrism: Multiculturalism and the media.* London, UK, & New York, NY: Routledge.

Silverstone, R. (2007). *Media and morality.* Cambridge, MA: Polity Press.

Simpson, R., & Coté, W. E. (2006). *Covering violence: A guide to ethical reporting about victims and trauma* (2nd ed.). New York, NY: Columbia University Press.

Sloan, W. D., & Mackay, J. B. (2007). *Media bias: Finding it, fixing it.* Jefferson, NJ: McFarland & Co.

Spark, N. (2006). *A History of Murphy's Law.* Lulu.com.

Ward, S. J., & Wasserman, H. (2010). *Media ethics beyond borders: A global perspective.* New York, NY: Routledge.

Wheeler, T. (2002). *Phototruth or photofiction? Ethics and media imagery in the digital age.* Mahwah, NJ: Lawrence Erlbaum Associates.

Williams, B. A. O. (2002). *Truth & truthfulness: An essay in genealogy.* Princeton, NJ: Princeton University Press.

Chapter 6

Ethical Challenges for the Cinematographer

Scott Sinkler

ABSTRACT

This chapter looks at the ethics of making media from the perspective of the photographer or the person behind the camera. When real-life issues arise, there will often be competing considerations that the cameraperson will have to weigh and balance. The camera is the portal between the real world and the media universe—the exact location where fleeting events are frozen in time and engraved into the permanent record.

> A photograph is a moral decision taken in one eighth of a second.
>
> Salman Rushdie (1999, p. 13)

Operating a film or video camera requires numerous choices and split-second decisions. Unlike ethical issues that come up during planning or editing, those that arise while filming often do so suddenly with little time for thinking through the implications. How the camera is used at those moments will determine the range of ethical or unethical uses the material can be put to later on. Questions of truth, distortion, context, fairness, exploitation, consent, doing harm, and privacy must be assessed and addressed in real time—so it's essential to have a good grasp of them before you pick up the camera.

In 2013, the number of mobile phones in use on the planet exceeded the world's population for the first time, and at least 85 percent of those phones had cameras. Some predict that in the near future, almost every human being will be able to record high-quality video and distribute it around the world with the push of a button (Pramis, 2013). This new reality means that the ethical dimensions of how images and media are created and used increase in importance every day. As channels of distribution morph and multiply, clear distinctions between news, entertainment, propaganda, surveillance, documentary, and home movies become blurred.

From 40,000-year-old cave paintings to this morning's viral video, the recording and sharing of images has allowed us to document, analyze, interpret, and shape our understanding

FIGURE 6.1   Fifteen-year-old Fabienne Cherisma, shot in the head by police after looting three picture frames in the wake of Haiti's 2010 earthquake. More than a dozen photographers captured images of her lifeless body. Several won awards for their work. Violating an unspoken rule, Nathan Weber stepped back to capture the larger context, unleashing a storm of controversy about media ethics. Credit: Nathan Weber/NBW Photo.[1]

of the world and of ourselves (Sample, 2014). With the invention of photography, the image became an almost perfect analogue of its subject and, based on its apparent veracity, is used today as evidence in crimes, for security and identification, for scientific research, to preserve history, and to report the news. The power of its realism gives us confidence that what we see in it is the truth. It's in the potential gap between truth and representation that some important ethical issues reside (Poe, 1840).

The First Amendment to the Constitution of the United States was written to protect free speech before the invention of photography, but it has expanded to encompass virtually all forms of expressive conduct and symbolic speech, including photography and motion pictures. It gives Americans who wish to document, explore, and explain our world to our fellow human beings a powerful tool, and in countries that have similar laws, important protections (U.S. Constitution, 1791).

But with power comes responsibility. Images can cause harm as well as express ideas. Just as free speech doesn't include a right to yell 'Fire!' in a theater, how we make and use images is, or ought to be, constrained by ethical considerations. From the perspective of the photographer or cameraperson, these considerations arise in four main areas: issues of truth, fairness, non-harm, and privacy.

BOX 6.1 THE NATIONAL PRESS PHOTOGRAPHERS ASSOCIATION'S CODE OF ETHICS

Visual journalists operate as trustees of the public. Our primary role is to report visually on the significant events and varied viewpoints in our common world. Our primary goal is the faithful and comprehensive depiction of the subject at hand. As visual journalists, we have the responsibility to document society and to preserve its history through images.

Photographic and video images can reveal great truths, expose wrongdoing and neglect, inspire hope and understanding and connect people around the globe through the language of visual understanding. Photographs can also cause great harm if they are callously intrusive or are manipulated.

(NPPA, 2015)

While filmmakers who work for media corporations may be contractually obliged to follow their employers' ethical guidelines, independent producers are constrained only by their conscience and a concern for their credibility and reputation. The documentary genre has broadened over the years to include a wide range of styles, enriching the field tremendously and finding a wide audience. But the blending of reportage and artistry makes it more difficult to apply hard and fast rules to media production, and competitive and commercial pressures can encourage producers to take liberties, cut corners, or push the boundaries of ethics and taste.

As a producer/director and director of photography since the 1980s, I've worked on documentaries and news as well as on cultural, non-profit, corporate media, and commercials. But it's in the area of documentaries where ethical issues have almost always arisen because the documentary implicitly promises to convey truths about the real world and real people.

My experience has led me to believe that while we should certainly lay out a set of ethical guidelines to operate by, when real-life issues arise, there will almost always be competing considerations that the cameraperson will have to weigh and balance before deciding how to proceed.

TRUTH

Misrepresentation

The expression, "the camera doesn't lie," has been a cliché since the invention of photography in the mid-19th century. Motion pictures can't be as easily retouched as still photographs, and cases of "photoshopping" or digital deception have, so far, not been a problem for documentaries. Up to now, it has been far easier to manipulate the meaning of the material through editing than through the filming process, but there are other ways that reality can be shaped and distorted by the camera itself.

Context

The widest lenses typically used in photography or motion picture production can take in less than 120 degrees of view horizontally, or less than one-third of everything you can see around you. A lens of standard focal length, which might be used for interviews or medium shots, takes in about 45 degrees, or one-eighth of the whole, horizontally. Zoom in further and you are viewing—and revealing—the world through a very narrow window indeed.

Where you point your camera, and how long your lens is, sets and limits the context of the reality you're capturing. By focusing on one thing, you're neglecting—concealing, in effect—everything else. Furthermore, where you position your camera determines what can be seen, how far away it is, and how visible it is. When you enter one room, you exit another. Where you choose to be, or not to be, and when, frames the reality you're representing and defines it.

When you decide to start and stop your camera slices reality across another dimension. Obviously, the editing process offers additional opportunities to limit the visual and temporal context of any event, but those decisions are often not within the cameraperson's control. So deciding what will be captured, and how, is an important responsibility, and if you're handing off the footage to someone else at the end of the day, your decisions may not be renegotiable.

Even when shooting a "talking head" interview, there are choices. We choose a room in which to film based on how it looks, either highlighting or downplaying evidence of the economic status of the subject, for example, or to frame him or her so as to bestow an aura of authority, respectability, or expertise. Lighting can easily and dramatically change the mood from upbeat and open to serious or even sinister. What we choose to use as the background telegraphs a message about the person being interviewed, and some producers and directors of photography (DPs) fuss endlessly with tiny details in the background for aesthetic or semiotic effect.

Staging

Standards of acceptability for staging events for the camera in documentaries have evolved over time. Robert Flaherty, considered by most to be the father of documentary film, made a huge impact with his 1922 film *Nanook of the North*, subtitled "A Story of Life and Love in the Actual Arctic." The first feature-length documentary, it depicted the daily life of an Inuk hunter and his community in the tundra of northern Quebec.

It was remarkable at the time for filming on location in remote and difficult conditions, and for providing a glimpse of an indigenous peoples' way of life that few in the developed world had ever seen. It was a huge critical and financial success and influenced documentary filmmaking for decades to come (Barnouw, 1974).

But, in fact, a great many of the scenes in the film were staged and directed by Flaherty—partly because of the bulkiness of the hand-cranked 35mm camera equipment he was using, and partly because it helped him tell the story he wanted to tell. For example, he asked the subjects to use harpoons for seal hunting as their forebears had done, though in reality they had been using rifles for some time. Nanook's real name was the less pronounceable Allakariallak, and his "wife" was actually the filmmaker's local girlfriend.

George Stoney's 1976 documentary *How the Myth Was Made* stunned audiences by exposing Flaherty's deceptions in detail, revealing scene-by-scene how he made the 1934 film *Man of Aran* about whalers apparently eking out a living on a remote and rugged island off the coast of Ireland. But, as with *Nanook*, many of the scenes reflected Flaherty's romantic imagination more than they depicted real life (Winston, 1999). Later generations of filmmakers have criticized Flaherty for his staging and romanticizing, and a documentary filmmaker trying to represent a different culture today using his methods would be considered beyond the pale.

Once cameras became more portable, filmmakers such as Robert Drew, Richard Leacock and D. A. Pennebaker set rules for themselves prohibiting staging and minimizing interaction with their subjects (O'Connell, 1992, p. 66). Jean Rouch, a French filmmaker influenced by Flaherty, coined the term *cinéma vérité* ("cinema truth") for his more interventionist approach to documentary making in which he freely interacted with and provoked his subjects from behind the camera. But, for whatever reason, the term "verite" has come to mean un-staged "real-life" material. "Direct cinema" and "observational documentary" are also terms associated with this method. "Fly-on-the-wall" refers to the filmmakers' total non-intervention and inconspicuousness to a point that almost denies their presence altogether (Nichols, 1991, p. 38).

But such a conceit raises a paradox. Is it really possible for "real life" to be recorded without the recording process influencing it? Common sense would suggest not. And, if not, are the conventions of the mute and unobtrusive film crew, and the subject who avoids looking into the camera, in some ways dishonest? On the other hand, how often is it possible to make an engaging film by merely sitting around waiting for things to happen? Rarely, in my experience—without the luxury of unlimited time and patience—and then only when the right subjects are chosen or stumbled upon, and when the situation is conducive to filming. Of course, timing is also key.

> We are really only successful in finding out anything when we are filming somebody who is more concerned with what he is doing than with the fact that we are filming him.
> Richard Leacock (quoted in Jacobs, 1971, p. 408)

On a practical workaday level, a balance is usually struck between, on the one hand, fostering situations in which an activity of interest can be recorded and, on the other hand, refraining from interfering. For example, this might mean planning to film a family dinner. A date is agreed upon. Some furniture may have to be moved, a light put up, and even the seating of the family members rearranged for best effect. Wireless microphones are hidden under clothing, or a boom mic is swung above the table just out of frame. In the finished scene, are we watching reality unfold, or the recording of a performance? Or some of both?

Most documentary productions operate on a tight schedule and budget. Skilled crew and professional equipment are expensive to hire and rent, so scenes are often scheduled and lightly staged for the sake of efficiency. The ethical questions arise in the degree to which what's happening is representative of reality. The filmmaker must judge what's appropriate—what's true to the subjects' nature, their relationships, and the larger reality they inhabit and exemplify.

In a verite documentary setting, putting words in the subjects' mouths is generally considered inappropriate, but often producers will ask someone to repeat what he or she has just said in the interest of catching it on camera. If the tone and context are the same, is that acceptable? Most documentary filmmakers I've worked with would say it is. Verite purists, on the other hand, may not.

Often, a stagey or artificial quality is conveyed by the subjects themselves. Some people are, or appear to be, able to ignore a camera and go about their lives as if nobody's watching. Others are self-conscious to the point where it's impossible to film them without their discomfort and unnaturalness being painfully obvious. Still others act for the camera, doing and saying what they think the filmmaker wants to see. So-called "reality television" has become a finishing school for this kind of "non-acting acting," where regular folks launch into character at the drop of a hat. In a documentary, it's up to the filmmaker to try to mitigate that tendency, shoot or cut around it, or incorporate it into the tone of the film by making the subjects' self-conscious, performative style obvious and part of their character.

FAIRNESS

Exploiting Tragedy/Voyeurism

> I usually enter people's lives at a time of crisis . . . I am keenly aware of the hypocrisy of asking someone for access that I myself would probably not grant.
>
> Joe Berlinger (Aufderheide, Jaszi, & Chandra, 2009)

Tragedy is a fundamental part of the human condition; one that, at least since ancient Greece, has been a reliable draw for audiences of theater, literature, and all media. Many, if not most, documentary filmmakers pursue their craft to expose injustice or to inform the public of human suffering in the interest of alleviating it, and it's at moments of crisis and pain that humanity in all of its dimensions is most starkly revealed. The fact is, there are few powerful documentaries about happy, well-adjusted families.

The ethical quandaries arise in the space between one person's suffering and another's benefit from it, whether it's advancing the filmmaker's career or affording the viewer some kind of voyeuristic pleasure or vicarious thrill. The documentary cameraperson must consider seriously the privacy and dignity of people who are suffering or disadvantaged, to gain their permission and participation when possible, and to try to bridge the gap between viewer and viewed. While paying subjects is usually not considered appropriate in documentaries, there are many ways filmmakers can be helpful or supportive to subjects in need; at a minimum, respect and empathy should form the basis of the filmmaker's attitude.

Hidden Camera

Most U.S. states and many countries have laws that restrict the use of hidden cameras, protecting our right to be free from being recorded without permission. But there are some gray areas, some possible exceptions, and a number of famous and effective uses of this technique in documentary film history.

Marcel Ophuls used a hidden camera and microphone extensively in his 1969 film, *The Sorrow and the Pity*, to interview former French Nazi collaborators. Claude Lanzmann did likewise in *Shoah* (1985), his ten-hour epic about the Holocaust (Bernstein, 1985).

In these cases, the usual rules might appear to be trumped by extraordinary circumstances. As Ophuls's goal was to film admissions of culpability by former officials, deception was the only method by which he could uncover and document their crimes, which rank among the worst in human history. His judgment was that the public's right to know outweighed the subjects' right to privacy and protection.

In 2012, a 4th-grader named Zachary Maxwell surreptitiously filmed his school lunches and made a short film called *Yuck* that went viral, won awards, and catalyzed a serious and constructive debate about the poor quality of New York City's public school lunches. His main point was that the meals served were nothing like what was advertised to parents. He broke school board rules that prohibited filming in school and would certainly not have been granted permission if he had asked. In the final film, the faces of other students are all blurred, so he broke no laws regarding privacy or consent. In the end, the New York Education Department approached Zachary and asked for his advice on proposed menus. Is breaking institutional or corporate rules an ethical transgression if no laws are broken? Was the public interest served in a way that would have been impossible otherwise (Sen, 2013)?

Cultural and Social Stereotypes

The visual media strive for—and one could argue, require—impact and efficiency to hold an audience's attention and get their point across which can lead to a kind of shorthand that can devolve into clichés or stereotypes. When capturing images of people from a different culture or social class, the cameraperson may ignore or frame out images that show commonality with his or her own background and focus on those elements which reflect difference. Sometimes the selection is calculated and deliberate; other times it's just about what attracts the eye. Often, contradictory signifiers can exist side by side. Context through framing is one way the stereotypical image may be emphasized, undercut, or neutralized. It's a responsibility of the photographer to consider whether his or her images might contribute to negative or narrow stereotypes, and if so, to resist that impulse.

NON-HARM

Invasion of Privacy

> What is the boundary between the society's right to know and the individual's right to be free from humiliation, shame and indignity!
>
> Calvin Pryluck (Rosenthal & Corner, 2005, p. 199)

Peter Davis's 1974 documentary masterpiece, *Hearts and Minds*, includes film footage of a nine-year-old Vietnamese girl, Phan Thị Kim Phúc, running down a country road, without clothing, severely burned, and wailing in pain shortly after being hit by napalm. A still of that moment by photographer Nick Ut became an iconic and influential symbol of the Vietnam War and the misery it inflicted (Harris, 2015).

A whole raft of ethical issues is raised by the image: Does it invade the girl's privacy? Does it exploit a tragedy? Does it abuse a power relationship? Should the cameraman have simply put down his camera to help?

The footage was taken in the context of news reporting, but was later used in a documentary film with a very strong point of view. The context is the immediate aftermath of a bombing in the midst of a brutal war. It's hard to imagine the cameraman being able to think through all of the ethical issues in that instant, and one could argue that it's understandable that he continued to film the dramatic scene. The question then is left to the editors and broadcasters: What to do with the material?

If they were applied rigorously, the recording and use of this image could easily fail all of our ethical tests. The question for the filmmaker is: Does the news value—or the public's right to be informed—outweigh normal, ethical standards to an extent that is justifiable?

The editors of *The New York Times* obviously thought so. They decided to publish the picture on the front page, and it went on to win a Pulitzer Prize. What does this say about the ethical standards of our journalistic institutions (Zhang, 2012)?

Public Disclosure of Private Facts

In this era of viral tweets and videos, disclosing private, embarrassing, or damaging information about a person can have profound repercussions. Suicides in the aftermath of private videos going viral have increased in recent years (Patchin, 2015). The thought that not only has one's secret been revealed but also that everyone in the world knows it and may be able to see it for the rest of time is an overwhelming proposition. It should go without saying that informed consent must be obtained when information is sensitive. For the cinematographer, consent becomes relevant when considering when to turn the camera on or off.

In 2014, Brett Zongker, an entertainment reporter for the Associated Press, interviewed Bill Cosby at the Smithsonian Museum of African Art about an exhibit based on Cosby's art collection. At one point in the interview, Zongker switched gears to ask the comedian about recent allegations of sexual abuse. Cosby awkwardly replied that he would not comment or answer the question. When the interview concluded, the camera operator left the camera running.

Not realizing he was still being recorded, or assuming that the material would not be used, Cosby asked the interviewer to discard the material that cast him in a bad light. When the reporter hesitated, Cosby went on for several minutes in a rather manipulative way, suggesting that if Zongker were to use it he would be betraying a lack of integrity and professionalism for having broken a kind of tacit agreement. Cosby then tried to go over Zongker's head by asking an assistant to contact the reporter's superiors. The entire interaction was captured by the still-rolling camera.

The Associated Press initially reported the story only in print, stating blandly that "Cosby declined to comment." After a subsequent interview with Cosby by National Public Radio's

Scott Simon garnered a similarly evasive response—but which NPR aired uncut, awkward pauses and all—the Associated Press decided to release their unedited interview including the post-interview footage. It immediately went viral, and the public's glimpse of Cosby's off-stage persona helped fuel a chain of events that included his loss of a television contract and a fresh wave of women emboldened to step forward with stories of having been drugged and raped. In the weeks and months that followed, more than 30 women came forward, many decades after the alleged attacks, and Cosby was ultimately arrested on charges of sexual assault (Folkenflik, 2014).

What ethical rules, if any, were broken? Or, was it just a violation of customary and unspoken entertainment industry etiquette? To what extent does Cosby's status as a public figure make a difference? If Cosby were to be found guilty of the numerous charges against him, would that change the ethical calculus? Was it right for the Associated Press to withhold the damning footage in the first place?

Different filmmakers and news organizations would arrive at different conclusions on all of these questions, and much has been written arguing the pros and cons of the AP's decision. Filmmakers such as Michael Moore have used similar material from pre- or post-interviews, when the subject has not expected the camera to be recording, to humorous and usually derogatory effect.

My personal rule is that if someone asks that the camera be turned off, I do so immediately. There have been several times when I've done that against the wishes of a producer or director. To me, it's a clear-cut case of consent. In journalism, a statement made "off the record" is not usable in a published report or distributed video or film. Yet neither of those clear directives was employed in this case. According to commonly accepted guidelines, invoking "off the record" must occur before the fact; it is never retroactive. Once again, we're faced with a possible crime weighed against giving a subject full control over his privacy and the use of his words and image (NYU, 2007).

INSIDE LIFE OUTSIDE (1988)

I co-produced, co-directed, and shot a one-hour documentary that followed a group of homeless people living in a shantytown on New York's Lower East Side over a two-and-a-half-year period.

The subjects of the film were incredibly charismatic people, but they were also addicts living on the street which meant that the power balance was significantly in my favor.

One scene created several ethical dilemmas. In it, I followed the main character, Michael, to visit his estranged son, who was about 11 years old, and who Michael hadn't seen in some time. I kept the camera running throughout. The kid was incredibly uncomfortable, both with my presence and with his father's, but he felt powerless to protest. Their fraught relationship and conversation was so powerful and revealing about Michael and his social environment that I kept filming and was later able to get a release from the child's mother. Although I covered my legal liability, I can't say in all honesty that it was the best example of informed consent, or respecting privacy for that matter. At this point in my career, I would handle the situation more sensitively.

FIGURE 6.2　Still photo from 1988 documentary, *Inside Life Outside*. Directed by Scott Sinkler and Sachiko Hamada. Courtesy of Scott Sinkler.

FED UP (2014)

I was director of photography on a feature-length documentary about childhood obesity and the food industry. The producers were duly rigorous about getting releases from everyone involved, including the parents of minor subjects. But I couldn't help feeling some discomfort with the assignment: filming kids—teenagers, mostly—who were morbidly obese.

The kids were all dedicated to telling their personal stories in an effort to help others like them, to draw attention to the problem, and, I would guess, to give themselves an impetus to lose weight. But as teenagers, opening themselves up for the world to see would surely invite negative attention from their peers. The ends were noble but were we, to some extent, exploiting tragedy by invading privacy and disclosing private facts?

When filming the kids, I chose camera angles that showcased their bulk—the opposite of flattering shots. I made every effort to catch them eating the worst possible foods and made framing choices that emphasized their size, their isolation, and, essentially, their unhappiness. Tasked with using my creative toolkit to tell the story of obesity, I looked for ways to convey that story dramatically, if honestly.

We had permission to film one of the kids at school. Following an overweight teenager around his high school with a camera crew is uncomfortable for subject and filmmakers alike—the opposite of inconspicuous. Kids snickered and made comments. Our subject was incredibly brave. As we followed him around, I realized that he wasn't, by far, the biggest kid in the school. I didn't have permission to film anyone else in an identifiable way, but I did try to capture images of other obese kids to show the pervasiveness of the problem. And, in the

Midwest, where we were shooting, it's a big problem. I realized I was skirting the line, but foremost in my mind was the goal of informing the public of the scope of the problem and trying to convey it in a visceral, visual way.

Fed Up spent many months as Amazon's best-selling documentary. It has informed the public in a meaningful way, and I believe it has helped change attitudes about a life-and-death issue facing families, our economy, and our healthcare system.

This example raises a number of important ethical questions. As a cinematographer, what other ways could you have shown the pervasiveness of the problem? What would you have done differently in this exact situation? Maybe more importantly, did the featured teenager think it was worth it?

A FAMILY UNDERTAKING (2004)

I was director of photography on a one-hour documentary about the funeral industry and the alternative practice of having funerals at home. We filmed in a casket factory and shot an embalming without fully explaining the intended message of the film: that there are legal and creative alternatives to the expensive and impersonal ceremonies the funeral industry has led us to accept as normal, and that embalming is an invasive, unnecessary procedure that is ecologically noxious as well.

Fully informed consent? I don't think so. Deceit? Maybe by omission—nobody was lied to, but the project was described in general terms that skirted the contentious themes that would have barred our access. At the time, I felt badly about misleading the friendly people who helped us and who maybe thought they would gain some useful publicity in the process. But I'm satisfied that we served the greater good by informing the public about an often

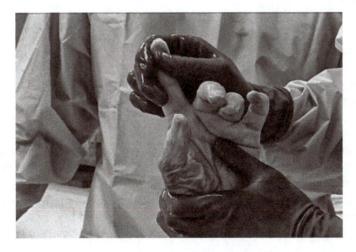

FIGURE 6.3   Still photo from documentary *A Family Undertaking,* directed by Elizabeth Westrate. Courtesy of Film Spot Films LLC, Scott Sinkler, director of photography.

manipulative industry and by offering alternatives to taken-for-granted practices that can exploit people in their time of grief.

Ethics and morality reside in the abstract realm of philosophy and judgment, and in and around the nuanced landscape of psychology, culture, and emotion. Society's problems involve complex human beings and encompass unpleasant realities, entrenched injustices, and outmoded traditions. Powerful corporations and public servants and institutions alike shield their malfeasance with rules and policies in the pursuit of profit or a good public image. The law draws a redline around clear-cut cases of ethical abuse and protects our freedom of speech. But there are gray areas.

An ethical code provides an important framework for our image-making decisions on a day-to-day basis. But my own feeling is that the most interesting documentaries often wander, and occasionally march, into the gray areas. Choices must be made, balances struck. Often it's complicated, and sometimes ends and means are in conflict.

We are all individuals with rights to privacy, safety, and respect—filmmakers and film subjects alike. But we are also members of larger groups, of society, and ultimately the human race. As makers of media, we have an obligation to humanity and history to explore, uncover, share, and analyze the problems and realities of life in order to improve society and the lives of others—to confront injustice and protect the vulnerable. And, as responsible media-makers, we have an equal obligation to respect and protect those who let us into their lives, and give us permission to capture and use their likenesses in the service of that goal.

When you pick up a camera and push the record button, you have a solemn responsibility to ask yourself: Is what I'm capturing true? Undistorted? Viewed in its proper context? Is it fair to the people I'm filming and the group they belong to? Am I exploiting them, invading their privacy, fictionalizing, or stereotyping? Have they given me truly informed consent? Will my use of the camera cause anyone harm? How your conscience and your reputation as a member of the media profession will fare depends on how you negotiate and resolve these critical questions.

TAKE HOME POINTS

- The photographer or cameraperson may face unexpected ethical issues, so it is important to have the principles in mind before shooting.
- It is the documentary cameraperson's responsibility to strive for truth, accuracy, and fairness in depicting people and events.
- Staging events as real is ethically problematic, but occasionally some intervention is required for the sake of filming. The important thing is that people or events are not misrepresented in the process.
- Context is important in framing reality. You can't film everything; what you exclude can be as important as what you include.
- Filming without consent with a hidden camera is against the law and is almost always unacceptable.
- The photographer needs to ask whether his or her images are perpetuating stereotypes of social groups.

- When weighing the public's right to know against institutional rules and policies against filming, consider the potential consequences to yourself and—especially—to the people in front of the camera.
- Encroaching on a subject's privacy or the public disclosure of private facts can be harmful and must be handled sensitively, particularly with vulnerable populations.
- Unless uncovering criminal or unethical behavior of sufficient public interest, filming that is harmful to individuals is always unacceptable.

NOTE

1 For more, see Peter Brook's (2010) remarkable, exhaustive analysis of the photographic coverage of this event.

BIBLIOGRAPHY

American Anthropological Association. (2012). *Principles of professional responsibility*. Arlington, VA. Retrieved from: http://ethics.aaanet.org/category/statement/

Aufderheide, P., Jaszi, P., & Chandra, M. (2009). *Honest truths: Documentary filmmakers on ethical challenges in their work*. Center for Social Media. Washington, DC. Retrieved from: http://archive.cmsimpact.org/sites/default/files/Honest_Truths_--_Documentary_Filmmakers_on_Ethical_Challenges_in_Their_Work.pdf

Austin, T., & de Jong, W. (Eds.). (2008). *Rethinking documentary: New perspectives and practices*. New York, NY: Open University Press.

Barnouw, E. (1974). *Documentary: A history of the non-fiction film*. Oxford, UK: Oxford University Press

Bernstein, R. (1985, October 20). Shoah (1985): An epic film about the greatest evil of modern times. *The New York Times*. Retrieved from: http://www.nytimes.com/1985/10/20/movies/an-epic-film-about-the-greatest-evil-of-modern-times.html?pagewanted=all

Brook, P. (2010, January 27). Fabienne Cherisma. *Prison Photography*. Retrieved from: https://prisonphotography.org/2010/01/27/fabienne-cherisma/

Chapman, J. (2007). *Documentary in practice: Filmmakers and production choices*. Cambridge, UK: Polity.

Cunningham, M. (2014). *The art of the documentary: Fifteen conversations with leading directors, cinematographers, editors, and producers* (2nd ed.). San Francisco, CA: New Riders Press.

Folkenflik, D. (2014, November 22). In NPR and AP Cosby interviews, a "No comment" that said everything. *NPR*. Retrieved from: www.npr.org/2014/11/22/365828829/in-npr-and-ap-cosby-interviews-a-no-comment-that-said-everything

Fox, B. (2009). *Documentary media: History, theory, practice*. Waltham, MA: Focal Press.

Gross, L., Katz, J., & Ruby, J. (Eds.). (2003). *Image ethics in the digital age*. Minneapolis, MN: University of Minnesota Press.

Hamper, B. (2007). *Making documentary films and videos: A practical guide to planning, filming, and editing documentaries* (2nd ed.). New York, NY: Holt Paperbacks.

Harris, M. (2015, April 3). Photographer who took iconic Vietnam photo looks back, 40 years after the war ended. *Vanity Fair*. Retrieved from: www.vanityfair.com/news/2015/04/vietnam-war-napalm-girl-photo-today

Hocking, P. (2003). *Principles of visual anthropology* (3rd ed.). Berlin, Germany: De Gruyter Mouton.

Jacobs, L. (1971). *The documentary tradition; From Nanook to Woodstock.* New York, NY: Hopkinson and Blake.

Kieran, M. (1999). *Media ethics.* Santa Barbara, CA: Praeger.

Koehler, D. (2012). Documentary and ethnography: Exploring ethical fieldwork models. *The Elon journal of undergraduate research in communications, 3*(1). Retrieved from: http://www.elon.edu/docs/e-web/academics/communications/research/vol3no1/06koehlerejspring12.pdf

Lester, P. (2015). *Photojournalism: An ethical approach.* London, UK: Routledge.

Maccarone, E. (2010). Ethical responsibilities to subjects and documentary filmmaking. *Journal of Mass Media Ethics, 25*(3), 192–206.

McLane, B. (2012). *A new history of documentary film* (2nd ed.). London, UK: Bloomsbury Academic.

National Press Photographers Association. (2015). *NPPA code of ethics.* Retrieved from: https://nppa.org/code_of_ethics

New York University. (2007). *NYU Journalism handbook for students: Ethics, law & good practice.* New York, NY. Retrieved from: http://journalism.nyu.edu/publishing/ethics-handbook/human-sources/

Newton, J. (2000). *The burden of visual truth: The role of photojournalism in mediating reality.* London, UK: Routledge.

Nichols, B. (1991). *Representing reality: Issues and concepts in documentary.* Bloomington, IN: Indiana University Press.

Nichols, B. (2016). *Speaking truths with film: Evidence, ethics, politics in documentary.* Oakland, CA: University of California Press.

O'Connell, P. J. (1992). *Robert Drew and the development of cinema verite in America.* Carbondale, IL: Southern Illinois University Press.

Palmer, C. (2015). *Confessions of a wildlife filmmaker: The challenges of staying honest in an iboxndustry where ratings are king.* Bluefield, WV: Bluefield Publishing.

Patchin, J. (2015). Summary of our cyberbullying research (2004–2015). *Cyberbullying Research Center.* Retrieved from: http://cyberbullying.org/summary-of-our-cyberbullying-research/

Pramis, J. (2013, February 28). Number of mobile phones to exceed world population by 2014. *Digital Trends.* Retrieved from: www.digitaltrends.com/mobile/mobile-phone-world-population-2014

Poe, E.A. (1840, January 15). The daguerreotype. *Alexander's Weekly Messenger.* Philadelphia. Retrieved from: www.daguerreotypearchive.org/texts/P8400008_POE_ALEX-WEEKLY_1840-01-15.pdf

Quinn, J. (2015). *Adventures in the lives of others: Ethical dilemmas in factual filmmaking.* London, UK: I. B. Tauris.

Rabiger, M. (2014). *Directing the documentary* (6th ed.). Waltham, MA: Focal Press.

Rosenthal, A., & Corner, J. (Eds.). (2005). *New challenges for documentary* (2nd ed.). Manchester, UK: Manchester University Press.

Rushdie, S. (1999). *The ground beneath her feet.* London, UK: Picador.

Sample, I. (2014, October 09). 35,000 year-old Indonesian cave paintings suggest art came out of Africa. *The Guardian.* Retrieved from: www.theguardian.com/science/2014/oct/08/cave-art-indonesia-sulawesi

Sen, I. (2013, May 10). The Michael Moore of the grade-school lunchroom. *The New York Times.* Retrieved from: http://cityroom.blogs.nytimes.com/2013/05/09/the-michael-moore-of-the-grade-school-lunchroom/?_r=0

Spence, L., & Navarro, V. (2011). *Crafting truth: Documentary form and meaning.* New Brunswick, NJ: Rutgers University Press.

Swimmer, J. (2014). *Documentary case studies: Behind the scenes of the greatest (true) stories ever told.* London, UK: Bloomsbury Academic.

This is 15-year-old Fabienne Cherisma, shot dead by a policeman after looting three picture frames. (2013, April). *Colors.* Retrieved from: www.colorsmagazine.com/stories/magazine/86/story/this-is-15-year-old-fabienne-cherisma-shot-dead-by-a-policeman-after-lootin

Thomas, G., Ibbotson, J., & Leonard, E. (2015). *Beyond the lens: Rights, ethics and business practice in professional photography.* London, UK: Proving House LLP.

U.S. Constitution, Amendment I. (1791). Retrieved from: http://billofrightsinstitute.org/founding documents/bill-of-rights/

Ward, P. (2006). *Documentary: The margins of reality.* New York, NY: Wallflower Press.

Winston, B. (1999). Documentary: How the myth was deconstructed. *Wide Angle, 21* (2). Retrieved from: www.der.org/resources/study-guides/how-the-myth-brian-winston.pdf

Winston, B. (2000). *Lies, damn lies and documentaries.* London, UK: British Film Institute.

Zhang, M. (2012, September 19). Interview with Nick Ut, the photojournalist who shot the iconic "Napalm girl" photo. *PetaPixel.* Retrieved from: http://petapixel.com/2012/09/19/interview-with-nick-ut-the-photojournalist-who-shot-the-iconic-photo-napalm-girl/

Chapter 7

Technical Framing

Annette Danto

ABSTRACT

This chapter offers you advice on how to make effective and ethical choices with technical framing. Your choices determine how subjects and objects are incorporated in specific shots: both directly and indirectly. For text-based media, selection of headlines and words become framing determinants. Technical framing choices always produce specific readings. Shot size, camera angle, composition, lighting and exposure, static or moving images determine patterns of inclusion and exclusion. In all media forms, technical framing regulates what the audience will see, understand, and experience.

CREDIBILITY, TRUTH, AND DECEPTION

With a hidden 16mm Aaton camera wrapped in a jacket and using available light, documentary director Stephanie Black and cinematographer Maryse Alberti sneaked into a Florida sugar cane plantation to document deplorable living and working conditions of Jamaican migrant workers.

Unable to get permission from the U.S. Sugar Corporation authorities in Florida, the director and her cameraperson often resorted to deceptive tactics to infiltrate tight security at the sugar plantation camps. Using cars with different license plates became a necessary part of the daily routine. This prevented the security guards from identifying the filmmakers' vehicle.

The resultant surveillance-style documentary, *H2 Worker* (1990), powerfully documents exploitive living and working conditions of Jamaican migrant workers who traveled to Florida because of a devastated economy at home. The documentary ultimately led to reforms.[1]

For media-makers, providing misleading information continues to be a controversial issue, especially when it comes to documentary filmmakers and journalists investigating sensitive subject matter. In the case of *H2 Worker*, the filmmakers shot on-camera interviews with migrant workers in locations other than their home barracks; shielding their identities and safeguarding their jobs.[2] This decision prioritized the protection of migrant workers. Filmmaker credibility was in no way compromised in this investigation of serious abuse and exploitation.

There are other situations where misleading representation can erode audience trust in media creators.

The Blair Witch Project (1999) seemed like a documentary but wasn't. Essentially a horror film written, directed, and edited by Daniel Myrick and Eduardo Sanchez, the film received acclaim from critics and grossed millions of dollars in worldwide ticket sales. The film opens with introductory text: "In October of 1994, three student filmmakers disappeared in the woods near Burkittsville, Maryland while shooting a documentary on the legend of the Blair Witch. A year later their footage was found" ("Blair Witch Project," 1999).

The legend of the Blair Witch[3] was invented by the film's writer/directors who hired three actors, explained the outline of the film's story to them, and then turned them loose in the woods with film equipment to shoot movie footage. The actors allegedly didn't know exactly what was going to happen once they embarked on their movie-making venture—thus the film feels like a documentary that captures events genuinely surprising to the filmmakers. When the actors/filmmakers purportedly disappeared, Myrick and Sanchez edited a film using alleged found footage from the cameras discovered in the woods while searching for the missing actors.

Publicity for *The Blair Witch Project* featured fake police reports and newsreel-style interviews with those who may have seen the missing filmmakers. This sparked debates across the internet about whether the movie was truth or fiction.

Publicity about the dead film students created buzz which, in turn, may have led to higher box office ticket sales. When the truth was uncovered and publicized, this created further buzz which generated lots of publicity for the movie and further increased ticket sales. Following the film's release, the "dead" film students gave interviews.

What can we take away from this example? As with Orson Welles's *The War of the Worlds* (October 30, 1938) broadcast[4] which reportedly traumatized radio listeners throughout the United States, the ambiguity as to whether *The Blair Witch Project* was documentary or fiction created audience confusion—though perhaps not to the same extent.[5] Did uncovering the deliberate intent to deceive the ticket-buying public generate questions about the trustworthiness of what the public sees on screen? One can wonder whether choices made in this instance may have served to erode public trust in media creators, filmmakers, and documentary producers.

For all media, what is included or omitted from audience scrutiny shapes attitudes and understanding of what is being viewed.

The technical frame bifurcates what is inside and outside. Defined by the edges as seen in a camera viewfinder or on a screen, a technical frame constructs and assigns meaning by emphasizing certain aspects while excluding others.

Technical reframing can entail reversals of foreground and background, sculpting audience perceptions and understanding of a story. Shifts in image emphasis, by highlighting different priorities, can manipulate viewer understanding of a narrative sequence.

A recent popular example is *The Affair*, a series on Showtime, which tells the story of an extra-marital affair from differing points of view. Various characters witnessing the same story provide alternative, self-serving, and contradictory versions of the same incident.

By playing with background–foreground emphasis, *The Affair* uses framing and reframing maneuvers to produce shifts in information provided to viewers. Similar events shot from divergent perspectives become the essential factor for illustrating alternative storylines.

VISUAL SHOT SELECTION AND ETHICS

Technical framing decisions form an audience's field of view by directing what the viewer sees and how. Since the eye of the media creator is the sole viewing perspective of the audience, it is essential to understand the emotion, purpose, and meaning behind each type of shot and to consider the ethical implications of specific shot selection.

With visual media, shot size, camera angle, composition, lighting, and exposure, static or moving camera are essential framing components. For journalists and news media creators, framing choices include headlines, words, and sources.

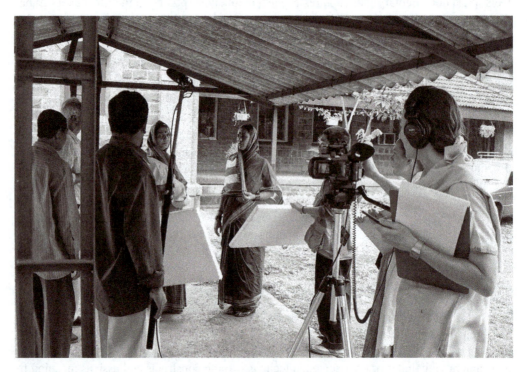

FIGURE 7.1   *Shanti's Story*, director, Annette Danto. Belgaum, Karnataka 2004. A preventive health-care narrative, developed for rural regions of Maharashtra, India. All story decisions were made with the target population in mind. In this specific image, we staged a sensitive abortion-related negotiation between two mothers in a private location with no other people in the background. Courtesy of Ilango Samuel Peter.

Word choice provides reference points for an audience by identifying the perspective of the media source. In influencing public opinion and political choice, this can be consequential. Usually viewers of news programs or readers of blogs and web-based articles are not even aware that the news is being framed.

Lawrence O'Donnell, an MSNBC journalist, recently lambasted journalists for being inconsistent with words used to describe mass murderers from different parts of the world. O'Donnell posed the question: Why do journalists choose words to characterize American mass murderers such as "psychopaths, criminals, deeply disturbed individuals," but use the word "mastermind" when referring to mass murderers elsewhere? He implored journalists to choose their words more carefully, warning about inadvertent glorification of terrorists in the global arena (Kordick, 2015).

CAMERA AS WITNESS: AVOIDING SENSATIONALISM

Images that depict degradation, mutilation, and pain can allure. The wish to see something gruesome is nothing new. Gladiator competitions and bull fights are legendary for drawing attention. Rubbernecking at traffic slow-downs is not dissimilar in spirit. We want to see

FIGURE 7.2   Do people have an appetite for visuals and activities that depict human suffering? Credit: Migel/Shutterstock.com.

whether anyone was injured; whether from compassion or schadenfreude. Does this suggest that people have an appetite for visuals that depict human suffering?

Our high tolerance for visual violence, destruction, and cruelty is showcased regularly on the internet, in films and television programs, and most dramatically in computer games. Even 30 years ago, this level of media violence would not have been tolerated. Today, 24-hour disaster news coverage, often in real-time, simulates an action movie. Mayhem is entertainment.

Has the excessive amount of media violence created emotional detachment for media-makers and audiences? If we have become somewhat indifferent to the suffering of others on screen, is it too late to reverse course? Is it possible to provide entertainment that stirs audience emotion without desensitizing viewers to human degradation?

Sparking the audience's emotions by intentionally shocking them with strong imagery and then allowing them to walk away is simply irresponsible. There are framing choices that can guide viewer reactions to violent, provocative, and/or divisive media.

Sparks can burn out; they can also ignite. Viewer reactions to violent and sadistic media vary widely. Viewers may feel deadened and desensitized, yet feel a thrill of addiction to violent imagery. Others may feel compassion toward victims. Painful images can also make people angry, inciting and provoking acts of violence.[6] Considering what happens to viewers after they leave the theater or walk away from their computer screen leads to questions of long-term ethical responsibility.

Ethical responsibility for media-makers needs to be considered on two fronts. First, when designing media with violent, pornographic, and sadistic content; how can the level of violence and sadistic content be reduced? Second, if we as media-makers retain the same level of violent content, do we bear any moral or legal responsibility once viewers leave the theater, turn off their television sets, and shut down their computers?

The answer to both questions is *yes*.

When working with graphic and sensationalized material, media-makers have a range of creative and technical options. Determining the major goals of the project is a first step. The relative importance of sparking or provoking an audience, desensitizing or deadening the audience, instilling compassion and humanity in an audience—all are possibilities and need to be clearly thought through and linked to technical framing selections.

The goal of terrorist propaganda videos can be to provoke an audience to violence. On the other hand, the goal of a video can be to instill compassion so viewers donate funds to charitable rescue organizations. Your decisions can propel an audience in any number of directions. Your determining influence on what the audience pays attention to, what they care about, and what they may choose to do, or not do, about it will be evident in your framing choices.

CAMERA AS WITNESS: HUMAN BARBARISM AND ATROCITY IMAGES

Historically, the camera has acted as a witness, documenting visual evidence of unfathomable episodes of human barbarism. In these situations, the graphic nature of visual footage serves an important purpose—to represent, as much as possible, the full horror of the atrocities.

Here, the ethical dilemma is, how does one visually capture human tragedy respectfully and without sensationalism? How do you choose between respecting a trauma victim's need for privacy on the one hand, and the public's need to know the truth of human suffering on the other? Will revealing the identities of the people on-camera harm them in any way? These questions pose compelling conflicts for any conscientious filmmaker.

There are no simple or clear-cut ethical strategies.

Atrocity images generate powerful emotional responses. In her book *On Photography*, Susan Sontag writes about her first encounter with Holocaust images: "Nothing I have seen— in photographs, in real life—ever cut me as sharply, deeply, instantaneously. Indeed, it seems plausible to me to divide my life into two parts, before I saw those photographs (I was twelve) and after" (Sontag, 1977, p. 17).

Sometimes atrocity images give birth to humanitarian concerns or activist responses by the viewer. Other times, witnessing atrocity footage might incite further violence. Can atrocity feed atrocity?

FIGURE 7.3 Bergen-Belsen was a Nazi concentration camp in northern Germany. The camp was liberated on April 15, 1945. Soldiers discovered 60,000 prisoners inside, most of them half-starved and seriously ill, and another 13,000 corpses lying around the camp unburied. Atrocity images always generate powerful emotional responses. Credit: Everett Historical.

Viewing non-stop distressing images in ignorance only shocks the senses. It does not teach meaning or historical truthfulness. Framing information provided by the media creator helps viewers interpret what they see.

We need to find out more about visual footage and images—no matter how familiar—before we use or recirculate them, or imply that they are representative of cultures, histories, or events.

In 1945, the U.S. Army shot 80,000 feet of 16mm film as they liberated Nazi Concentration and Prisoner of War Camps in Europe. Images of survivors are as distressing as those of the dead. Prisoners and victims of extreme torture, starvation, and Nazi medical experimentation look directly into the lens. Many appear dazed, confused, disoriented.

Footage of emaciated and starving concentration camp victims eating their first meal in days is difficult to watch. Close-up footage brings an uneasy intimacy between the viewer and victims. Mountains of corpses being bulldozed into open pits is intercut with footage of robust and healthy-looking Nazi guards and community residents sightseeing the camps. Close-ups of Nazi guards show their expressionless faces as they carelessly toss decomposing corpses into open pits.

Theatrical re-enactments illustrate how prisoners were restrained while being tortured. A Nazi officer calmly explains how chains, barbed wire, and ropes were effectively used to secure prisoners.

Used as evidence, the graphic U.S. Army footage led to the conviction of 19 Nazi officers at the Nuremberg trials in November, 1945. The documentary made of this footage includes a detailed introduction at the opening of the documentary framing the material. This enables viewers to think about what it means to look at these images. Now, 70 years later, this introductory frame helps audiences assimilate what they are seeing.

When we point and click our smart phone cameras at our family and friends, we rarely think we are committing a crime or doing anything wrong. However, when it comes to atrocity images, is the violence perpetrated on the victim repeated through the fidelity of the camera? In other words, does recording images of victimization perpetuate the degradation by creating a permanent record?

Marianne Hirsch has discussed this idea of camera violence. In discussing Holocaust images, she considers how "subjects looking at the camera are also victims looking at soldiers whose guns help herd them off to trains and extermination camps. As they face the camera, they are shot before they are shot" (Hirsch, 2012, p. 136).

Technical framing decisions about how to cover stories about human suffering are never easy or straightforward. Media-makers must always weigh and calculate what to present and how best to present it while always keeping in mind the potential long-term impact on those in front of the camera lens.

FURTHER FRAMING ISSUES

Photographs . . . are simply a crude statement of fact addressed to the eye . . . the eye is connected with the brain; the brain with the nervous system. That system sends its messages in a flash through every past memory and present feeling. This sleight of hand allows

> photographs to be . . . both a faithful copy or transcription of an actual moment of reality and an interpretation of that reality.
>
> Virginia Woolf (Sontag, 2003, p. 26)

Virginia Woolf points out here that viewers bring every past memory and present feeling to bear on how they interpret, or misinterpret, what they are watching. When viewers watch media—episode by episode, scene by scene, sequence by sequence—they are often looking at hundreds and hundreds of individual shots each of which reflects a directorial choice.

One way to mitigate diverse audience readings and misreadings is by making careful shot selections. The impact of each individual shot along with the sequencing of shots operates on viewers without them being aware of it. Operating subliminally on audience emotional reactions, shots convey more than overt story content. Conscientious storyboarding and planning of shot lists helps translate story and emotional subtext into the concrete building blocks of visual communication.

Establishing shots, lasting only a few seconds, introduce new locations allowing audiences to become oriented to a story's environment. Travel documentaries often make

FIGURE 7.4 A wide shot of a market in the ancient section of Madurai, near Meenakshi Temple (2015). Courtesy of Ilango Samuel Peter.

ethically compromised decisions when selecting establishing shots that highlight the exotic. This feeds into negative and often inaccurate cultural stereotyping. Innocently, a cinematographer may select images that are instantaneous in their stereotyped associations. These choices can be ethically consequential. Aestheticizing poverty, for example, attempts to create beauty in images of human tragedy.

Wide shots are used to emphasize location. An aerial wide shot of Hiroshima after the August, 1945, atomic bombing emphasizes widespread geographic devastation after the nuclear holocaust. We are unable to see any individuals—only the broad sweeping image of a destroyed landscape. How does this impact the audience? By avoiding closer images of disfigured faces or burned children's toys, wide shots can protect the viewer from too much emotional content.

But a wide shot alone is insufficient in showing the human suffering over generations of families harmed by radiation exposure. Medium shots, close-ups, and insert shots are needed to disclose the personal consequences of such events.

Master shots are designed to record the entire action in a given scene. Often wide shots, they allow for a complete run-through of the scene or sequence, from beginning to end, from the exact same camera position using the exact same lens. Master shots include all the characters in the scene. Master shots can present challenges for actors as well as crew. Since they encompass more action in the frame, they place more technical demands on everyone.

Full shots provide separation and distance between character and audience. The psychological reality of a character is diluted and carries less emotional weight than closer shots. Useful for diffusing emotions, it is not the best choice during emotionally intense sequences. However, in situations involving human pain and suffering, it is often best to use a long lens[7] at a distance. This is less intrusive than pointing a camera directly in the face of a crime victim or the suffering.

Close-ups provide no sense of context or environment. They highlight emotionally consequential moments by having a character's face occupy the frame. Sensationalized media always uses close-ups to highlight human suffering, loss, or pain. Intrusively pointing a camera in the face of a crime victim has become a conventional technical framing choice for sensationalized network news coverage. If it bleeds; it leads.

Insert shots emphasize objects used to create associations between characters, events, or actions. Highlighting a specific object brings significance to that object. Associations between characters, events, or actions can be invented and then solidified by the placement or selection of an insert shot.

Reaction shots are usually close-ups of faces. A reaction shot reveals the emotional reaction of an actor or subject, and thereby moves a story forward. Sometimes, if the reaction shot is not part of a continuous sequence, it can be added to alter a story's meaning. This alters an audience's understanding of a character's motivation.

Camera movement is often motivated by story content. A hand-held camera, for example, generates a feeling of uneasiness for an audience. It also provides greater freedom of motion for a cinematographer; a necessary requisite in observational documentary.

Camera pans and tilts require decisions about when and where to start/stop a pan, when and where to start/stop a tilt. Revealing partial information to an audience through a pan or tilt that stops before additional information is covered can mislead viewer perception.

FIGURE 7.5   Ryo Murakami, cinematographer, in Liberia shooting *Out of My Hand* (2014), directed by Takeshi Fukunaga. Courtesy of Donari Braxton and Takeshi Fukunaga.

EYE LINE AND ETHICS

Being intentional with eye lines can communicate a theme to your audience quickly and with intensity. Camera positioning makes a difference. It alters the relationship between the subject and the audience.

Should the subject or actor look directly into the lens (on-axis), or to the left or right of the camera (off-axis)? When an actor or interviewee looks directly into the lens, it appears as though the subject is addressing the audience directly. It creates an intimate, one-to-one relationship between the person on-camera and the viewer that is more intense, immediate, and powerful.

In Errol Morris's documentary *Fog of War* (2003), Robert McNamara looks directly into the camera lens as he discusses the hardships of the Vietnam War. Without the intervention of an interviewer, the impact of this on-axis style is intense and powerful. Adding to a feeling of intimacy is the background. The white background is evenly lit, with no shadows. There is no sense of context. The only thing for an audience to focus on is the image of the person on screen and his words.

Errol Morris said of his decision:

> I interviewed over a hundred people on a white background . . . I'm not the first person to film someone on a white background. It's been done by a whole number of photographers, August Sander, Avedon, etc. I have no patent, no trademark, on shooting someone on a white background. Of course, when you try to do something that's free of artifice, somehow that becomes artificial as well.
>
> (Chappel, 2004)

With off-axis eye lines, the interviewee looks either to the left or right of the camera lens and is assumed to be speaking to an interviewer. This is standard with news-style interviews, where the interviewer may be on- or off-camera asking questions. Regardless of whether the interviewer is visible to an audience or not, viewers are aware of the interviewer's presence and influence on the interview. Michael Moore, for example, is generally on-camera and always an active participant in the interview process. His role and influence is open and transparent.

In fiction filmmaking, technical framing decisions create meta-messages, exerting covert influence on viewer understanding of what is being presented. In Jonathan Demme's film *Silence of the Lambs* (1991), a struggle for dominance between characters is established using shot size and on-axis eye lines. Agent Starling and serial killer Hannibal Lecter confront each other repeatedly in this movie. Confrontational scenes between the agent and serial killer are framed with agent Starling in a medium shot, intercut with Hannibal Lecter in a close-up. Both look directly into the camera. This technical framing and eye-line choice highlights the struggle for dominance between the two characters. The editing of these two shots brings forth feelings of heightened tension and struggle for the viewer. Even without dialogue, the visual framing choice conveys an intense subtext between these two characters.

Other eye-line angles with ethical implications include:

- *Eye level*: camera is placed at the subject's height, so the actor is looking at the lens and doesn't look up or down. This is a neutral angle with no dramatic power.
- *Low angle*: camera placed below the actor's eyes, looking up at them. This makes characters look dominant, aggressive or ominous. This gives a character power.
- *High angle*: camera is placed above the subject and is looking down on them. This makes characters look weak, submissive, or frightened. This would be the point of view of an adult looking at a small child. This takes away power.
- *Dutch angle*: camera is tilted, skewed, and at an odd angle. This disorients and disturbs the viewer.

COMPOSITION

Composition is always a matter of selection. What is the camera position? What will be included and excluded? When will the camera be turned on and turned off?

FIGURE 7.6 A low angle of authority figures always intensifies the power differential. Credit: arindambanerjee/Shutterstock.com.

Composition can be misleading. For example, war photography can show an expansive scene involving corpses, while ignoring all the people who are physically unharmed. This manipulation of audience perception is a key ethical consideration.

The cinema verite approach of Albert and David Maysles, Frederick Wiseman, and Nicolas Philibert attempts to show life as it unfolds by selecting the most "objective" camera position. The camera is a "fly on the wall," attempting to be unobtrusive. The frame is considered neutral, objective, unbiased. The media-makers are supposedly invisible.[8] There is minimal, if any, interaction between filmmakers and subjects in this approach to production.

But is there ever a truly "objective" camera position? Choices always need to be made. Where do you place the tripod? How do you choose to frame the characters in the situation being documented? While cinema verite practitioners claim their cinematography is neutral, when you come right down to it, there really is no such thing as a truly objective camera position.

AESTHETIC DETERMINANTS

Aesthetic decisions can be intuitive, with little forethought: a spectacular sunset over a sparkling blue lake, children splashing at an open fire hydrant, a cat stalking a canary. At other times, aesthetic framing choices are technically laborious, demanding coordination of complex lighting set-ups, zooming in to a character's face as they move through the frame.

Albert Maysles had an instinctual way of observing with a compassionate eye. For documentary cinematographers in particular, the technique of simultaneously observing through the camera lens and outside of the camera frame is essential in determining what the story is and how best to capture it as it unfolds. Often relying on intuitive choices, the cinematographer makes deliberate and instinctive visual selections—all flowing from his/her perception of the moment.

It is important for the cinematographer to remain open to unfolding events. Pre-determined aesthetic choices sometimes lead to a "closing off" of possibility. This means that ethical choices and decisions must be made, at times, instantaneously and instinctively.

SUBLIMINAL STORYTELLING

The documentary *Forest of Bliss* (1986), produced by Robert Gardner and Akos Ostor, is considered a classic of ethnographic cinema. It provides a useful extended example of technical framing. The documentary follows life in Benares (Varanasi), on the Ganges, and has been described as notable for the "virtual absences of awareness on the part of the living subjects of the film that they are under surveillance by the camera" (Cavell, 1996, p. xii).

Marvin Barrett (1986) writes:

> Gardner's camera is unblinking-unhurrying-nerveless. It never fusses or intrudes, although it is present at the most intensely private moments. The result is that one sees life (and death) with a steadiness and concentration . . . The lack of subtitles or voice over narration further enhances this sense of unmediated reality.
>
> (p. 91)

The ethnographic approach to media creation uses no subtitles or voiceover narration. In *Forest of Bliss*, this limits the ability of non-Hindi-speaking audiences to comprehend what is being communicated between characters on screen. The viewer seems to be watching reality unfold but with limited access to what is being communicated.

There are sequences in the film when the on-screen characters refer to the media production process. Early in the film there is a sequence showing laborers carrying logs. They seem aware of the camera, though never look directly into the lens. One of the men says in Hindi, "lift the wood and stop watching the show" (Gardner & Ostor, 1986). At other times, the audience can see on-camera spectators watching bargaining sequences and the filmmaking production process.

The film creates the impression of India as mysterious and magical. This orientalist construction results from presenting Benares as a visual narrative without sufficient attempts

FIGURE 7.7   When composing an image, richness of detail can simply exoticize or it can inform the viewer if contextual information is provided. In this image, a man is worshiping the Shiva Lingas with a back drop of the majestic Ganges. Ananda vana was the name of Varanasi long, long ago, which means "Forest of Bliss." The Hindu belief is that if a person is cremated on the banks of the Ganges in Varanasi, that person will attain Moksha—the transcendent state attained as a result of being released from the cycle of rebirth. Courtesy of Balakrishnan K. Anat, photographer.

to contextualize the rituals, religious practices, and cultural activities presented on-screen. The use of voiceover narration or subtitles would frame what is going on for the audience and would erode the fantasy of filmmaker invisibility.

All styles of media production, including ethnographic and cinema verite, involve creative and deliberate technical choices. As the above examples illustrate, these technical decisions influence the meaning which the audience receives and interprets. While the general viewing public may accept the visuals at face-value, media-makers know better.

DIRECTING ACTOR PERFORMANCE

What an audience witnesses on screen is shaped by a director's style and approach to working with actors. What are directorial limits in extracting a desired performance? Is mistreatment of an actor or actress as a method for generating a performance ever justifiable? Should the director be concerned with possible adverse effects upon the actor as a person and artist?

The moral relativist answer is: sometimes. The moral absolutist answer is: always.

BOX 7.1 *THE SHINING* (1980)

On the set of the 1980 film *The Shining*, director Stanley Kubrick paid excruciating attention to performance detail reportedly over-analyzing every single move actress Shelly Duvall made. The stress of the movie took a physical toll on Duvall, who is said to have lost some of her hair and become seriously ill during filming. Kubrick's tactic was to make Duvall feel utterly hopeless and ensure she received no sympathy at all from anyone on the set. Although Duvall understands that this was Kubrick's way of pushing her to the limits to get her best performance, she would never want to repeat the experience.[9]

Unfortunately, all too often in the history of male directors and female actresses, off-camera manipulation is justified as a method for achieving desired performances on-camera.

Some directors believe that getting the best on-camera performance requires off-camera methods. In the production of *9½ Weeks* (1986), as a way of facilitating the character's mental breakdown on camera, director Adrian Lyne allegedly used questionable off-screen tactics to humiliate and isolate actress Kim Basinger so that her on-camera performance would be more authentic and powerful for the audience.

Before shooting began, the director purportedly instructed Kim Basinger and her co-star to ignore each other off-camera. A warm, supportive, and friendly relationship between the two lead actors might lead to a less compelling performance on camera.

The crew was also told to limit interaction with the actress when she was on and off set. No reasons were given for these orders, but it led to an atmosphere in which the lead actress felt marginalized and alone during the entire production.[10]

Gender often plays a role in this directorial dynamic and approach. Sadly, male directors often torment female actresses in order to break them down emotionally on screen, and this is more common than one would expect. Threats and actions designed to impose power as a way of creating a more compelling on-camera performance is unethical, to say the least.[11]

TECHNICAL FRAMING AND DOGME 95

Various moviemakers have implied that their technical approach is morally superior. Can this be true? Does the technical frame determine ethical content? Or, is ethical content determined by the eyes and mind of the individual behind the camera?

Dogme 95 was a film movement aimed at removing glitz and glamour from the process of filmmaking. It appealed to independent filmmakers with small budgets whose sole desire was to create authentic, raw pieces of cinema.[12]

The goal of the Dogme approach was to purify filmmaking by refusing special effects, postproduction modifications, and any other technical manipulation of footage.

BOX 7.2 DOGME 95: THE VOW OF CHASTITY

I swear to the following set of rules drawn up and confirmed by Dogme 95:

1. Shooting must be done on location. Props and sets must not be brought in.
2. The sound must never be produced apart from the image or vice-versa.
3. The camera must be handheld. Any movement or mobility attainable in the hand is permitted.
4. The film must be in color. Special lighting is not acceptable.
5. Optical work and filters are forbidden.
6. The film must not contain superficial action.
7. Temporal and geographical alienation are forbidden.
8. Genre movies are not acceptable.
9. The film format must be Academy 35mm.
10. The director must not be credited.

Furthermore I swear as a director to refrain from personal taste! I am no longer an artist. I swear to refrain from creating a "work", as I regard the instant as more important than the whole. My supreme goal is to force the truth out of my characters and settings. I swear to do so by all the means available and at the cost of any good taste and any aesthetic considerations.

("The Vow of Chastity," n.d.)

The filmmakers emphasized story and actors' performances. Created by Danish film directors Lars Von Trier and Thomas Vinterberg, Dogme 95 required adherence to strict technical limitations.[13]

Do specific technical restrictions, like the ones listed above, have any real connection to moral superiority? Can "vows of chastity" in religious orders always guarantee moral conduct? The feature film *Spotlight* (2015),[14] about the massive scandal of child molestation and cover-up within the local Catholic Archdiocese might suggest otherwise.

In many ways Dogme 95's "Vows of Chastity" blossomed as a reaction to the political economy of Hollywood. Unable to compete with Hollywood productions, Danish filmmakers invented the Dogme 95 Manifesto as a way of reframing the economics of moviemaking.

All of this occurred shortly before the era of smartphones and the full explosion of digital technology. Adherence to the Dogme 95 approach allowed lower-budgeted productions the opportunity to compete with Hollywood. It gave independent media creators hope and validation.

The link between technical limitations and economics seems valid. Working with a low budget, a media creator must reconcile themselves to what is possible to accomplish with limited funds. But economic resources by themselves do not make something more or less ethical.

Manufacturing a link between technical limitations and moral superiority is not valid. Furthermore, specific technical restrictions emphasize the means of production rather than the content or substance of a story. This guides primary audience attention to how that media was created, rather than what was created. A $40 million CGI feature film or a zero-budget smartphone movie both draw viewer attention overwhelmingly to the tools of production. Whether a media project is well funded or not, drawing audience attention to technical innovation by itself, is unrelated to and has no bearing on the ethical content of the story.

The technical frame is one part of a media creator's toolbox, and is best used thoughtfully when conveying information and creative story content. Allowing the tool to determine what can or cannot be communicated draws primary attention to the means of production rather than the content or substance of the story.

Technical framing choices have strong ethical implications. What is included/excluded, how images are framed, and other stylistic choices impact what an audience will see, understand, and experience.

Ultimately it is the eyes and mind of the person or persons making these choices that is responsible for the parameters of the technical frame and the ethics of what is being presented.

TAKE HOME POINTS

- You don't have to tell all the details of the project's goals when investigating injustices.
- When misrepresentation is used for publicity purposes, the results often backfire. Once an audience learns they have been deceived, their trust in media creators erodes.
- Shot selection is consequential in how an audience understands and experiences media content.
- Being intentional with eye lines can communicate a theme to your audience quickly and with intensity. This positioning matters. It alters the relationship between the subject and the audience.
- Aesthetic decisions can be intuitive and made with little forethought. Ethical choices and decisions must be made, at times, instantaneously and instinctively.
- By playing with background–foreground emphasis, technical framing and reframing maneuvers produce shifts in information provided to viewers. Technical framing of similar events becomes the essential factor for demonstrating shifting perspectives.
- When working with actors, threats and actions designed to impose power as a way of creating a more compelling on-camera performance is unethical.
- Creating media on a low budget does not by itself determine moral superiority.
- Whether a media project is well funded, or not, drawing audience attention to technical innovation by itself, is unrelated and has no bearing on the ethical content of the story.

NOTES

1 Personal communication with director, Stephanie Black, October 30, 2015.
2 The director of *H2 Worker* initially wrote a letter to the sugar plantation management requesting permission to shoot a documentary on the plantation. This led to a follow-up meeting with one of the managers of

the camp/plantation. Her request was denied. This then led to deceptive tactics and methods to get the filming done.

3 The storyline revolves around a fictionalized legend: in 1785, a woman was accused of witchcraft and was banished from the village of Blair, Maryland. A year later, her accusers and half of Blair's children vanished. The town of Burkittsville is established at the site of the abandoned village about 40 years later. Over the next 150 years a series of child murders and mutilations take place there.

4 *The War of the Worlds* is an episode of the American radio drama anthology series, *The Mercury Theatre on the Air*. It was performed as a Halloween episode on October 30, 1938, and aired over the CBS radio network. Directed and narrated by actor and future filmmaker Orson Welles, the episode was an adaptation of H. G. Wells's novel *The War of the Worlds* (1898).

5 For a detailed description of the impact of *The War of the World*'s radio broadcast on October 30, 1938, see Martin Gilbert (1999, p. 223).

6 These three articles in *The New York Times* discuss the impact of cameras and social media on the escalation of public protest, with specific reference to numerous recent cases of police violence in the United States: "A stark image of a shooting carries impact," by Francis Robles and Alan Blinder (April 9, 2015); "Citizen's video raises questions on police claims: Rising use of cameras," by Matt Apuzzo and Timothy Williams (April 9, 2015); and "Right time, right place, right app for capturing interactions with police," by Farhad Manjoo and Mike Isaac (April 9, 2015).

7 Long-focus lenses are best known for making distant objects appear magnified. This effect is similar to moving closer to the object, but is not the same, since perspective is a function solely of viewing location.

8 For an amusing fable about the invisibility of the cameraperson, read Elliot Weinberger's essay, "The camera people" at www.scribd.com/doc/159480203/The-Camera-People-Elliot-Weinberger

9 The long list of directors who purportedly tortured their actresses as a way of generating "authentic" performances and strong emotional subtext on-camera include Eric von Stroheim, Alfred Hitchcock, Lars von Triers, Rainer Werner Fassbinder, Stanley Kubrick, Adrian Lyne, and, recently, Abdellatif Kechiche. There are many others, and much has been written about directorial methods that create a great deal of angst for actors and crew; all in the name of trying to get the best possible on-camera performance by the actors. The issue of directing "subtext," the emotion underlying the words, is, according to some, enhanced by working conditions. For further reading about this, see Billson (2013).

10 *New York Times* reporter Nina Darton conducted an illuminating interview with Adrian Lyne in which he explains and justifies his approach to directing actors the way a moral relativist might. Seeing no dilemma whatsoever with his off-camera approach of marginalizing actors or isolating them, the limits according to Adrian Lyne are defined by your participants. He is stating that it is all relative to the participants. But is humiliation and marginalization ever really relative?

11 Sexual harassment fueled by power differentials is never justified on- or off-camera. Rainer Werner Fassbinder was well known for tormenting actresses in order to break them down. Alfred Hitchcock's obsessive relationship with Tippi Hedren, on and off the set of *The Birds*, was notorious. Sadly, this dynamic has been all too prevalent in the history of male directors and female actresses. For more about Hitchcock, see Oglethorpe (2012).

12 Dogme 95 led to increased public interest in Danish cinema and provoked debate. Many have questioned the motivation behind the vow of chastity. Was it really a serious attempt to produce a pure form of cinema, or was it simply a clever gimmick? In the late 1990s, the Danish government did offer increased financial support to Danish filmmakers. Many films were created using the Dogme approach including *Dancer in the Dark* and *Dogville*.

13 Dogme also reached into Danish architecture, reminding practitioners of the need to focus on human dimensions. By the mid-1990s, many mainstream Danish architects had become obsessed with detailing, and less concerned with how their buildings fostered human interaction.

14 Directed by Tom McCarthy, this film is a docudrama about the 2001 investigation by a team of journalists assigned by *The Boston Globe* editor Marty Baron to investigate allegations against John Geoghan, an unfrocked priest accused of molesting more than 80 boys.

BIBLIOGRAPHY

Adams, A. (2014, July 14). The celebration. *Examiner.com*. Retrieved from: www.examiner.com/article/idie-gold-the-celebration

Aufderheide, P., Jaszi, P., & Chandra, M. (2009). Honest truths: Documentary filmmakers on ethical challenges in their work. *Center for Media & Social Impact*. Retrieved from: www.cmsimpact.org/making-your-media-matter/documents/best-practices/honest-truths-documentary-filmmakers-ethical-chall

Bainbridge, C. (2007). *The cinema of Lars von Trier: Authenticity and artifice*. London, UK: Wallflower Press.

Barrett, M. (1986). Images of death. *PARABOLA: The Magazine of Myth and Tradition, 11*(3), 90–93.

Barth, K. (1932–1967). *Church dogmatics* (Vols. 1–4). London, UK: T. & T. Clark.

Benson, T. W., & Anderson, C. (2002). *Reality fictions: The films of Frederick Wiseman*. Carbondale, IL: Southern Illinois University Press.

Billson, A. (2013, November 4). Why do some film directors abuse their actors? *The Telegraph*. Retrieved from: www.telegraph.co.uk/culture/film/10411273/Why-do-some-film-directors-abuse-their-actors.html

Black, S. (Director). (1990). *H2 Worker* [Motion Picture]. United States: Lionsgate.

Cavell, S. (1996). Words of welcome. In C. Warren (Ed.), *Beyond document: Essays on nonfiction film* (pp. xi–xxviii). Hanover, NH: University Press of New England.

Chappel, B. (2004, October 27). As time closes in: A conversation with Errol Morris. *Gothamist. Errol Morris*. Retrieved from: http://errolmorris.com/content/interview/gothamist1004.html

Crane, S. A. (2008). Choosing not to look: Representation, repatriation, and Holocaust atrocity photographs. *History and Theory, 47*(3), 309–330.

Danto, A. (Director). (2004). *Shanti's story* [Motion Picture]. Belgaum, Karnataka, India: Pathfinder International.

Danto, A. (Director). (2011). *Reflections on media ethics* [Documentary]. San Francisco, CA: Forwardintime.com.

Danto, A., & Ilango, S. P. (Director). (2003). *A daughter's letter* [Music Video]. Madurai, Tamil Nadu: Gandhigram Institute of Rural Health and Family Welfare Trust.

Darnton, N. (1986, March 9). How *91/2 weeks* pushed an actress to the edge. *The New York Times*. Retrieved from: www.nytimes.com/1986/03/09/movies/how-9-1-2-weeks-pushed-an-actress-to-the-edge.html?pagewanted=all

Demme, J. (Director). (1991). *Silence of the lambs* [Motion Picture]. United States: Orion Pictures.

Dogme95.dk—A tribute to the official Dogme95. (n.d.). *Dogme95.dk*. Retrieved from: www.dogme95.dk/

Gardner, R., & Ostor, A. (Directors). (1986). *Forest of Bliss* [Documentary]. United States: Film Forum Distributors.

Gilbert, M. (1999). *Descent into barbarism: The history of the twentieth century, 1934–1951*. London, UK: HarperCollins.

Goss, B. M. (2009). *Global auteurs: Politics in the films of Almodóvar, von Trier, and Winterbottom*. New York, NY: Peter Lang.

Grundberg, A. (1990, August 12). Ask it no questions: The camera can lie. *The New York Times*, p. 1.

Hirsch, M. (2001). Surviving images: Holocaust photographs and the work of postmemory. In B. Zelizer (Ed.), *Visual culture and the Holocaust* (pp. 214–246). New Brunswick, NJ: Rutgers University Press.

Hirsch, M. (2012). *The Generation of postmemory: Writing and visual culture after the Holocaust*. New York, NY: Columbia University Press.

Hüppauf, B. (1997, October). Emptying the gaze: Framing violence through the viewfinder. *New German Critique* (72), 3–44.

Kapur, J. (1997). The art of ethnographic film and the politics of protesting modernity: Robert Gardner's forest of Bliss. *Visual Anthropology, 9*(2), 167–185.

Keilbach, J. (2009). Photographs, symbolic images and the Holocaust: On the (im)possibility of depicting historical truth. *History and Theory, 48*(2), 54–57.

Kordick, G. (Producer). (2015, November 18). *The last word with Lawrence O'Donnell* [Television broadcast]. New York, NY: MSNBC.

Lumholdt, J. (Ed.). (2003). *Lars von Trier: Interviews.* Jackson, MS: University Press of Mississippi.

Maysles, A., Maysles D., & Zwerin, C. (Directors). (1969). *Salesman* [Documentary]. United States: Maysles Films.

Maysles, A., Maysles, D., Hovde, E., Meyer, M., & Froemke, S. (Directors). (1976). *Grey gardens* [Documentary]. United States: Maysles Films.

Morris, E. (Director). (2003). *Fog of war: Eleven lessons from the life of Robert S. McNamara* [Motion Picture]. Sony Classics, USA.

Myrick, D., & Sanchez, E. (Directors). (1999). *The blair witch project* [Motion Picture]. Lionsgate and Haxan Entertainment.

Nitrategeek. (2011, October 23). The shining [web log post]. *Stories Behind the Screen.* Retrieved from: https://storiesbehindthescreen.wordpress.com/tag/shelley-duvall/

Nussbaum, E. (2015, March 23). What about Bob? The strange allure of Robert Durst and "The Jinx." *The New Yorker, 91*(5), 96.

Oglethorpe, T. (2012, December 21). Hitchcock? He was a psycho: As a TV drama reveals his sadistic abuse, *Birds* star Tippi Hedren tells how the director turned into a sexual predator who tried to destroy her. *The Daily Mail Online.* Retrieved from www.dailymail.co.uk/tvshowbiz/article-2251425/Tippi-Hedren-tells-Alfred-Hitchcock-turned-sexual-predator-tried-destroy-her.html

Ostor, A. (1989). Is that all that forest of bliss is about? *Society for Visual Anthropology Newsletter, Spring 5*(1), 4–9.

Rabiger, M. (2015). *Directing the documentary* (6th ed.). Burlington, MA: Focal Press.

Roberts, J. (1999, November–December). Dogme 95. *New Left Review,* I/238.

Russell, C. (1990). Cane fields bearing an ugly harvest. *Sun Sentinel.* Retrieved from: http://articles.sun-sentinel.com/1990-11-04/features/9002230466_1_migrant-workers-jamaicans-sugar

Scott, A. O. (2004, May 26). *The Five Obstructions* (2003): A cinematic duel of wits for two Danish directors. *The New York Times.* Retrieved from: www.nytimes.com/movie/review?res=9C02E4D6143EF935A15756C0 A9629C8B63

Sontag, S. (1977). *On photography.* New York, NY: Farrar, Straus and Giroux.

Sontag, S. (2003). *Regarding the pain of others.* New York, NY: Farrar, Straus and Giroux.

The director must not be credited: 20 years of Dogme 95. (2015, August). *Museum of Art and Design.* Retrieved from: http://madmuseum.org/series/director-must-not-be-credited-20-years-dogme-95

The vow of chastity. (n.d.). Retrieved from: www.dogme95.dk/the-vow-of-chastity/

Treem, S., Levi, H., Reiner, J., Overmyer, E., & Epstein, A. (Producers). (2014). *The affair* [Television Broadcast]. New York, NY: Showtime.

Truffaut, F. (1954). Une certaine tendance du cinéma français. *Cahiers du cinéma, 31,* 15–29.

Utterson, A. (2005). *Technology and culture, the film reader.* London, UK, & New York, NY: Routledge.

Williams, M. E. (2014, June 13). Horror's first viral hit: How "The Blair Witch Project" revolutionized movies. *Salon.* Retrieved from: www.salon.com/2014/06/13/horrors_first_viral_hit_how_the_blair_witch_project_revolutionized_movies/

Wolf, D., & Stern, J. (Producers). (1990). *Law & order* [Television Broadcast]. New York, NY: National Broadcasting Company.

Chapter 8

To Zoom or Not to Zoom?

Jon Alpert

ABSTRACT

This chapter is an edited transcript of the keynote address by Jon Alpert at Brooklyn College on March 14, 2013, as part of the Global Media Ethics Conference. Alpert explores the role of cinematographer/journalist in documentary production with a focus on war photography. Through numerous examples, he explains the complex ethical decision-making that often occurs when you try to find a balance between obligations to your subjects and an audience's right to know.

RESPECT, RESTRAINT, AND THE RIGHT TO KNOW

Have any of you had to make spontaneous ethical decisions when you were in the field? Often, as a cameraperson and documentary filmmaker, ethical decisions need to be made instantaneously, without warning. I would like to share ethical decisions I've had to make around the world, often without any preparation, without any training, without any time.

There is the issue of privacy and whether people have the right not to be in your film. There is also the public's right to know. We've had public figures that didn't want to be in our documentaries, but are in our documentaries. This is the sort of thing you have to figure out while actually filming.

We made a documentary on Section 60 in Arlington Cemetery (Alpert & O'Neill, 2008). This is where they bury the dead (military personnel) from Iraq and Afghanistan, and a very, very sensitive place where families grieve. We didn't even take the camera out for the first two weeks. We saw things. As a documentary filmmaker, you see something and feel compelled to film it. You see a mother throwing herself on a grave and weeping. You want to film it, but have to restrain yourself because of ethics and mores. You have to win the

FIGURE 8.1 As a documentary filmmaker you sometimes see things and want to instantly turn the camera on. But sometimes you need to restrain yourself in part because of ethics, and also because it is important to win the trust of the people you are filming, especially in sensitive situations. Credit: Cheryl Casey.

trust of the people that you're filming in these types of sensitive situations. In many cases those same grieving families have also been abused by the aggressive media, reporters, and journalists.

People in Newtown, Connecticut, hate the media right now.[1] Media camped out on their doorsteps, hid in the bushes—one guy dressed up as a clown so that he could lure the kids over to his camera, "Hey, kids, come on over here. Do you know anybody that was killed?" Newtown, Connecticut, is a place where people are very, very sensitive right now. I think some members of the media behaved unethically in the way they covered the massacre at the Sandy Hook Elementary School.

We all have a right to know. We want to know and understand what happened there. We also want to understand how we can prevent something like that from happening again, but there are certain boundaries you have to acknowledge. An important one is just common respect for people. Eventually, we decided not to make a film in Newtown.

MY BEGINNINGS AS A FILMMAKER

When I started filmmaking, I didn't start out thinking I was a reporter. I didn't start out thinking I was a journalist. We were living in Chinatown, still live in Chinatown. Downtown Community Television Center (DCTV) is always in my heart. It has been in Chinatown for 40 years.

We started filming because we wanted to change our community and make it better. The schools were terrible, housing was terrible, healthcare was terrible. We were doing community organizing, but were very, very ineffective.

When we began to document some of these problems: the cheating happening in school board elections (ballots being thrown in the garbage), or the health conditions in Kings County Hospital where the cancer therapy machine was called "The Killer" by the staff because it was so old and killed so much healthy tissue. By documenting and letting the public know about these problems, we were able to move things in a better direction.

We realized documentary filmmaking and using a camera could help improve our lives and improve the lives of other people, so we started DCTV. We began giving classes to train other people. We wanted to build a big posse of people who could do this work. We gave equipment to them. In the beginning, we just showed our films from a post office truck. There was no cable TV back then. There was no internet, and we had an old post office truck with a couple of black and white TV sets. We parked it on a street corner and screened our films.

If our films got boring, people would walk away. That was our classroom. That was how we learned. There wasn't a classroom for ethics. There wasn't a classroom where anybody taught us what the correct behavior for a journalist was. We had to learn this on the job, and sometimes, I think, we made the correct decisions, and sometimes, I think, we made the wrong decisions. I'll share some examples of both.

THE VIETNAM WAR

I'd like to start out with an example from Vietnam. After the Vietnam War, there were a lot of people who wanted to escape Vietnam and come to the United States. People were chaotically commandeering boats and going out to sea and it was just a big mess. The United States started something called the Orderly Departure Program (ODP), except it wasn't really orderly. Once a week, a big jumbo jet would fly into Vietnam. People pre-cleared to leave would have one final screening by the State Department.

If they gave the right answers to a number of questions, they would be allowed to get on the plane, finally get out of Vietnam, and come to the United States. It was a pressure-filled, very emotional one hour in which these State Department officials would fly in, ask questions, and the door would either open or close on your chance to leave Vietnam.

Often, in journalism and media production classes, the instructors talk about the fact that reporters and filmmakers aren't supposed to participate in the story. We're supposed to be neutral. We're not supposed to get involved, and we're not supposed to influence what's happening.

What do you do when somebody comes up to you as a human being and needs your help and asks you questions? Do you ignore that?

Sometimes the role of journalist/filmmaker and the role of human being come into conflict. That is what happened to me in this specific circumstance. A Vietnamese woman came up to me because she was terrified of giving the wrong answers, of actually telling the truth, and of being denied the opportunity to leave Vietnam. I didn't want to become her confidant, but all of a sudden, I became her confidant. How do I deal with that?

This is an example in which I participated in the story, but I participated in the story in a way that was obvious to the viewer. That was the way I decided to deal with it. I was able to help this woman and give her information. A complexity was that I also knew she was lying. But I didn't say anything. You can see, in this particular story, that there are three or four different conflicting ethical universes colliding with each other. I had about two minutes to try and figure it all out. I filmed both sides so the viewer knew what was going on.

This is an example of the kinds of things you'll encounter when you actually go out into the field. This is a case in which, if I'd behaved differently, perhaps the woman would still be in Vietnam. Who knows? These are the things that you have to think about when you're filming because it's not only the viewers and what the viewers are going to know, but also the people that you're filming that are also being affected. I don't think this was a case of life and death, but it still had a major impact on someone's life.

This next example is also a story about Vietnam, also after the war. When the South Vietnamese army was defeated, the officers of this army were put into what they called re-education camps. They were basically concentration camps. These officers just disappeared and nobody knew what happened to them. After about five or six years, it became known that these guys were still alive and they were in the camps. There was actually a friend of a friend who was a former colonel in the South Vietnamese army. He was in one of these camps: Z30C. I began petitioning the Vietnamese government to let me visit this camp.

Nobody had been in any of these camps. No-one had any idea what the condition of the prisoners was. The Vietnamese government liked me, thought I was an honorable, ethical reporter, and one that they could trust to tell the story truthfully. Among all the reporters and international observers who were asking to visit these camps, they selected me. We showed up at the gate of this camp. It was a very internationally controversial issue because these people had basically disappeared for a dozen years. I looked up at the sign, and realized I was in trouble because it wasn't camp Z30C. It was camp Z30D. They took me to a different camp, and I realized I might not get to see the person I was looking for.

What do you do? If the soup kitchen knows you're coming with a camera, what are they going to do? They're going to sweep the floors. If they have advance knowledge of your visit, they're going to make sure that everything is sanitary. As a reporter or a documentary maker, you are going to encounter situations in which people have basically cooked everything in advance in order to make sure that it looks really good for your cameras. What do you do, especially if it's in a place where everybody's been trying to get in, and you're finally the one let in the door? And what do you do when you realize that this thing is like a big Disneyland and they've just tilted everything.

How do you deal with that? How do you deal with it in a way that you don't actually lose access to the place you've been trying so hard to see? Also, how hard do you push? If you push past a certain point you might be endangering people. How do you decide whether you want to get more information or whether you need to back off because you're putting somebody in danger? This all happened in this particular case. One interesting technique that I used is asking questions and being aggressive on camera.

The man conducting the tour knows he's being recorded, and all of a sudden, he's under pressure to let me do what I want to do because if he says no, he knows that I've recorded that. Here we are, we're visiting camp Z30D where they have prisoners, supposedly 1,000 prisoners, but it's obvious that they've set this thing up for me. Everything's been prearranged, and I have to figure out how to handle it.

They had cleaned this camp out prior to our arrival and taken all the inmates and brought them up to the mountain to cut timber so that I couldn't find them—so I couldn't talk to them. The fellow that speaks at the end, Major Kung told me what things were really like. They couldn't crack him. If he didn't want to go out to the forest, he just said, "Beat me. I'm sitting here." They had taken the guys like him who they couldn't hide from me and left them in a barracks that they thought I would never get into. But you saw that basically I was pushing my tour guide to let me see things, and I wound up getting to see the major.

Major Kung was obviously crying out, hoping that somebody would help him, and as much as he was willing to talk under the circumstances, I had to decide how far to push him. Also, I was certainly leaving the camp and he was staying there. What would be the repercussions for him? While speaking to him, it was important to be cautious about being overheard. At times I used music as a cover to speak with people and try to get information.

The right-wing media groups labeled me a murderer and said that I would be responsible for the death of Major Kung, and that he certainly would have been executed as soon as I left the camp. The only thing I could do as a reporter was to contact the Vietnamese who had let me in and said

> For the rest of my life I will always pay attention to what happened to Major Kung. If I find out that you hurt him, I will do everything I can to scream at the top of my lungs and will use my position as a journalist to let other people know what you've done to him. You'd better not punish him for speaking the truth.

That was the best I could do. This was a very difficult situation for a journalist to be in, when you're so far away from a subject that could be hurt as a result of your report. But I also had a responsibility to the public, which was to show the American government what was going on in those camps. I tried to get some action started so that people would pay attention to these folks that got left behind. I called the Vietnamese up once a month and said, "I'm asking about Major Kung. What's going on?" I never really got an answer, but about ten months later I got a phone call, and it was Major Kung.

He was in San Diego and was very thankful to me. I had brought attention to his case. He felt that, after my visit, things in the camp began to change. And, shortly thereafter, the camps were emptied out. Everybody was released. We got lucky on that one. When you're in a combat situation, there are lots of decisions you have to make, and some of them affect not only the way in which you tell the story and the truthfulness of the story, but also affect your own safety. I had never been in a wartime situation before I began doing international reporting.

FIRST REPORTERS IN THE KILLING FIELDS OF CAMBODIA

Growing up, the closest I got to anything that was really dangerous was a hockey fight where I was picking on somebody who was about three times bigger than me.

As a filmmaker/journalist, all of a sudden, you're in a situation that is extraordinarily dangerous and loaded with international interest. Maybe you don't even begin to understand the different players in that situation who are tugging you this way and that, because they're hoping that they can influence your story.

Are you guys old enough to know who Pol Pot was and what happened in Cambodia? After the Vietnam War, there was a very bizarre government that took power in Cambodia. They decided that any connection to Western economies and Western cultures was evil. They emptied out the cities and sent everybody out into the countryside to work on farms. This was a very paranoid regime that killed many people (1.7 million by some estimates) and caused mass starvation of others. About a quarter of the population of Cambodia died over a four year-period. One of them was my friend, a professor in the New York state college system named Sokum Hingh.

The Vietnamese forces and Cambodian forces allied against the Americans during the Vietnam war and helped defeat the American military, but afterwards they resumed their ancient rivalry and began fighting with each other. This bizarre regime in Cambodia began attacking the Vietnamese. Finally, the Vietnamese had enough. They invaded Cambodia, pushed Pol Pot out of the capital, and were in the process of taking over the country.

We were the first reporters in there. These were the killing fields of Cambodia. This is where we saw fields of skulls and bones as far as the eye can see: thousands and thousands of people who had been killed under the Pol Pot regime. It's an extraordinary feeling to walk over skeletons and try to figure out how to photograph them so you can capture the full horror. You realize you are walking on skulls and they are crunching underneath your feet. We wanted to be there, to see the fight. This was an international controversy. We wanted to know who was doing the fighting and whether it was voluntary.

A lot of the other reporters who were there were frightened and wanted to stay in the hotel. Most reporters want to stay in the hotel during wartime. We, on the other hand, wanted to get out to the actual battlefield and see things for ourselves. We didn't trust anything that the government officials were telling us. Here's an example of the military and the government trying to trick a reporter like me, so that I'll report a story the way they like it. In the following story, I never got to the real front lines.

I always got stuck in this city called Battambang. But I held a mirror up to what was going on. You go halfway around the world to be a combat reporter, and you don't get to see any combat. I was certainly aware that there were other reporters who would accept a situation like that and make it seem like it was a real dangerous battlefield. I'm not going to name any names. But, there're some famous, "brave reporters" who spent most of the time on their hotel balconies. Sometimes they never even went out into the field. They had cameras, but they never really got close enough to the battle.

I always worked as an independent. I was never on staff any place, yet in those days, my reports were being shown on NBC. When you're a reporter, not only are you battling to try to get access to the story, battling to try to tell the truth, but also sometimes you're fighting

FIGURE 8.2   Photojournalists documenting war and conflict can get drawn into the action. Credit: KANIN.studio.

with the other reporters. On a nightly newscast, by the time the commercials are done, it's 20 minutes' worth of air time, and you've got 200 correspondents all over the world fighting to get onto that news cast.

All of a sudden, some kid from Chinatown, who has no background in journalism, who has a squeaky voice and is yipping around behind a camera is knocking your report off the air—and is out in the killing fields of Cambodia while you're in your hotel room.

WITH GUERRILLAS IN THE PHILIPPINES

The Philippines had a terrible dictator named Marcos who stole, threw everyone in jail, and was just a horrible guy. He also happened to be an ally of the United States. We supported him for many years. Some of the media reports, ours included, were part of helping push Marcos out. But, after he left, there was still a guerrilla war going on in the Philippines, and a tremendous inequity between rich and poor. People were wondering, now that Marcos is gone, is the war going to stop? We found ourselves up in the mountains with a group of guerrillas who were terrible fighters.

Every time we went out with them, we almost got killed. They forgot the bullets. We went out in a boat with them. The boat had a hole in it. I'm bailing water and holding my camera up thinking, "Gee, I'm going to get killed with these guys." Plus, we're not seeing any fighting. I said, "Listen, who's doing the fighting?" They said, "Well, it's the Combat Brigade. Do you want to join them?" You've got to really be careful what you wish for, so of course I say, "Yeah, I want to join the Combat Brigade." They walk us three days and three nights up and down the mountains, and they finally bring us to this group of guys.

The first group of guerrillas were warm and fuzzy, and we had a lot of fun with them. The Combat Brigade; they don't talk. These guys were killers, and that's all they did. They would ambush government convoys. When the convoy is driving along the road, they block the road in the front. They block the road in the back, and they just keep shooting until everybody's dead. Then they take the weapons. That's how they furnished their army. These were the guys that I was with. The night before the raid, they explained to us what they were going to do. Then we walked down to the side of the road and waited for the ambush to happen.

Here's the ambush in which they attacked this government convoy. This was an ambush; 14 government soldiers got killed. They basically kept shooting into the trapped army truck until they turned these guys into hamburger. Then they stole the guns.

I don't know how we could have warned anybody that the attack was taking place other than to run down in the road before the first car of the convoy came in and start shouting, "Ambush! Ambush! Ambush!" We certainly would have been killed but, again, this is an example of a split-second decision that we had to make when we were out there. In this case, it was a life or death decision.

Our story aired on American TV and was very controversial. John Chancellor was the anchorman at NBC at that particular time. His buddies who were in the Philippines—the big-shot, handsome reporters that got the big salaries, but never went out into the battlefield—had whined to him and said that this story had to be fake. Nobody had ever filmed a battle that close up before.

I confess that I had just come back from Robert Redford's Sundance Filmmaking camp. In the middle of the battle, I'm thinking all the time, "I'm going to shoot this angle, then I'm going to go over there and get that angle." You see we edited this thing. It's a little too nicely edited with some of the reverse shots and things like that. It was a very well-photographed battle, and there hadn't been anything like that on TV before. NBC thought it might be fake so they sent down a truth squad to look at the raw tapes because they thought that this might be true.

Three executives from NBC who had combat experience—all had been soldiers in previous wars—went into the editing room and watched about three hours' worth of raw tape from this battle. I was a little bit nervous, sitting outside the room, wondering what they're going to think. When they came out, shaking their heads, I asked, "Uh-oh, what is it?" They said, "Well, we know two things. One, this stuff's real. We've never seen anything like this before and, two, you're crazy." But when it was ascertained that the footage really was true footage, they changed their criticism of us. They attacked us for basically allowing the murder of these 14 soldiers and questioned whether or not we had done everything we could to prevent this attack.

I had to say, "Listen, I . . ." When we had been with those keystone cop guerrillas, the ones that were really bad fighters, we actually saved one guy's life. He was a fish thief who was going around to the different fish pens that they had in this lake and stealing everybody's fish. Their plan was to lure him into a trap, say they wanted to meet with him, capture him, and kill him. They wanted to do this to demonstrate to the local fishermen that the guerrillas would safeguard locals against crime and protect their fish. I thought, "Yeah, I guess the guy should be punished," but I didn't think the penalty for stealing fish should be the death penalty.

In a way that was different from the way in which we normally behaved, we made ourselves very visible in the village. We began asking a lot of questions, wondering where this guy is, and wondering if he was ready to die. He was hiding somewhere in the village, and word got back to him that the guerrillas were seeking to execute him. He managed to escape. That was an opportunity for us to save somebody's life. I don't know whether that's what reporters should do, but we decided that we needed to do this as human beings.

"I HURT A LOT OF PEOPLE"

We made a report from Cuba at the time of the Mariel Bay Boatlift. I don't know how many young people know about this, but there was a time in Cuba when a group of dissidents jumped over the walls of two embassies in Havana. Normally, the embassies are very well protected. For some reason, these people were allowed to get over the walls. When nothing happened to them, and when the Cuban government didn't try to get them out and punish them, a lot of other folks thought that they might be able to seek asylum in these embassies as well, so they jumped over the walls too.

After a week, there were hundreds and hundreds of people crowded into these cramped areas, all demanding to be allowed to go to the United States. Jimmy Carter was the president at the time and he says, "These people are all freedom fighters, and we welcome them to America. Fidel let them go." Fidel thought about this, and said, "You know, these people are the scum of the earth. I don't like these people. I think I really want to get rid of them." So he says, "All right. You want these people? Send the boats. Anybody who wants to leave Cuba is free to leave. Anybody who wants to pick people up, just sail right into Mariel Bay with your boat, and we'll load up your uncle, your grandma, your cousins. We'll stick them on the boats, and they can come to the United States."

It turned into the biggest zoo you ever saw in your life. There were hundreds and hundreds of boats. Anything that could float was coming in from Florida, shrimp boats, tug boats, water skiing boats; and they were all there in the harbor waiting for their relatives to go through this system and be released to go to the United States.

Thousands of people, and they're all coming. There were some rumors that something was wrong and that maybe it wasn't all grandmas and grandpas, that somehow Fidel was tricking Jimmy Carter and was sending other people as well: murderers, rapists, and people with psychiatric problems. Even people who didn't want to go were being hauled down to Mariel Bay. Nobody could prove this.

There were many, many reporters all asking for the same thing. The Cubans allowed one reporter to go, and that was me. This is what I saw in Mariel Bay when I got there and who I saw being loaded on the ships: they actually backed buses up to the psychiatric institutions and said, "Who wants to go to the United States?" Everybody did. They emptied out the prisons.

You saw the movie *Scarface*? That's about the Marielitos. It is the singular greatest immigration of hardened criminals in the history of the United States, and we didn't know what to do with them. In any case, my report aired. NBC had sent a jet, and the jet was waiting on the runway in Havana for this report. They figured it was going to be of great importance.

While I'm editing, the phone rings, and it's Fidel's secretary. In those days, you didn't edit on laptops. The machines were pretty big, and you couldn't—at least, we couldn't because we didn't have any money—carry these things around the world. We were dependent on editing at the local TV station where we were editing our report, and they're looking over our shoulders. The Cubans didn't know this either, and they're going, "Oh my God, look at what this guy's filmed. This is unbelievable. Fidel's going to go crazy."

So Fidel's office calls and says, "Jon, what are you doing?" I said, "Well, Fidel said that only the *escoria* [scum] wants to go to the United States and, you know, I saw the *escoria* out there and I filmed it."

They said, "OK," and that was it. So, the report goes to the airport. The jet flies to Miami. There's a helicopter waiting. The helicopter picks it up, brings it to the Miami Bureau of NBC. This is the lead story on NBC news that night, and 30 minutes after the broadcast is over, Jimmy Carter goes on national TV. He more or less quotes word for word from my newscast and decides to stop the boatlift. It's over, and nobody else can come to the United States. What I didn't know is that the Cuban government was so anxious to get rid of people who were unhappy, people who would be dissidents, people who were unwilling to be part of the revolution. They were cleaning house, and Cubans who were not perfect revolutionaries were systematically being told by state security guards, "We just want to let you know that tomorrow morning there's going to be a bus to Mariel Bay, and we're not telling you to get on it. We're not telling you not to get on it, but we just want to let you know the bus is going to be there and you're free to go."

Some 300,000 people, in addition to the 80,000 people that left, had signed up to go to the United States. But when the boatlift stopped, these people could no longer leave Cuba. When they made the decision to leave Cuba, they basically declared that they were against the revolution. Many lost their homes and their jobs. They could no longer go to the United States. All of a sudden, these 300,000 people had to be reabsorbed back into Cuban society because of this report.

I hurt a lot of people. I think, perhaps, as an American I helped the United States because I helped stopped the flow of criminals into the United States. There was an extraordinary repression against gays in Cuba in those days. I think life outside Cuba was better for them, and it's good that they had the opportunity to leave. But the criminals were criminals. The ones that came here to the United States hurt many, many people. We put them all in the Krome Detention Center in Georgia, and they burned down the prison. They were so incorrigible that they just couldn't be housed even in the American prison system.

This is an example of unknown consequences of the work that you do. You always have to be questioning yourself even when you're wondering, "Is my audio working? Is my F-stop correct?" You also have to be asking yourself the moral and ethical questions while you're filming, and you don't have a lot of time to make these decisions. Good luck!

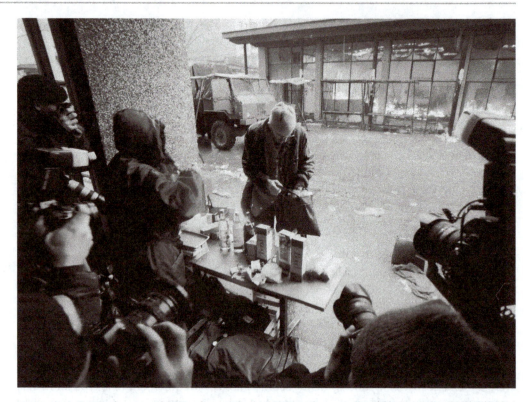

FIGURE 8.3   Press photographers gather around a man buying supplies from a market stall engulfed in flames during the final days of the siege in Sarajevo, Bosnia, in March 1996. Credit: Northfoto/ Shutterstock.com.

TAKE HOME POINTS

- Unpredictable things happen when you are in the field as a reporter, or working on a documentary. Nonetheless you must be prepared to quickly consider the ethical complexities even when you don't have a lot of time.
- When covering breaking news, you often have to make instant decisions about the public's right to know and an individual's right to privacy. These decisions have to be made with restraint and sensitivity.
- We want to understand what is happening in different parts of the world. We want to understand how people are feeling in conflict zones. But we need to recognize that there are certain boundaries media-makers need to understand and honor.
- When covering war and conflict, it is sometimes hard to stay neutral. You must decide when you have to do something to help another person. This reality can put your role as a reporter tasked with "getting the story" and being a human being into conflict.

NOTE

1 In Newtown, Connecticut, at the Sandy Hook Elementary School a mass shooting occurred on December 14, 2012. Twenty-year-old Adam Lanza fatally shot 20 children and six adult staff members. To read more about this, see Sanchez (2013).

BIBLIOGRAPHY

Alpert, J., & O'Neill, M. (Directors). (2008). *Section 60: Arlington National Cemetery* [Documentary]. United States: HBO

Alpert, J., & O'Neill, M. (Directors). (2009). *China's unnatural disaster: The tears of Sichuan Province* [Documentary]. United States: Downtown Community Television (DCTV) and HBO.

Alpert, J. & O'Neill, M. (Directors). (2012). *In Tahrir Square: 18 days of Egypt's unfinished revolution* [Documentary]. United States: HBO.

Danto, A. (2011). *Reflections on media ethics* [Documentary]. San Francisco, California: Forwardintime.com

Sanchez, R. (2013, December 29). Conn. police release final report on Newtown school shooting. *CNN*. Retrieved from: www.cnn.com/2013/12/27/justice/connecticut-newtown-shooting-report/

Chapter 9

Hidden Camera

A Conversation on Surveillance

Samir Chopra with Mobina Hashmi

ABSTRACT

This chapter is an edited transcript of a conversation with philosopher and computer scientist Samir Chopra. In it, Chopra describes how the asymmetrical power relations between the observer and observed that define surveillance structure our experiences as citizens, consumers, and media practitioners and audiences or users. He identifies transparency, accountability, and consent as the core ethical concerns raised by pervasive media surveillance. Instead of the exclusive focus on privacy, he suggests that a more productive line of thinking centers on asking what kinds of lives are enabled or made impossible by surveillance?

THE ASYMMETRY OF POWER IN SURVEILLANCE

MH: We're talking today about new media technologies that connect cameras and computers in a way that allows for new forms of surveillance. So, as we start, could you give us a simple definition of surveillance?

SC: I would define surveillance as information-gathering activities, with the added twist being that the information is meant to be used to further some ends which the observed subject might or might not be in agreement with. There is information gathering over an extended period of time, there is some analysis of the information involved, and this information will then be used to make possible some further political, social, economic, or criminological objective.

You could label the observation of animals by naturalists a kind of surveillance, but what distinguishes surveillance from this kind of observation is that it typically happens in some political or legal context where one of the kinds of objectives I mentioned above would be furthered by that kind of observation, as opposed to some simple categorization in a natural scheme.[1]

MH: Would you say that one of the issues that comes up there is that of asymmetrical information gathering and asymmetrical power relations?

SC: Yes. In the information gathering, whether the consent of the observed subject has been taken or not is a very important factor in our judging if the relationship is proceeding according to appropriate parameters of power distribution and power sharing. Who is interested in the information? How are they taking it? How is the person whose information is being taken negotiating that particular relationship? These are relatively advanced concepts about the way in which surveillance takes place.

The other concept that you mentioned about the asymmetry of the observation is also a relatively advanced concept in that it's about whether the observer and the observed are transparent to each other. There's a sense in which the subject who's being observed becomes transparent to the one observing them. They are being surveilled, information is being gathered, it's being analyzed, processed, and then used to further observe and surveil them. In all of this, the observed subject can remain unaware of the surveillance, of the grounds on which that surveillance is proceeding, and of what's being done with the information.

FIGURE 9.1 Closed-circuit television cameras are ubiquitous in many urban settings. Credit: Vasin Lee.

So these two concepts you just mentioned, asymmetry and the relative autonomy of the observed subject to negotiate the parameters of the relationship; these are very important concepts in surveillance activities.

VISUAL AND DIGITAL SURVEILLANCE

MH: The title of this chapter is "Hidden Camera." You've talked about how people being observed don't know they're being observed. Is thinking of surveillance as vision-related still a useful way of thinking about surveillance? As we see visual and other media converging with computation in social media, what might be a better metaphor for thinking about surveillance than "big brother is watching"? Or, do you think that still works?

SC: There's a distinction to be made here between the question of whether the kinds of data that will be gathered and found to be useful will be more than just visual data and the question of what language people will use to describe their sense of the usefulness of this data, or the vividness or efficacy of this data. They will still largely rely upon visual metaphors, because that's just how our language is. People will still speak of having gathered "insights," of having come to "see something" or having been "enlightened"

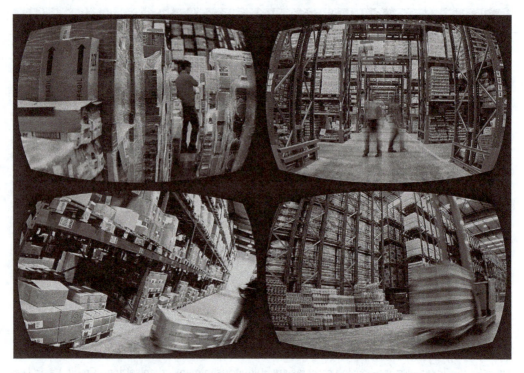

FIGURE 9.2   Although digital surveillance is much more powerful, visual surveillance, of workers for example, continues to be a powerful tool for monitoring behavior. Credit: bikeriderlondon.

by a set of data or something "dawning" upon them. These sorts of visual metaphors will dominate. Vision is a dominant sensory modality and it powerfully affects the way we speak.

But the kinds of data that will be gathered will go beyond the visual. In fact, mere observation by cameras is just a small subset of the kinds of observations that people will carry on. In fact, what is really interesting is the number of sensors now that make possible what one could call promiscuous data gathering. They sense information about our diet, about our various bodily parameters, about our shopping patterns, about the kinds of trails we leave on social networks, the kinds of consumption trails we leave online, the kinds of things we buy offline, the kinds of people we meet, the kinds of things we say, the kinds of things we write in various comment spaces online. So the interactions we have with people in this world, all of whom in turn are leaving various data trails, can then lead to these kinds of very rich analytical lenses being brought to bear upon these data signatures and data footprints we leave all over the place.

It means that visual data is just one small subset of these information trails, but I think people will still speak of surveillance largely in the framework of cameras and opaqueness and transparency and "seeing is believing" kinds of metaphors will still dominate.

CONSENT AND TRANSPARENCY IN THE CREATION OF DIGITAL IDENTITIES

MH: What would you identify as some central ethical issues as you think about surveillance specifically?

SC: Some of the most important ethical issues have already been mentioned in the earlier discussion we had about the asymmetry of power relations between people being observed and those observing them. Also, ultimately the ethical considerations at play are influenced by the fact that data that is gathered about us is used by someone to further very particular ends. There's an inescapable political angle in this, which is revealed by asking, "Why is this data being collected?" and "What is being done with it?"

There are times when we give up information about ourselves in order to further some part of ourselves or our life's projects. For instance, we might write memoirs in which we reveal intimate details of our lives, but we do it in such a way that that transaction is negotiated by us, and the ends that we further are indeed the ones that are furthered and not the ones that somebody else with agendas that we might or might not agree with wants.

The broadest ethical issue at play in this information sharing, as we give and take and enter into different kinds of transactions and relationships, is: What do the two partners in a transaction bring with them? How do they get to actually meet with each other and come to know various things about each other that they need in order to be able to drive that transaction?

The biggest problem is the asymmetrical nature of modern surveillance. For example, three or four pieces of information about us are enough to uniquely fix our identity and remove our anonymity.[2] But, we know very little about who's collecting our information and what they're doing with it. You have very little say about withholding that information.

And we know that this information is used to further some ends in ways that can negatively impact our lives. There're credit scores, no-fly lists, and mortgage ratings. There might be information used by your future employers against you. It's not too hard to imagine somebody writing a software app that would scour social media networks to find out whether there were frequently embarrassing or insulting references made to you in social media. If the results exceeded some particular numerical coefficient, the company could simply decide to not call you for an interview.

These kinds of applications are not so bizarre, given the ways in which people are talking. For example, now you have this app, Peeple, on which your friends can rate you and give you likes and dislikes. You could get an overall likability index. It's not impossible to imagine that some social club or some employer might decide that people who have low ratings like this on their Peeple index might just not qualify for jobs with them.[3]

We even see this dynamic playing out in the artistic world. If budding authors, and I know this because I have looked this up, contact a literary agent who is supposed to represent non-fiction authors, they want the authors to come to them with established social media presences and profiles. That means if you want to write a book on subject *X*, you should be recognized as a go-to authority on social media for subject *X*, and you should be able to provide numerical data analyses that speak to your standing as a social media authority on this topic.

The word "algorithm" is often bandied about. What that simply means is that there is some finite, computable, step-by-step method for calculating some quantitative score connected with you which measures you on some scale devised by someone else to further their ends, which will establish your worth. When you think about it, that's bizarre. If you read Stephen Jay Gould's book *The Mismeasure of Man*, you will find it is a sustained critique of various attempts to reify intelligence by assuming: a) that there was *one* thing called intelligence; and b) that it was the kind of thing that could be numerically measured. I wonder if similar problems exist with the various kinds of numerical scores that are being created to measure things like your creditworthiness or potential criminality.

Some of these numerical indicators have very interesting tales of successes associated with them, and I don't want to knock statistical methods *tout court*. But, I just don't know on what terms these transactions are taking place. If you think of this as a political issue, the issue at heart has to be power, and it has to be the terms on which this transaction is taking place.

SECRECY AND DEMOCRACY

MH: Two of the main critiques of surveillance have been that it's antithetical to a democratic society in that idea of shutting down openness, and that it is also antithetical to a democratic society because it is bureaucratic in the sense of, like you said, constructing and reifying categories that are meant to be predictive perhaps, but instead become prescriptive.

SC: Yeah. Think about the first one, about what the damage to democracy is from surveillance: there is all this information, which is being used for political ends, which is being applied for the deployment of power, well then, the taking of information is a kind of power grab in a way, because my control over how my information can be used is a form of my political power. And so, for that to be taken from me in a kind of non-negotiated power-taking is fundamentally problematic in the political sense, which is that given the efficacy of information, the fact that people can take my information without asking my permission or telling me what they're going to do with it is a form of political usurpation.

The other thing is that it's taken, and then it becomes sacred, then it becomes a trade secret. Proprietary algorithms are applied to it and then these databases cannot be shared with people. What I find interesting is that the information is grabbed by people without paying a proper price for it, and then, the moment it happens, all of a sudden it becomes clamped down. The parameters of this transaction are, "Give us everything that you have, but don't ask us for a single thing about what we have and what we do with it." I think that's a fundamental problem for a democratic society.

The second point about bureaucracy is especially important, because it implicates an entire machinery of secrecy. People have to cooperate in certain ways and form political alliances for this surveillance to take place. Certain kinds of legal regimes have to be negotiated by corporations with the government that say, "You give us protection for certain kinds of data." Then impenetrable guards and locks and barriers have to be set up. Citizens have to be told that they cannot enter these certain domains and have to go into other domains, and entire ministries of secrecy have to be set up in order to protect us, and then a whole culture of blaming and vilification has to take place when people actually dare to breach these citadels. Unsurprisingly, people who do dare get hit very hard. So, if you look at the treatment of Chelsea Manning or of Edward Snowden, you see how we are told that the people who are 'giving away' these secrets are complete villains. So we are supposed to be giving up our secrets to the government, we are supposed to be giving up our secrets to the corporations, but we're never told what this secrecy is for and how our information is to be used.

By the way, there's one important distinction I want to make. People, even senior journalists, will sometimes say about Edward Snowden wanting to expose the government: "Doesn't Snowden realize the value of privacy? After all, he wouldn't want anybody wanting his personal secrets to be open." And, of course, this is a completely misguided notion, because you're talking about the transparency of a government entity as compared to the transparency to be attached to a private entity.

The ethical dispute or the ethical issue at hand is that of power. Power's an ethical business. For my mind, everything actually boils down to just this one issue. That's all. What gets done with the data? Who does it? How do they do it? Do you have any say in the matter?

MH: Surveillance is the idea that somebody with more power than you is watching you. The concept of "sousveillance"[4] is the observed turning around and now watching

FIGURE 9.3   Protesters hold up signs in support of Edward Snowden at a demonstration against mass surveillance in Washington, DC on October 26, 2013. Credit: Rena Schild/Shutterstock.com.

the observer. This concept has been used to discuss citizen journalism and we can use it to think about people like Chelsea Manning and Edward Snowden. Basically, we have this idea of people using the techniques of surveillance to surveil those usually doing the surveillance. If we think of public media and journalism as the means by which a democratic society makes power transparent to the people, do you think this idea of sousveillance or citizen journalism can work as a counterbalance? What are some of the ethical issues involved? Can, as Audre Lorde asked, the master's tools be used to dismantle the master's house?

SC: I think it's the only option we have. Thinking of privacy as wanting to control what information you gave up is a losing battle, and what you should be fighting for now is total transparency going in the other direction, that is, to find out who is spying on you and for what ends. What we need are more exposés and more exposures like the kinds we got from Chelsea Manning and from Edward Snowden. They are considered bigger villains than they might be because it's very easy to say things like, "They had access to three million classified documents." Part of the problem is that too much is classified. You could say, "One million classified documents!" Well, if I classify everything as secret, well then you are breaking laws all the time. One issue is that too much is considered secret, too much is kept classified. It's too easy to fall afoul of the law in that case, which is a convenient trap for those who would maintain secrecy about their activities, and that creates an atmosphere of greater secrecy, greater lack of trust, greater caution on the part of people when they are handling governmental documents. I think there should be some declassification.

There should also be an increase in the kinds of things that are covered by the Freedom of Information Act. In today's society some of the older limits on when information could be released are ridiculous. So much information is coming out that it's better that information come out quicker now than it be submerged for as long as it can.

Citizen journalism ties into this by turning the lens back on those who would surveil you, demanding clarification of what the procedure is, finding ways to make sure that people know what at any given point is happening to them, relying on moles within the establishment or on future Mannings and Snowdens, but also making it so that they can't be threatened with things like, "Oh, you'll go to jail for two hundred years." Instead, the offense would just be something like, "Yeah, you'll go to jail for six months." There's a big difference, and one that makes a difference in the kinds of activity that people are willing to undertake as well.

FIGURE 9.4 A protester uses a tablet computer to photograph an anti-government rally organized by the nationalist Pitak Siam group on November 24, 2012 in Bangkok, Thailand. Credit: 1000 Words/Shutterstock.com

PRIVACY IN THE AGE OF SOCIAL MEDIA

MH: Following up on your points about the excessive penalties that, if I heard you correctly, are the result of a culture of secrecy that automatically removes so much from the domain of the public into the domain of the privacy of the state, we could say that we have an increasingly insecure government that is obsessed with its privacy. On the flip side, when we talk about ordinary people today and about the contemporary media landscape, we're really talking about social media and we're talking about the ease with which people can become media producers and, importantly, the ease with which all forms of media creation can be shared. One issue that comes up, especially with the younger generation, is having to deal with a very different notion of privacy. One of the central ethical questions that it raises for us is, "What is your understanding of privacy in this environment?" And then, "What are some of the issues that we need to keep in mind as media creators and consumers?" given that we're constantly engaged in some form of surveillance. We're participating in and we're drawing others into this web of surveillance as part of our everyday life.

SC: In order to better deal with privacy in this particular domain, you need to understand its value in different terms. Not just from the informational aspect, but also the value that privacy has in allowing us to live certain kinds of lives. Some kinds of relationships are not possible without privacy. Some aspects of personal relationships like intimacy are not possible without privacy. In this thinking, privacy is not just a space in which you can do illegal things without people coming to know.[5]

Privacy allows you to construct spaces in which you can find yourself in ways that are not possible when you're not private. People say things like, "Well, why are you worried about surveillance if you aren't doing anything illegal?" The reason I'm worried about surveillance, even if I'm not doing anything illegal, is because I want to live my life in a particular way and I want privacy in order to do that.

Most of the time we deal with privacy from that purely penal, punitive, secrecy model. I think of it as having a great deal to do with intimacy and as part of a personality construction model, and I think you should have a chance to talk about the value of privacy in your life; why you should have it; why you might want to cherish it in the lives of others; and, why you might want to retain it as a personal value such that even when people bring considerations of political need and demand, you can at least understand the value of your privacy and understand it in its fullest context. What does it mean for you to be sharing the details of your personal life with everybody? Does that make you susceptible to certain kinds of pressures, and people giving you feedback, and then thereby influencing the kind of life you might want to lead?

If we only talk about surveillance by the state and we only talk about surveillance by corporations for marketing or for law enforcement, we might not get to thinking about the ways in which we are willing to be surveilled or we are surveilling others and our friends, and as a result, being influenced by them, alas, in ways we might find uncomfortable or not genuinely respectful of other people's needs to find a space within which they can conduct their lives on their own terms.

MH: I don't like this word, but is this reworking of privacy part of the "price" of being social and participating in these social networks? That is, is part of the price of being social, of having human relationships now, to consent to or to agree with these forms of sharing of information? When it comes to decisions about posting your pictures of your friend's wedding, or the privacy settings on your Facebook account, what are some questions you would like people to ask as they engage in these practices?

SC: First, why are we here in these spaces? Social networks are a good thing from the point of view of us wanting to stay in touch with our friends. To communicate. To have ways of communicating with people using the tools that social media gives us, some of which we find very useful. I want to tell my friends what I did because my friends are interested in knowing what I do. I want to know what my friends are up to because that is a very natural form of curiosity.[6]

But beyond that, we have to be a little bit careful and ask if, by participating in social media, are we entering a space which is configured in such a way that our interactions with other people become a kind of performance? A performance that is choreographed and facilitated by the tools and the interface of the space that we use to produce certain kinds of interactions, and spectacle, and to generate certain kinds of data that is useful to those who make the system.

Then what happens is that this life that we're living, it also becomes something that always has value for other people in terms of what they're getting out of watching us, observing us, and doing something with what they see. Perhaps that's fine. Perhaps that's something you just can't help if you are online. But the extent to which we are just willing to forget about these questions of how much our interactions are choreographed by this space to produce a kind of data these guys want should make us a little bit uneasy. I should strive to have better control over it and to know more about what is going on so that, maybe, I can be more authentic in my dealings with other people.

MH: We talked a little bit about what questions we should keep in mind as we act as media producers and the kinds of media literacy we need. It seems like you're saying that as an ethical participant in this media environment, we should think more about what the platforms that we're using enable and what our acts of creating and sharing media imply?

SC: There are more and more kinds of lives they are making possible, but we should also ask what kinds of lives are they making difficult to live. I think that negative way of framing the question is a very good way of framing it. It's to say, the way in which we use or deploy media to tell stories to people and to serve political ends make possible certain ways of living. They also make impossible certain other ways of living. We should also think about the loss they induce.

MH: That's a great way of putting it.

SC: Yeah. This always comes up when people talk about things happening online. My favorite example is whenever people talk about online education as compared to physical education. Everybody talks about the promise of online education, and the response to that is pointing out the benefits of physical education, and how online education will never get there. But there are also some things which physical education doesn't make possible which online education makes possible.

For example, some kinds of voices are silenced in face-to-face encounters which find expression in online encounters. We should recognize that as well. Similarly, journalists and others are using new media to extract certain kinds of information to use, to combine information in certain ways to tell stories that might be invasive to privacy or that might enable certain forms of surveillance on their own. So, we should also think about what kinds of ways of relating to each other as human beings we are making more difficult.

MH: Along those lines, I want to mention a couple of recent examples and ask if you could help us think through them. What are the kinds of questions we should be asking as we think through the ethical issues raised by these examples? There is the story of the Rutgers University student who killed himself after finding out that his roommate had used a webcam to spy on him making out with a man. Then, there are websites that engage in "Twitter shaming," which is publicly naming and criticizing people who make racist, homophobic, or other kinds of biased comments on Twitter. Mitt Romney's presidential campaign was seriously damaged by a hidden camera video taken at a fundraiser of him disparaging the 47 percent of voters who would support Obama. For me, though, the example that brings all these issues together is the Sony hack, which revealed a lot of valuable information about the practices of a very important studio. At the same time, it clearly violated the privacy of public figures. So, as we work with these examples, how do we get beyond the "good/bad," "yes/no," "right/wrong" labels? What are the right ethical questions to be asking as we engage with these examples?

SC: These examples can be illuminated by analogy with something that seems unrelated but which is actually about the same issues: the nature of certain interactions between players is fixed by the relative power of the participants.

For example, take some behavior you call racist. When you call it racist, you are saying something about the relative power and the history of the participants in the issues. When a white actor puts black polish on their face and acts as a black actor, it's not the same as a black actor putting white polish on their face and acting like a white person with black people at some party, right?

At one level of description, the act is the same. But the power of the participants makes a big difference. Something similar happens in the case of these kinds of information sharing and information taking and surveilling transactions. We need to ask in each of these stories that you've told me, which side had the greater power? What kind of power imbalance was being addressed by the transaction at hand? Was there a power inequality that was being exacerbated? Was there a power imbalance that was being addressed? What was it? Why do those imbalances exist?

I think the real question is, "How is it that we have come to a situation that such large institutions of power have such concentrations of power that their information has become so valuable that people can be sent to jail for it?" As in the case of corporations and trade secrets. In the case of private citizens, people exchanging information with each other typically becomes problematic when there is a power imbalance.

For example, a tape of a gay person having sex is only problematic in a society in which gay sex is problematic. Otherwise, it's just another boring sex tape and who cares? Somebody's having sex in their campus dorm. Who cares? The only reason the video is significant, and why somebody felt compelled to commit suicide, or somebody was sent to jail, is because it's gay sex. It says something about the laws of criminalization and bigotry toward gay sex.

It's the inquiry into the power equation that is the generally interesting question in each case. If you look at Sony, I think that's why your instinctive reaction is that the leaks are a good thing because this is a large, secretive corporation which has a lot of control over our lives and we want to know more about it.

Then you're forced to deal with the fact that this corporation has, over the years, managed to convince governments that its secrets need protection. It needs the criminalization of activities of our citizenry in order to conduct business in the way that it wants. We should be asking, "Why is it that business needs to be conducted in terms which would criminalize certain kinds of behavior by citizens?"

MH: To wrap up, I'm going to put some words in your mouth and tell me if you agree. In a strange way, traditional forms of media representation actually created a real divide between who was doing the representing and those being represented, which is the traditional form of surveillance. Social media actually does bring us more into contact with each other and brings social relations to the fore. The kinds of questions that you're asking about what power interests are served, what the nature of the power imbalance is, are brought home in a more immediate way in our current environment than they were in an earlier environment because we're involved in constructing those relationships in such a direct way.

SC: One might even say that social media has laid bare some of the fabric of social power. For instance, when I notice through social media that some friends of mine are having a dinner to which I was not invited, I am brought face-to-face with a subtle aspect of our daily social relations. I realize that when we look at the field of our friends, all our friends are not the same. There are networks and sub-networks of influence, and attraction, and compatibility.

Our interactions online will ultimately bring these to the fore. They highlight the faults within our social strata. For instance, within a family, one sibling might have a certain amount of attention paid by the family to her page and this might be revealing of a larger kind of profile that she has or doesn't have within her family.

TAKE HOME POINTS

- Surveillance is the gathering of information in the context of an asymmetrical power relation about people for uses that may not be clear to them. It thus violates the ethical principles of transparency and informed consent.
- Keep the principle of respect for others' privacy in mind even when there is no legal requirement to do so.
- Commercial social media platforms are designed to encourage the kinds of interactions and sharing that generate data that will be valuable to advertisers and marketers. As media creators, choose a social media platform that best reflects your own ethical commitments to privacy. Inform your audience of how their information will be used.

- Social media platforms also make it easier to engage in peer-to-peer surveillance. Just because you can gather information about friends, colleagues or even strangers does not mean you should.
- Ordinary citizens and media creators can sometimes reverse the gaze and engage in surveillance or monitoring those in positions of power. If you do this, be mindful of the consequences to yourself and to those whose information or images you collect and share. Carefully consider if your actions are necessary for the public good.
- When the government or corporations gather information about us through tracking our online behavior, we cannot give informed consent. It is detrimental to democratic participation because while your information might be taken from you, information about the government or corporations is increasingly protected in the name of security or through the creation of intellectual property.
- New media technologies can enable new forms of community, creative expression, and lifestyles. But, altered notions of privacy, including the pressure to live more and more of our lives in public, can also make certain other forms of identity and community more difficult. Be respectful of different ways of creating and managing online identities and communities as you craft your own social media presence.

NOTES

1 For more on the topic of surveillance, including case studies, see Samir Chopra's blog: http://samirchopra. com/tag/surveillance/
2 See Cheney-Lippold (2011) for a detailed analysis of how our online activity is monitored to create "algorithmic identities."
3 Peeple gained a lot of publicity and was widely ridiculed before it was even released. As a result, the developers changed direction. It remains to be seen if it will change further and survive or vanish. For more, see Farivar (2015).
4 Developed by computer scientist Steve Mann, "sousveillance" literally means vigilance from below. To learn more about this concept, see Mann (2005).
5 For more on the topic of privacy, see Samir Chopra's blog: http://samirchopra.com/tag/privacy/
6 For more on Facebook, see Samir Chopra's blog: http://samirchopra.com/tag/Facebook/

BIBLIOGRAPHY

Cheney-Lippold, J. (2011). A new algorithmic identity soft biopolitics and the modulation of control. *Theory, Culture & Society, 28*(6), 164–181.

Chopra, S., & Dexter, S. D. (2008). *Decoding liberation: The promise of free and open source software*. London, UK: Routledge.

Chopra, S., & White, L. F. (2011). *A legal theory for autonomous artificial agents*. Ann Arbor, MI: University of Michigan Press.

Farivar, C. (2015, October 5). Facing a strong backlash, person-rating app Peeple seemingly vanishes. *Ars Technica*. Retrieved from: http://arstechnica.com/business/2015/10/yelp-for-people-app-if-it-exists-disappears-from-the-internet/

Gould, S. J. (1996). *The mismeasure of man*. New York, NY: W. W. Norton.

Lupton, D. (2013). Quantifying the body: Monitoring and measuring health in the age of mHealth technologies. *Critical Public Health, 23*(4), 393–403.

Mann, S. (2005). Sousveillance and cyborglogs: A 30-year empirical voyage through ethical, legal, and policy issues. *Presence, 14*(6), 625–646.

Chapter 10

The Ethics of Sound

John Gurrin

ABSTRACT

This chapter provides a framework for the ethical use of dialogue, music, and sound effects in narrative and non-fiction media-making. How do technical and creative sound choices influence audience perception of a story? By examining the use of sound in public/private space, location recording, sound design, and sound editing, this chapter will offer guidance in the ethical use of sound for media creation.

> The different arts reach our brains in different ways; they lodge there with differing ease, at different speeds, with different degrees of inevitable simplification; and for different durations.
> Milan Kundera (2010, p. 54)

Sound is all around us and always present. We cannot close our ears the way we can close our eyes. It requires conscious attention to listen closely, while looking in different directions and focusing requires almost no thought. I must use textural adjectives to describe sound—grainy, soft, edgy, smooth, bitter—whereas I can use adjectives to describe the visual world exactly: I see a small, blue wooden table with metal scissors, paper, and a black stapler.

What does this mean in terms of our experience of watching a film? First and foremost, it means that our conscious focus is mainly on what we are seeing, while our subconscious is tuning in to the sounds we hear, the music, the tones of voices (whispering, angry, warm), and the ambience that surrounds the action. The media narrative is constructed through visual language while sound provides the emotional framework establishing what we feel moment to moment.

FUNDAMENTALS

When we discuss film and media sound we are referring to dialogue, music, sound effects, and ambience; all used to create a convincing aural experience that mirrors the way we experience the world. Collaboration of numerous people working at various stages of a project form the sound department. This can include sound designer, production recordist, boom operator, sound editor, foley engineer, and automated dialogue replacement engineer (ADR).

Generally coming on board during the early stages of a media production, a sound designer's main task is to plan the construction of a soundtrack that creates a seamless experience for the viewer. The visual edits, the jumps from close-up to wide shot, the compression of time, the shifts from one location to another are masked or smoothed over with sound. If the sound design is effective, it flows into the viewer's experience and doesn't draw attention to itself. If not done well, then it is noticeable and can interrupt the viewer's experience.

During the production of any media project, the person responsible for gathering sound on location is the production sound recordist. Working closely with a boom operator, the

FIGURE 10.1 Jan McLaughlin, production sound mixer, at work on the set of *Nurse Jackie*, Season Seven, New York City, 2015. Courtesy of Alex Milne.

production recordist is the key crew member making technical decisions as to how the sound will be recorded while on set—whether in a studio or on location.

The sound editor's job is to create a sound world that feels as if it is real. This is accomplished by building tracks containing all the discrete sounds chosen or recorded. This is a highly artificial process. The miscellaneous sounds collected by both the production recordist and the foley engineer[1] can be from things and places that have nothing to do with the actual objects and locations that were filmed. Everything—from footsteps to the rustle of clothing, from door creaks to street ambiences—is chosen, not for its verisimilitude, but for what it sounds and feels like.

The sound environment that the editor constructs is an attempt to represent a film-maker's vision through sound selection. Care must be taken not to disrupt or distort the filmmaker's aural vision through audio-track misrepresentations, distortions, and substitutions.

PRODUCTION SOUND

Production sound is, most importantly, the recording of dialogue on set or location. Incidental sounds like footsteps, clothing rustle, and ambiences are not the focus of the effort and are often minimized so that the dialogue is as distinct and isolated from the environment as

FIGURE 10.2   Production sound mixer using a sound mixing board. Courtesy of Alex Milne. .

possible. This gives the editors the most flexibility in building the sound environment in postproduction.

A production sound recordist needs technical skills that include knowledge of acoustics and the basic physics of sound; and an understanding of recording devices, microphones, pre-amplifiers, mixers, radio transmitters and receivers, headphones, cabling, and connectors.

A production sound recordist also needs the separate—but equally important—relationship skills that have an impact on the quality of the filmmaking experience. Any job involving people has an ethical component simply because how one treats other people is a function of understanding one's role. Film crews have their own particular hierarchy and culture. They are often skilled and resourceful, competent, and creative. The intensity of the experience of making a film requires a great deal of collaboration and communication.

The production sound recordist, by the nature of the job, is close to the actors: he/she often holds the microphone inches from the actor, or attaches it to their skin or clothing. This physical proximity requires being in the emotional space of the actor. The actor's job is to be open and vulnerable; to experience profound emotions in the middle of the artificial

BOX 10.1 STRESS, COMPETITION, AND FATIGUE

> The moral mind is not a default mind. In very competitive environments, where you're under a lot of stress, a lot of cognitive load, you won't even necessarily see that there is a moral consideration at all.[2]
>
> John M. Darley (Darley & Heffernan, 2011, p. 159)

I hate to tell this story, but I was once on a film set for a music video in the middle of winter. We were on the shore of the East River in Queens, New York. It was late at night and the shoot had started early in the morning. There was a baby in the shot. His parents were safely in a trailer, hundreds of feet away. It was freezing cold, wet, and windy; and there was the director, an assistant director, the cameraman, the baby, and me. The assistant director had set the child down on a blanket, but he would keep sitting up when the shot required that he lie down. After several unsuccessful attempts to get the shot, the director turned to the assistant director and said, "Can't we just knock it out?"

There was a moment of silence—a huge pause—and then the assistant director continued, as he had before, trying to coax the child to lie down. Everyone, including the director, acted as if nothing had happened, nothing had been said, and this moment was never referred to again. It seems crazy and unbelievable, but for a moment, long enough to verbalize it, this thought had actually entered the mind of this competitive, stressed, and tired man. Insane. It's important to note that this was a completely professional and experienced crew. That's an extreme case of something that is obviously unethical. But there are often little things that happen, small transgressions that dehumanize the situation and the people in it.

environment of a film set with the "same" performance potentially shot several times. The sound team needs to be respectful of the actor's process, remembering that in the midst of all the technical chaos and activity, the actors are making themselves vulnerable, not for the crew, but for the unseen audience that the actors have in their imagination.

PUBLIC AND PRIVATE SPACE

Whenever wireless mics are used, the production sound recordist has a responsibility to turn off the mics when the actor leaves the "public" space of the film set and is in need of privacy. This is significant simply because it is really easy for the actor to forget that he is wearing a mic. It happens all the time.

On an independent feature a few years ago, I noticed that the boom person was wandering over to the sound cart whenever there was a break in action, listening to the actors who had retreated to their trailers. This is clearly unethical; the actors are assuming that they are in private and should be treated that way. They should be free to do anything they want: cut their toe nails, fart, whisper to their mother, whatever they want to do. I began muting the transmitters every time the actors left the set. What was alarming was that the boom person, who had noticed that I had interrupted her eavesdropping, acted annoyed, as if what she was doing was normal. I don't know where this attitude comes from, but it is similar to the notion that celebrity actors have lost their right to privacy, and photographers can feel free to hunt

BOX 10.2   PUBLIC AND PRIVATE SPACE IN DOCUMENTARIES

I was one of the sound mixers on the documentary *Capturing the Friedmans* (2003), a great film that was edited and structured in a way that allows the audience to come to their own conclusions regarding the material being presented. When the project started, however, we were making a film about children's entertainers and had been shooting for about a year. As the film developed, we began to focus on two men, one of whom was David Friedman. In an effort to understand more about him, we visited his childhood home and interviewed him sitting on the stoop. After a while, we took a break and he wandered off, ending up talking with a neighbor, well out of earshot and clearly off-set. I had not stopped recording and heard his neighbor refer to Friedman's father dying in jail. This was a pretty dramatic moment. I stopped recording because I realized that I was intruding into a private conversation that David Friedman did not intend to be on-camera. I rewound the tape, cut off the section involved and did not hand it in with the rest of that day's footage. It turned out that a couple of weeks later the story about his father was revealed in a different context. The story came out anyway, but it might not have. This was an ethical dilemma, and I resolved it by carefully considering that my responsibility to the director did not outweigh my responsibility to the subject, David Friedman. I believe I made the right decision under the circumstances.

them down in any detail of their private lives. The sound person can actively address this at the start of a shoot by speaking with the actors and explaining exactly how and when she will use the different mics and when she will mute them. This is a great opportunity to establish rapport and a relationship of trust with the actors.

The same rules apply for documentary production. When the documentary participant leaves the filmmaking space and the "filming" has stopped, the wireless mics will still be on and the production sound recordist could continue to record. The ethical action for the production sound recordist is to turn off the mics.

MUSIC IN FICTION FILMS

Music can be used to heighten drama, to increase tension, to foreshadow conflict, and to lighten or darken the mood of a scene. It can also be used comically and as a dramatic or comic punchline. It has a powerful and important place in films because of its ability to elicit nuanced feeling. It changes the way we experience what we are watching, and it does this in ways that we may not be aware of. It happens unconsciously: our prejudices and needs powerfully affect our experiences in ways we do not understand and cannot access.

Filmmakers can take the existing work of composers and songwriters and introduce it into an entirely new and much more specific context. This changes the meaning of the piece of music and changes the experience of that section of the film. The ready availability of music online, and the simplicity of copying and editing, seemingly remove all barriers. All we seem to need to do is to obtain the appropriate copyright clearance and mechanical rights license, and we are good to go. There is no legal requirement to understand anything about the music.

In many scenes, the music carries the narrative, giving it depth and scale. In such scenes, the primary author of the work is the composer or sound designer, but that truth is never credited in a meaningful way.

In biographical filmmaking or biopics, the filmmaker has an obligation to portray the creative work of subjects in an ethical manner. In *Testaments Betrayed*, Milan Kundera (1996) traces the unforgivable misrepresentations that have been made about the work of novelists and composers. He quotes from the works of scholars who bend and cheapen the words of writers who can no longer defend themselves. It is a powerful and tragic book that makes it clear how cruel and insulting it is to have words put in our mouths, or to have our work taken out of context and made to serve a different master.

The ethical dimension, the ethical requirement, is to do what can be done to understand something about the composer, the composition, and the time and context in which it was composed.

A very real challenge to the filmmaker is to initially make the film work without any music to support it. Successfully creating tension or sadness in a scene without music is difficult. Music adds dimension to a scene or story. It can also tell us what we are supposed to feel or experience. Music can add nuance to our viewing experience. It can also manipulate our reactions.

MUSIC IN DOCUMENTARY FILMS

Using music to create sympathy or antipathy, while a normal part of fiction films, must be done with care in a documentary.

Documentary filmmakers have an ethical obligation to take greater care not to manipulate the audience through music. Just as lawyers cannot program background music for their arguments before the court, documentary filmmakers should avoid undue manipulation. In fiction films we are accustomed to music being used to manipulate emotions, but documentary filmmakers should maintain a stricter standard.

The Inconvenient Truth (2006) is an excellent example of successful ethical use of music in a documentary. The evidentiary scenes are free of music, while portions of the film that follow Al Gore's personal relationship to climate change have music. An appropriate distinction is made between the objective presentation of facts and the personal/subjective story.

DOCUMENTARY INTERVIEWS

Audiences like to believe they are being presented with "truth" when they watch documentary interviews. Audiences want to be able to trust the filmmaker.

In documentary production, a goal is to provide the circumstances that will enable an individual or group to speak freely and honestly, on camera, about the subject under discussion.

If we approach an interview with preconceptions, or ask leading questions, we are interfering with that encounter. The possibility of a documentary participant wanting to please the filmmaker or, simply, to bring the interview to a close can mean they say something they would not ordinarily say.

There is no such thing as a truly objective film because of the realities of placing the camera, recording the sound, and the selection that goes into the editing process. No documentary is truly objective; nevertheless, sometimes the filmmaker strives to create an experience that is as truthful as can be accomplished given the circumstances.

Shooting a documentary involves numerous people and production gear. If I am going to shoot, I need to have appropriate lighting which might mean I ask the participant to sit in a particular place near a window, or I might need to set up lights that point at him. At the very least, I need a cameraperson, a lighting person, and a sound person. I might also need an assistant cameraperson. I might need three or more lighting and grip people. I may also have producers and production assistants. Even on a small crew there are several people involved, all of whom, in doing their jobs, are likely to distract the participant.

Some documentary participants might be very comfortable with having cameras and crew around and may be able to give spontaneous and natural interviews. Other documentary participants may be very uncomfortable with cameras and crew around. If we consider this for a moment, keeping in mind that the primary goal is an honest and unmediated encounter, then a new and important role for sound-only interviews comes into play.

Sound-Only Interviews

A director by him/herself, or with only a sound person, is less threatening and less disruptive than a crew with camera, assistant camera, gaffer, grips, electrics, hair and make-up, producers, production assistants, etc.

One of the most interesting qualities of film is that the sound and the image can be separated, moved around, and used independently. Splitting image and sound in this way reveals how a film truly is a constructed object. This means that we can be listening to an interview recorded on one day while watching footage shot on another day: our participant could be walking along a river, packing a bag, or anything else, while we listen to them tell their story.

The director can record the initial interviews either alone or with a single sound person. These interviews can be recorded anywhere your participant is comfortable; they don't have to worry about how they look or what clothes they should wear, and you don't have to worry about setting the light in a particular way.

Once this sort of interview has taken place (maybe once, maybe several times), then our participant may be less disturbed when the additional crew arrives to set up lights, tripods, and the camera. Recording a sound-only interview can enable a certain quality of truthfulness because it's a less technologically and socially complex situation. These interviews which are recorded without cameras rolling can then be cut with images that fill out and add dimension to what is spoken.

Wild Sound

Wild sound refers to sound that is recorded without the camera rolling. We can record all the sounds that are specific to a location environment—doors or drawers being opened or closed, jackets being taken on and off, the hum of an air conditioner, or creaking of a floor—that will help the editors create a sense of place.

These sounds are valuable in helping the editor create an accurate representation of the sounds of a space without having to record Foley or to rely on sound-effects libraries. The idea is to use the props and objects that are actually in the space, rather than trying to recreate them later. The same thing holds true for ambience. The actual noise of the street outside, through that particular window, may prove to be the ambience that works very well in the scene. Of course, it also might not work, and the great thing about postproduction is that you can change or add to the ambience and make it work in a different way.

SOUND EQUIPMENT AND ETHICS

One might think that equipment choices don't have ethical dimensions, but they do. If we take as our premise that we are looking to create a situation where our participants feel free to speak openly and honestly, then our equipment choices become ethical choices.

Earlier we discussed reasons why we might choose to record an interview rather than shoot it. Here we are going to look more closely at our sound equipment:

- Boom-mounted microphones versus wireless lavaliers.
- Shotgun microphones versus super-cardioid microphones.

FIGURE 10.3   Sound equipment can have ethical implications. Courtesy of Alex Milne.

Boom-Mounted Microphones Versus Wireless Lavaliers

If we go to a camera store or conduct an internet search for film sound equipment, what will be suggested is a shotgun microphone mounted on a camera and a wireless lavalier attached to the participant. I disagree with both of these choices for several reasons.

An important thing to understand is that a microphone on a boom pole will always sound better than a lavalier. The diaphragms in lavalier microphones are miniaturized; it's difficult to reliably make a miniature diaphragm that meets a very high specification. On the other hand, the diaphragm in a standard super-cardioid capsule can be manufactured to a very high tolerance (simply because the diaphragm is significantly larger). Although lavaliers can sound excellent, they are no match for even a standard small-diaphragm condenser microphone like the one contained in a super-cardioid capsule.

A boom microphone is suspended in the air, away from any surfaces, whereas a lavalier is mounted on the body. In normal conversation, people stand about two to three feet away from each other. The boom-mounted microphone is at roughly the same distance. If I were standing and talking to someone from a couple of feet away, what I hear, and what the microphone would hear, is the natural sound of a voice.

The lavalier is placed near the chest: it's on a tie or attached to a piece of clothing. That is a very unnatural place from which to listen to a voice. The sound coming from the chest has more low frequencies and less presence. The manufacturers introduce a speech equalization

FIGURE 10.4   Honoring the boom operator:
A bronze statue of a boom mic operator on the
Avenue of the Stars at Kowloon Promenade,
Hong Kong. Credit: Iryna Rasko/Shutterstock.com.

boost that pulls out the high-mid-frequencies in order to make the speech more intelligible. A lavalier microphone is equalized to make it sound more natural whereas the free-field microphone already sounds natural because it's placed in a better position. From an ethical standpoint, the pursuit of the authentic brings us closer to a more realistic portrayal of what is going on, and therefore, the truth.

A boom microphone is in a better position and is a better-sounding microphone for producing authentic production tracks.

The next disadvantage to a lavalier is that it is mounted on or underneath clothing. There is a possibility of clothing rustle whenever the participant moves. The microphone itself is rubbed by cloth which produces scratching sounds very close to the diaphragm. These objectionable sounds become a problem in themselves. Furthermore, mounting the mic becomes a fussy and intrusive process. It involves touching and arranging the participant's clothes and mounting equipment on them. Clearly this is not part of anyone's normal experience. Not only is it obtrusive and physically uncomfortable for people to be wired with

FIGURE 10.5 Production Sound Mixer William Kozy placing a radio microphone on Richard Topham III. Mounting a radio microphone can be a fussy, intrusive process. Courtesy of Greg Sextro and William Kozy.

a microphone, but it also creates the possibility that there will be clothing noise which will either make individual takes unusable or will require extra work in postproduction.

Another dimension to this difficulty is that the transmitter/receiver combination on a lavalier can be interrupted if the environment is not free of radio interference. Radio stations and taxicabs broadcasting nearby can be picked up and ruin a recording. Also, of course, the battery can stop functioning in either the transmitter or the receiver. Any of these things will interrupt the transmission, create another technical delay, and possibly ruin a take. We have multiple extra problems that are introduced to the filmmaking situation by using a wireless microphone. We end up with inferior sound quality, potential clothing rustle, problems with radio interference, and the possible discomfort caused to the participant.

Ethically speaking, all of these problems get in the way of capturing honest moments (whether fictional or real). Lavalier mics can ruin takes—which preemptively cuts out footage that otherwise could be considered. The narrative can be skewed by omission.

A boom microphone is easier, simpler, and better. It is also less obtrusive and less distracting for those being recorded.

BOX 10.3   CAMERA MOUNT OR BOOM-MOUNTED MICROPHONE?

Mounting a microphone on a camera may seem like a good solution, but is inferior to using a boom for several reasons. Using a boom mic and an independent sound recording device means that one person's full attention is given to recording good sound. They can adjust the gain as needed and will not have to rely on Automatic Gain Control circuits (which are problematic because they can't differentiate between dialogue and ambience), and they are focused on listening rather than splitting their attention between camera and sound. The cameraperson is then also free to concentrate solely on the image, focus, and visual coverage.

A microphone mounted on the camera is generally not in a good position relative to the participant. A microphone on a boom pole that is held above the frame and pointing at the participant is closer and will, therefore, provide a recording where the voice is louder relative to the location ambience and the noise of the microphones themselves.

If you have the budget, the skill, and the experience to use a multitrack recorder and multiple lavaliers as well as a boom microphone, then that is the most flexible way to go. It gives the postproduction team the possibility of completely re-mixing the scene. It is important to understand though, that using lavalier microphones successfully is probably the skill that takes the longest for any production sound recordist to master.

Shotgun Microphones Versus Super-Cardioid Microphones

A standard small-diaphragm condenser mic with a cardioid polar pattern is typically about six inches (150mm) long and 3/4 inches (19mm) in diameter. Sound coming from in front of the mic (0°) reaches the diaphragm cleanly. Sounds coming from off-axis are increasingly attenuated the further off-axis they get.

A super-cardioid or hyper-cardioid microphone is slightly more directional (it attenuates off-axis sounds more than a cardioid) but, as a result of this increased attenuation at the sides, is more sensitive to sounds from directly behind the mic (180°) than the cardioid.

For recording dialogue, both the cardioid and the super-cardioid provide a natural, authentic sound.

A shotgun microphone is a super-cardioid microphone with a slotted tube attached to the end of the capsule. This slotted tube serves as a phase-interference or line-interference device. The idea is that sound (moving as a wave) enters all of the little vents on the side of the tube (at different times) and, by bouncing around within the tube, eventually runs into itself 180° out of phase and thus cancels acoustically before it reaches the diaphragm. This phase-cancellation concept works fairly well; however, what tends to happen is that if you point a shotgun microphone straight at something, the sound enters, goes through the tube and hits the diaphragm. We have good, natural sound. But, as soon as you're slightly off-axis, the sound starts to shift in tone. This creates a complicated situation: rather than the voice simply being attenuated when it is off-axis, the tone quality now shifts as well.

In a super-cardioid microphone *not* mounted on a boom, the off-axis frequency response is less compromised: the attenuation is smoother.

Sometimes a shotgun microphone is said to have more "reach," but this is misleading. No mic can "reach" better than another. The difference is in how much attenuation of off-axis sound occurs. If the mic attenuates off-axis sounds significantly, then the direct sound will be stronger relative to the off-axis sound, not stronger in itself.

Shotguns are effective, especially in exteriors. But as soon as we move close to the participant, the shotgun microphone loses many of its advantages. First, the diaphragm in a shotgun microphone is about 4–6 inches (100–150 mm) further away from the participant than an equivalent super-cardioid microphone. Those extra 4–6 inches make a significant difference to the gain necessary to record the sound. The voice-to-ambience ratio will therefore be better with a super-cardioid microphone than with a shotgun microphone.

The shotgun microphone is less forgiving. As we noted earlier, the signal is attenuated and the tone is affected if you move slightly off-axis. With the super-cardioid microphone, the off-axis sound still sounds natural, and the attenuation happens more smoothly. If I have two people who are talking in a two-shot with a shotgun microphone, I would be moving the microphone from one to the other and back again. That's fine except that in most dialogue scenes there are overlaps with both people speaking at the same time. The boom operator has to choose between one character and the other. Rather than having to pan back-and-forth from one to the other with a shotgun microphone, I can place a super-cardioid with the microphone aiming straight down the middle and just leave it there. Both actors will be picked up equally; there'll be no need to move the microphone. The wider acceptance-angle of the microphone works to my advantage when I have overlapping dialogue.

A super-cardioid microphone is generally the best choice for interior locations. Remember that films, regardless of whether they are fiction or documentary, are mostly close and medium shots. A wide establishing shot at the beginning of a scene orients the audience, and then the camera will move to a medium close-up or a close-up. Two-shots and singles are the meat-and-potatoes of any film. A super-cardioid microphone on a boom pole works very well for these shots.

THE QUEST FOR AUTHENTIC SOUND

Given that films are artificial, created objects that use every trick available to *seem* real, where does the effort to be authentic come in? Is this an irrelevant consideration given that our media world today is filled with so much that is false, so much that is virtual, so much that is misleading? Is the quest for authenticity a lost cause?

Today, with the advent of sampling and the ability to appropriate any image or sound from anywhere, we are in a strangely unaccountable and slippery environment. I would argue that something authentic is therefore all the more powerful. Mirroring what we intuitively know as true, representations of authentic emotion stand out against the mainstream.

If I look at films from many years ago, what astonishes me is how stodgy and stiff they can be, how contrived and two-dimensional. The great films transcend that of course, because they transcend their culture. It is important to realize that today's films will appear equally stereotypical to future generations, except for those pieces of art that manage to transcend today's cultural imperatives. Despite all that we have learned about power and language and relativity, and our awareness of subjectivity, *the authentic is still the ethical*. It's up to you to decide what that means for you.

Sound is an important and often little-understood part of new media, fiction, and documentary projects, yet it has a significant impact on the viewer. Decisions about manipulating or influencing audience reactions through the soundtrack have powerful results and media creators should make them with care. Careful reflection on potential consequences of certain "sound" choices, whether technical decisions about recording or creative decisions about the use of music or effects, are critical guideposts of ethical practice for the media creator.

For the sound designer, production recordist, boom operator, and sound editor, respecting and being sensitive to people whether crew members, documentary participants, actors, or composers is an important part of ethical practice.

I hope this introduction to the ethics of sound becomes the beginning of a personal exploration of sound and a primer for ethical practice.

TAKE HOME POINTS

- Dialogue, music, and sound effects are powerful creative tools for media-makers; often affecting the audience on an unconscious level. Sound has a direct impact on visual storytelling and can effectively manipulate audience reactions.
- When selecting music, be sure to carefully consider the emotional subtext of the music itself as well as that of the lyrics. Keep in mind that when dealing with global internet distribution, there are cultural variations in the interpretation of musical tone, expression, and lyrics.
- Equipment selection can have ethical implications. Hidden microphones, wireless body mics on actors, and camera microphones need to be used with care.
- Remember that music is not simply an "object" to be used. It is the creative work of an artist who should be respected.
- Hidden cameras and planted microphones can present significant ethical dilemmas. Issues of disclosure, recording when someone is unaware of the camera/sound, and consent are important elements for the sound recordist to carefully consider before participating in productions requiring surveillance-style/covert media-making.

NOTES

1 The Foley engineer is involved in the creation and recording of sound effects in postproduction.
2 John Darley is a professor of psychology at Princeton University and a researcher into bystander behavior.

BIBLIOGRAPHY

Darley, J., & Heffernan, M. (2011). *Willful blindness*. New York, NY: Bloomsbury.

Guggenheim, D. (Director) and Gore, A. (Writer). (2006). *An inconvenient truth* [Documentary]. United States: Paramount Classics.

Holman, T., & Baum, A. (2013). *Sound for digital video* (2nd ed.). Burlington, MA: Focal Press.

Jarecki, A. (Director). (2003). *Capturing the Friedmans* [Documentary]. United States: HBO/Magnolia Pictures.

Jarecki, A. (Director). (2015). *The Jinx: The life and deaths of Robert Durst* [Documentary]. United States: HBO

Kundera, M. (1996). *Testaments betrayed: An essay in nine parts*. New York, NY: Harper Perennial.

Kundera, M. (2010). *Encounter: Essays*. New York, NY: HarperCollins.

Miles, D. (2015). *Location audio simplified: Capturing your audio . . . and your audience*. New York, NY: Focal Press.

Saltzman, S. (2014). *Music editing for film and television: The art and the process*. Burlington, MA: Focal Press.

Tompkins, A. (2002, July 28). *Sliding sound, altered images*. Retrieved from: www.poynter.org/uncategorized/1466/sliding-sound-altered-images/

Section Three **Postproduction and Distribution**

Introduction to Section Three

Postproduction and Distribution

Annette Danto and Mobina Hashmi

IMAGINE you are editing a film that is set on the outskirts of Nevada, near a Shoshone reservation. A brawl breaks out among drunken teenagers. You have been instructed to edit the footage at a fast and furious pace to convey maximum violence using a frenetic sound-track, even though the footage itself isn't particularly violent. Should you appeal to the viewers' lowest common denominator, even though that is likely to intensify negative stereotypes of the Shoshone community?

When editing a slow-moving documentary interview, you are faced with the need to speed things up. This can be done by removing words, sentences, and phrases. However, such cuts are likely to distort what the interviewee intended. Similarly, in journalism, situations occasionally arise where a timeline might be condensed to make a series of events more dramatic at the expense of what actually happened. These are a few of the ethical complexities that may arise during the final stages of media completion.

Postproduction is our final opportunity to determine what viewers will see on screen, for how long, and from whose point of view. For journalism, it is the final opportunity to determine what the readers will read and understand about a given story.

Once a project is done, we need to think about where and how the completed work will be seen. Distribution options vary depending on the target audience desired. Is your media project designed for educational outreach? Will you self-distribute through a film collective, or will you enter into a contractual agreement with an independent distributor?

Determining which content is circulated and which is suppressed has important consequences for democratic participation. For example, as Lawrence Lessig (2004, 2008) argues, intellectual property laws developed for print culture actually stifle creative expression in today's digital remix culture.[1]

On the other hand, the infinitesimal lag between creative concept and distribution in new media forms such as livestreaming or tweeting can mean we are immersed 24-7 in a torrent

FIGURE S3.1   A plethora of social media platforms make it easier than ever to distribute content today. Credit: Miss Ty/Shutterstock.com.

of information, opinions, and stories. This information ecology demands that we remain perpetually critical and informed.

MEDIUM-SPECIFIC POSTPRODUCTION AND DISTRIBUTION

In conventional three-stage media-making, it is not uncommon to face conflicting directives between directors, executive producers, and distributors in postproduction. Opposing intentions can push you toward creating a specific message that may not be apparent in the existing footage, telling an alternative story that may not be the story you believe is true, or altering footage by removing specific lines of dialogue or sequences.

Sometimes final editing decisions are contentious, involving power differentials. For example, when a newspaper editor decides which story will be on the front page, is s/he influenced by pressure to improve circulation figures? Sometimes the editing actually begins in the development phase when we self-censor to accommodate censorship codes.

Who decides what is in the best interests of an audience? How do these decisions translate across cultural contexts? For example, although the BBC is linked with "quality television" in the United States, it has been criticized for elitism and paternalism within the U.K. The Motion Picture Association of America's ratings system is meant to enable audiences to make informed decisions about the suitability of content, but it can also mean that films that challenge social norms are denied widespread distribution.

Who guides the completion of a media project, and what is that individual(s) primary motivation? Does the writer/director decide, or are final decisions made by the executive producers and/or funders?

Negotiating opposing perspectives and understanding divergent priorities is confusing and stressful. For the postproduction picture editor entrusted with the important task of combining visual imagery, dialogue, sound effects, and music to convey a story or deliver a media message, the demands can be intense. Editors of mainstream television programs often walk a fine line between demands made by network standards and practices, what the ratings reveal, and what the writer and showrunner have in mind.[2]

Ethical action requires understanding and defining various perspectives, analyzing the pros and cons of alternative approaches, and making final editing decisions that are in the best interests of the project. This is rarely a simple or straightforward process.

POSTPRODUCTION AND DISTRIBUTION ETHICS

Regulation and Censorship

Media regulation and censorship are always influenced by historical, cultural, and social sensitivities. As a way of securing or promoting their vision of co-existence in diverse pluralistic societies, government authorities engage in media censorship.

FIGURE S3.2 Censorship can mean preventing people from speaking or it can mean limiting how and where their speech can be heard. Credit: benjaminec.

This type of governmental intervention is often at odds with the interests of media creators and proponents of freedom of expression. However, most agree that certain controls or limits generally serve the public good. But, who decides how much control should be exercised? Who defines what is in the best interests of the public? As K. Hariharan's chapter on censorship in India shows, the public good is often decided by national elites who have their own investment in shaping public life. As political theorists Nancy Fraser (1990) and Seyla Benhabib (1992) point out, minority groups—ranging from women, ethnic and racial minorities, and political minorities—are often forced to either conform to what national elites think is in the public interest or are simply prevented from participating.

Further complicating media regulation today is the pressure of globalization and the emergence of new technologies. The internet continues to stay one step ahead of regulatory agencies because of the lack of a clear national location, loose forms of control, and elusive and evolving technology.

In some countries technological innovation has generated potential markets that can only be opened up by relaxing old forms of regulation and providing new, more welcoming regulatory frameworks. In this way new technologies challenge rationales for certain regulations while introducing needs for new forms of regulation.

Copyright

For media-makers there are often many questions about copyright law, individual rights of ownership, and fair use. Ethical concerns include not only how we use copyrighted material from others, but also how people use our copyrighted material. In both situations: there are laws, and there are ethics. As discussed by Annette Danto and Tami Gold, legal agreements and ethical concerns do not necessarily go hand-in-hand and can sometimes be at odds.

Entertainment law and copyright experts, Jaime Wolf and Neil Rosini, discuss the intersection of copyright law and ethics, and present case studies illustrating ethical complexities related to ownership of media.

Distribution

Where and when something is screened can have great impact on the ethics of that media.

When George Stoney was the executive producer at the National Film Board of Canada (NFBC), he oversaw the production of a series called *The Things I Cannot Change* (Ballantyne, 1967). This documentary series told the story of the Bailey family, a so-called "multi-problem family."[3]

For three weeks, the NFBC crew lived in the Bailey family's house, documenting their intimate difficulties with alcoholism, unemployment, and child management. When the film was completed and released on television, the family saw it for the first time. After the program ended, neighbors stopped by with their reactions and surprise, saying that they had been unaware of all the troubles the Baileys were experiencing.

The Bailey family became so embarrassed that they had to move out of the neighborhood. They were deeply ashamed that the neighborhood now knew their private troubles.

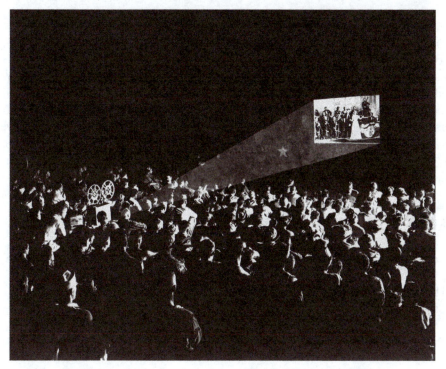

FIGURES S3.3 AND S3.4 How, where, and what we watch may have changed dramatically, but the powerful appeal of visual media persists. Credit: Monkey Business Images and Everett Collection respectively.

The impact of the nationally televised documentary had a significant impact on the family's sense of privacy and dignity.

Upon reflection, the producer, director, and editors determined that, had they prepared the family more effectively regarding the implications of participating in a nationally broadcast documentary, the family might have made a different choice. At the very least, had this family been forewarned of the potential impact of the program, their embarrassment and humiliation when confronted by the neighbors might have been less.

This is the type of distribution circumstance that presents important ethical lessons, leading back to both preproduction and postproduction. When an individual agrees to be a part of a documentary series, it is important for the media creators to insure that the individual understands where and how the material will be seen.

Finally, distribution can have as much of an influence on the ethics of a media text as the content of the text. As we discussed in the introduction, we can think of media as an object or as a practice. Although Stoney and his crew might have asked for the official consent of the family members being filmed, they appear to have considered their documentary series as a "media object" they produced rather than seeing themselves as engaged in the practice of media production that implicates them—and their subjects—in an ongoing relationship with each other and the audience. From this perspective, the documentary series itself is not a discrete media object, but the occasion for the expression and development of these relationships.

In contrast to this model, we can turn to the infamous U.S. reality television program *Keeping up with Kardashians* (E! 2007–present) which chronicles the lives of a family that has become famous through being on television. Part of the success of this television series, and the financial rewards it has produced for the family, lies in how the television program started a relationship with the audience. The Kardashian family actively rely on distribution beyond their television audience for the success of their reality show. To fully enjoy and understand the series, you have to look at all the ancillary texts such as the program's website, the Kardashians' social media accounts, tabloid coverage of the family, appearances on other television programs and films, and personal relationships with other celebrities in sports and music.

OVERVIEW OF CHAPTERS

This section is divided into four chapters.

- The Editor: A Story's Advocate
- Case Study in Regulation and Censorship in Indian Cinema
- Copyright and the Right to Copy
- Digital Distribution Ethics

In the initial chapter, "The Editor: A Story's Advocate," Terilyn Shropshire presents the ethical challenges for postproduction editing. Interviews with award-winning media editors present best practices for fiction, documentary, and reality television postproduction.

K. Hariharan's chapter, "Case Study in Regulation and Censorship in Indian Cinema," analyzes the role of India's Censorship Board. In their chapter "Copyright and the Right to Copy," Annette Danto and Tami Gold discuss ethical dilemmas related to ownership of one's creative work. Interviews with Jaime Wolf and Neil Rosini, entertainment lawyers specializing in copyright law, shed light on fair use, ownership, and media ethics. Finally, Mobina Hashmi's chapter, "Digital Distribution Ethics," examines how considerations of audience, cultural contexts, and financing shape media producers' distribution decisions. She draws our attention to the ethical values expressed in the regulatory and technical infrastructures that allow certain kinds of media to circulate in certain ways and not others.

Sometimes it is difficult to recognize or predict an ethical minefield; and at other times self-interest clouds one's vision. Regardless, media-makers can learn to make creative, effective and principled choices.

Media ethics are not determined by religious belief, historical context, or technological innovation. They can be taught. Recognizing ethical complexities is a first step. Figuring out ways of unpacking those complexities requires a little patience, critical thinking, and an ability to anticipate consequences.

As you get ready to share your work with others, keep these ethical fundamentals in mind:

- When faced with competing directives, strive to keep the best interests of the project in mind.
- The Golden Rule, "Do onto others as you would have them do unto you," applies in a very concrete way to intellectual property and how we negotiate copyright clearances and fair use.
- When and where something is screened can have as much impact on the ethics of that material as anything else.
- Setting limits on what content is distributed can be done with the best of intent. However, it is important to remember that acting in the public good can reinforce the power of dominant groups.

As we lead you into the final section of our book, we want to reiterate that creating ethically enriched media that communicates without offending, entertains without unduly provoking, and educates without misleading is an integral element in working toward a pluralist global society.

NOTES

1 Lessig's 2004 book, *Free Culture*, is appropriately enough, available through a Creative Commons license at www.free-culture.cc/freeculture.pdf
2 For examples, see Gray (1991) and Lotz (2004).
3 This documentary stirred a great deal of controversy with regards to the treatment of the poverty-stricken family at the center of the story. The embarrassment experienced by the family featured in the documentary inspired producers and filmmakers at the NFB to rethink the ethics of documentary filmmaking. George Stoney, who was an executive producer at the NFB, discusses this in his interview in the documentary *Reflections on Media Ethics* (2011).

BIBLIOGRAPHY

Ballantyne, T. (1967). *The things I cannot change* [Documentary]. Canada: National Film Board of Canada.

Benhabib, S. (1992). *Situating the self: Gender, community, and postmodernism in contemporary ethics.* New York, NY: Routledge.

Danto, A. (2011). George Stoney Interview, *Reflections on media ethics* [Documentary]. United States: Forwardintime.com.

Fraser, N. (1990). Rethinking the public sphere: A contribution to the critique of actually existing democracy. *Social text, 25/26,* 56–80.

Gray, H. (1991). Recodings: Possibilities and limitations in commercial television representations of African American culture. *Quarterly Review of Film & Video, 13*(1–3), 117–130.

Gross, L. P., Katz, J. S., & Ruby, J. (2003). *Image ethics in the digital age.* Minneapolis, MN: University of Minnesota Press.

Lessig, L. (2004). *Free culture: How big media uses technology and the law to lock down culture and control creativity.* New York, NY: Penguin Press.

Lessig, L. (2008). *Remix: Making art and commerce thrive in the hybrid economy.* New York, NY: Penguin Press.

Lester, P. M. (1991). *Photojournalism: An ethical approach.* Hillsdale, NJ: Erlbaum.

Lester, P. M. (1996). *Images that injure: Pictorial stereotypes in the media.* Westport, CT: Praeger.

Lotz, A. D. (2004). Textual (im)possibilities in the U.S. post network era: Negotiating production and promotion processes on *Lifetime*'s Any Day Now. *Critical Studies in Media Communication, 21*(1), 22–43.

Pearlman, K. (2016). *Cutting rhythms: Intuitive film editing.* New York: Focal Press.

Purcell, J. (2014). *Dialogue editing for motion pictures: A guide to the invisible art.* Burlington, MA: Focal Press.

Smith, R. F. (2008). *Ethics in journalism.* Malden, MA: Blackwell.

Chapter 11

The Editor

A Story's Advocate

Terilyn A. Shropshire

ABSTRACT

Whether editing your own project or working as a hired editor facilitating a filmmaker's vision, your creative skills, personal instincts, professional behavior, and moral compass will be called into action on a daily basis. This chapter will explore the various ethical dilemmas editors encounter as we take a story through its unpredictable evolution in the editing room. This includes the importance of an editor's point of view during production, defining and redesigning the visual narrative, the politics of collaboration, boundaries of accuracy, and navigating the ratings board.

In this chapter, editors working in fiction, documentaries, and reality television will share their perspectives on how ethics shape stories, impact collaborations with filmmakers, and affect how editors navigate uncharted political waters. Through our experiences and stories about how we faced certain situations, you can, hopefully, begin to consider how you might solve your dilemmas when faced with creative and ethical challenges.[1]

EDITING: DWELLING IN THE "WHAT IF?"

At the very heart of editing is dwelling in the "what if?" Your choices are derived not from thinking in terms of what the problems are, but from knowing that there are solutions.

The script is not the film. The footage is not the film. Both are part of the evolutionary process of a filmmaker's journey to bring a story to the screen. The journey will take a significant turn when the editing process begins. Choices made by many others must now be evaluated, narrowed, and redefined by you, the editor. A large number of people are counting on you to select the best of their efforts. They are expecting you to hone in on the best performance; the correct camera angle; the perfect look for the costume, hair, and make-up;

FIGURE 11.1   A video editor operating an editing system during a political rally in June 2013, Bangkok, Thailand. Credit: 1000 Words/Shutterstock.com.

and the appropriate use of sound and music. This task seems an easy enough goal to achieve, right? Just simply leave in the good stuff. Some would say that defines your job, in a nutshell. But, what happens when all of those "best" and "perfect" moments are not in the same take or camera angle? How do you make your selects?

An editor has the power to manipulate visual and audio information to influence the audience's perception. When you watch a movie, you see only what the filmmaker has chosen to show you. The decisions may originate on the page and get further defined on a set, but they get solidified in the editing room. Where you look in the frame, for how long, and from what point of view you experience a moment are filtered through the watchful eye of an editor. The combined use of visual imagery, sound, music, etc., to convey the story is the primary responsibility of the editor.

THE FIRST AUDIENCE

Depending on the schedule and budget of a project, an editor may begin working at different stages of a film's development. If you have a long-standing relationship with a director, your input may begin during preproduction. On the other hand, you may be hired on a project after the material has been shot.

FIGURE 11.2 Terilyn A. Shropshire ACE, at work. Courtesy of Michael Chernak.

The stage at which you come on board can influence the nature of your collaborative relationships with the other creative people involved. But, no matter when you step into the process, it is your responsibility, from that stage on, to ensure that you have the necessary elements to tell the story. The editor must always be the advocate for the story.

Relatively early in my career, I was editing the film *Eve's Bayou* (1997) in Los Angeles, and I received a call from the director Kasi Lemmons, who was shooting on location in New Orleans. She had filmed a scene that she was not sure was going to work. It is my experience that directors have a good idea at the end of the day whether or not they achieved the scene they intended to shoot.

I was asked to prepare a cut as quickly as possible for review. The result of this first cut would determine whether or not the scene would need to be reshot. The possibility of a reshoot has immense repercussions for any production schedule. An additional day may need to be added at considerable cost. In some cases, other scenes may be eliminated to balance the time and cost of reshooting the scene. The actors or locations may no longer be available, and sets may already be struck down.

Eve's Bayou was a low-budget, independent film on a 36-day shoot schedule with the completion bond company closely monitoring the set.[2] The ramifications of our potential reshoot were more severe. The production was awaiting my cut to inform them how they would proceed. It was important that I reviewed the dailies as quickly as possible. I had to trust my first emotional response to what I experienced on screen to construct this particular

BOX 11.1   THE EMPEROR'S NEW CLOTHES

It is crucial to be honest with your creative collaborators. Be forthright about what works and what doesn't. I use Hans Christian Andersen's tale of the "Emperor's New Clothes" to make my point. A very vain emperor has been convinced to walk proudly amidst his subjects adorned in non-existent finery, but no one is brave enough to tell him the "naked" truth. I am not ethically serving the filmmaker if I tell them they are "dressed" beautifully when they are, in fact, exposed.

moment in the film. Was this scene serving its purpose in the film successfully as shot? Was I cutting it correctly? In this situation, I did not have the luxury of fine-tuning my work or second-guessing the outcome.

No editor wants to tell a director that a scene is not working or is incomplete. It is your responsibility to the filmmakers and the film to be the first audience. Any issues you see in the dailies are not going to disappear magically, and once it enters your editing space, it becomes your problem to solve. You must trust your skills as a storyteller to be decisive and confident in what you communicate to the director and producers.

In the end, we agreed that the scene was not working. Kasi made the decision to do a rewrite and shoot another scene with more emotional resonance for the characters and the story of the film.

"HOW IS IT LOOKING?"

As editor, your particular line of sight or intimate knowledge of all the material will inevitably place you in a position in which above-the-line personnel—that is the producers or the studio—will ask you the question, "How's it looking?" What they want to know is, do they have a film? Is the script in which they have invested large amounts of money becoming a reality in the editing process?

Prior to the filmmaker's input on the cut, you are seen as the keeper of the big picture. How you communicate what you see—and to whom—is as important as what you communicate. Assistant editors are often put in a position of being the first to answer the phone when a producer or studio executive calls the editing room, eager for information. It is important that any feedback about a work in progress comes from the person who has first-hand knowledge of the cut—the editor.

During the shooting of a feature film, we are often put in the position of being asked to "see something" prior to the director's direct involvement in the edit. It is natural for a producer or an executive to be curious. At the same time, you are building the foundation of a cut on which the filmmaker will ultimately put their stamp.

Most directors do not want the studio viewing edited scenes that they have not first seen themselves, or on which they have not given input. It is not uncommon or unreasonable for them to be cautious as to who has early access to the work, prior to their time in the editing room. An editor can be placed in a sensitive position of both needing to assure the studio that the film is coming together smoothly, and honoring the trust that the filmmaker has in you to protect early perceptions or judgments of a work in progress.

Prior to the beginning of any project, I have a discussion with the filmmaker about how they want to handle these inevitable requests during the course of the production shoot. As a rule of thumb, my response to these requests is to tell a producer or studio executive that I am happy to show them any material they need to see, as long as they have a prior discussion with the filmmaker to gain their approval. Even if a young director is pressured to show an early cut and feels powerless to prevent this access, I try to make sure that the director puts his or her eyes on any cut of a scene prior to anyone else.

When it is time to open up your process to feedback—no matter what stage of the journey—it is essential that you make the best presentation of the material you can. People will say, "Oh don't worry, I have seen early or rough cuts before." Disregard this statement and use all the tools at your disposal to present the best cut visually and sonically. As the saying goes, "You only have one chance to make a first impression."

DEFINING THE VISUAL NARRATIVE

If you are editing a film that began with a screenplay, you have a narrative roadmap introducing the intent of the story that you are building in the cut. What the script cannot tell you is how this roadmap will be interpreted and shaped visually during the filmmaking process. The choices of the director, cinematographer, production designer, and other creative collaborators will color and layer the footage arriving in your editing room. A character on the page will be brought to life by the emotional and physical nuances of an actor's performance, revealing unforeseen, unwritten layers of the story. What the script also does not reveal is the unpredictability of events during production. It does not tell you what adjustments may need to occur when the director runs into overtime and is unable to complete his or her intended day of shooting. What if the film is running over budget and scenes must be lost to cut overages?

If you are editing a documentary, your cut is the visual script. What if the footage or new information reveals the possibility of altering the storyline? Who decides? How might your work be affected by this decision?

THE PLAYGROUND, THE PENDULUM, THE POLITICS: ETHICS OF COLLABORATION

> The film should have the biggest ego in the room.
> Barney Philing, editor, *Grand Budapest Hotel* (2014)

Remember when you were a school kid, heading out to the playground for recess? You found yourself in a defined amount of space with a variety of classmates, some of whom you were

BOX 11.2   MATHILDE BONNEFOY

FIGURE 11.3   Mathilde Bonnefoy. Courtesy of Dirk Wilutzky_2014.

Academy Award-winning editor and producer of *Citizenfour*, Mathilde Bonnefoy has edited both fiction and documentary, collaborating with directors such as Wim Wenders (*The Soul of a Man*) and, most prominently, Tom Tykwer. Her first feature editing credit is the director's time-bending international hit *Run Lola Run*, and she has continued to work with Tykwer on *Heaven*, *Three*, and *The International*, among other films.

Bonnefoy discusses working with director Laura Poitras to shift the storyline on *Citizenfour* after the unexpected appearance of Edward Snowden:

> When Laura asked me to edit the film, Edward Snowden had not contacted her yet. She had spent the past years shooting her film about surveillance with several other characters, and we had set to work with this material. So when she started receiving what was, at the time, anonymous, encrypted emails that later turned out to be from Snowden, we already had a quite advanced cut of the film. And so when she returned from Hong Kong having shot with him and brought back this extraordinary footage, we had to rethink the film completely from scratch, and from there on, also react to what the world was doing in reaction to the revelations. There were many dramas that unfolded . . . And these were historic events that were potentially extremely relevant for the film. So, one of the aspects of my work that I would say was more the producer aspect of it was to decide with Laura what to shoot, for example. Very

often we would say, "Oh, this is happening. Should we shoot it? Should we try to get someone on the ground to shoot it?" Or Laura would write, "I'm here in Hong Kong. What shots do we need?" These were decisions that we were making and more or less conceiving of how the film should become as things were happening . . . I've always felt that if you're an editor that really expresses his or her opinions forcefully and as much as I think is necessary, you're—how can I say?—you're spilling over in many other job definitions. Because you're not just cutting, you're saying, "We need this for the film. We shouldn't actually be shooting this. The script should be different. We should be cutting this scene out." You're intervening on many levels. So when Snowden appeared in the picture, we understood relatively quickly that he would take central place. And in doing so, what happened necessarily was that he pushed other characters aside that we had in our footage and that had been central to the film before, but that we ended up having to completely recut.

How does an editor draw the line between shaping the dialogue and distorting it? When does the practice of shortening or enhancing a subject's thoughts for efficiency infringe upon the initial meaning? Mathilde Bonnefoy shares her perspective on the difference between maneuvering the "truth" in fiction versus documentary:

There is indeed a big difference between fiction and documentary which is that in fiction I will have absolutely no hesitation to re-cut a scene and change its meaning completely, if it serves the story. And to have a person say the opposite of what was planned. It happened many times in films that I've edited. I have absolutely no qualms about altering what they say because these are fictional characters, and they're the product of our mind's creation. In a documentary situation, on the other hand—no. Depending on who the director is, I would say there is a prevailing standard of ethics that demands that one does not distort in any way the expression of characters because they are real, and you cannot with good conscience make them say things that they did not and change the meaning of what they have said. Of course there will be situations where you can shorten what they say, edit it in some way that the general meaning is not only kept but maybe even enhanced because it's shorter, more efficiently expressed in a way or another. But to change the meaning would be disloyal towards the protagonist and the audience. And so this is, of course, something we've completely forbidden ourselves to do.

friends with and others, quite the opposite. We relive the dynamics of this playground in our professional lives every day. Who is on your playground? How do you navigate around the "bullies" to serve your purpose in the editing room? You may not like the person playing next to you, but you do have to coexist for a certain period, so how do you make this work? How do you raise the bar on appropriate behavior rather than lower your standards of conduct?

On any given film project, there are positive forces that are pushing a story forward and opposing forces impeding progress. I have a mantra that I share with my crew: your involvement is about flow vs. impedance. You are either helping the film get to where it needs to go, or preventing it from getting there. What is your intent? On any given day, and depending on who may be stepping into the process at any given point, your "work pendulum" may swing from a ratio of 90 percent creative/10 percent political to opposite extreme. As the editor, what is your role in navigating the project through unpredictable, uncharted territory? How do you honor your responsibility to navigating the story? What happens when you reach a point in your editing process where you are not in agreement with the choices that your director or filmmaker is asking you to implement? How do you communicate your perspective without jeopardizing your relationship with your collaborators or risking your job?

If you ask an editor what the best part of their job is, many will tell you that it is in the early stages of the cut, when they are sitting in a solitary space shaping the film. The raw material is in front of you to play, to discover to shape out of the watchful eye of others. What did *you* like about that take? What performance emotionally affected *you*, made *you* laugh, made *you* cry. You are creating a cut based on how you responded emotionally. It is a very intimate time when you have the freedom to explore the material in a direction that speaks to your connection with the characters.

As the postproduction progresses, you will encounter a broader influx of feedback that will influence that initial direction. The first voice will be that of your director who has emerged from one phase of the journey, ready to begin to see the film they envisioned. It is time for them to enter into your process. As an editor, you cannot help but feel a certain amount of pride and ownership in your work. You would not be a craftsman or an artist if you did not. Now, if you ask editors the opposite question, as to what is the least favorite part of their job, they are most likely to tell you: making a change to a cut they feel is working, or seeing a cut get worse. Of course, what constitutes better or worse is an ongoing subject of negotiation in the editing room.

A common mistake young editors make is to take ownership of the cut to the point where they become resistant to entertaining another perspective. In other words, they forget why they are in the room in the first place. When you are working in a collaborative art, it is important to always remember that you can take pride in your work, but you cannot covet it. Your influence on a film is integral to the storytelling, but it is not your vision alone that will determine its ultimate outcome. As confident as you are in the decisions you make, if you choose to become overly possessive or protective of your work, you cease to be useful to the filmmaker, and more importantly, to the film.

The director and you are there to provide perspective to each other in service to creating the best possible visual version of the story. It isn't uncommon for editors to hear their inner voice saying, "No, the cut is working the way it is." It is important to try to overcome that "No." It is your responsibility to the film to "dwell in the possibility," no matter how counterintuitive that prospect can feel at times.

Often the exploration might take you to places you did not consider. Sometimes you will discover a version that both of you can agree is better. Other times the exploration may not change your conviction. The short-term solution may lead you to push temporarily past the section and revisit it later. When you return to this section, you may still feel strongly that something in the cut is not working as well as it did, or could. It is important to speak your truth as best you can and move on. Trust your voice, but know whose voice is ultimately responsible for the story.

As the postproduction process continues, more voices and perspectives will enter your collaborative environment. Producers, studio execs, and even test audiences will add their feedback to the process. You may encounter a familiar sense of resistance from your director, as he or she now must face the presence of a multitude of perspectives. It is the nature of making commercial art. The director, you, and the rest of the crew were all hired for your creative skills in order to deliver a viable product to your investors. As an artist, your relationship to the film is more complex than simply regarding it as a commodity. Nevertheless, there are others who have much riding on its critical and financial success; it is necessary for you and the director to not disregard their desire to have their voices heard.

Sometimes, if the people who have financed a film feel their feedback is not acknowledged or considered, they will push back harder on the filmmakers. This situation can result in a less than optimal creative environment for improving the film. You may not agree with their opinions, but it is always important for you to be open and to listen to these perspectives in service to the story.

It is not uncommon for the delivery of feedback to be accompanied by directives on how to fix a perceived problem. Often you will be offered ideas that range from the sublime to the ridiculous—with the latter being the most debilitating to have to consider. However, if different notes are all pointing to the same area, pay attention to what they are saying: there is an obstacle preventing the audience from seamlessly flowing through the story. Some executives are better at articulating a note than others. It is the director's and your task to filter through the thoughts, opinions, and directives of others and isolate the real problem. In a best-case scenario, the problem is expressed, but it is left up to the director and you to find the necessary solution.

But what if it you are asked to cut something in a way that conveys a message that does not feel right to you? How might you communicate with your director? What are the possible repercussions?

WHOSE TRUTH? POINT OF VIEW BETWEEN THE FRAMES

> As soon as you're editing something, you're recreating reality. If it's a documentary, it is in a way that it will condense it, and in the best case, present the essence of a situation. And so, of course, each editing decision is a decision of, "Am I truthful to the situation or not?" It's an ideal that you need to keep yourself close to.
>
> Mathilde Bonnefoy

> If it feels wrong, it is wrong.
>
> Lillian Benson

If a fictional story and documentary are both defined to a large extent in the editing room, does the editor face a greater ethical dilemma in selecting and manipulating the footage with a

BOX 11.3   LILLIAN BENSON ACE

Editor of the acclaimed civil rights series *Eyes on the Prize II* (1988), Lillian Benson's professional body of work as a television, video, and feature film editor spans almost 30 years. In 1990, the native New Yorker was nominated for an Emmy for her work on *Eyes on the Prize II*. She has contributed to films that have garnered five Emmy nominations, four Peabody Awards, and numerous other honors. Recent films she has edited include the documentary *Get in the Way: The Journey of John Lewis* and the narrative short *Progress*, part of the HBO Access series. She also directed *Amen: The Life and Music of Jester Hairston*, an educational film about the composer-arranger.

Lillian Benson recounts a time early in her career when she was editing a project about juveniles in the prison system:

FIGURE 11.4   Lillian Benson ACE. Courtesy of American Cinema Editors.

One of my early editing jobs was a documentary series about crime. The director wanted to end the tease of an episode with "a" prisoner who was serving a long sentence for a serious crime he committed when he was young. But he had really changed and spent much of his time counseling young people to keep them out of trouble. He was African American. The other alternative was to end the tease with a 17-year-old boy who was serving time in Juvenile Hall. He climbed into his neighbor's window at night, raped her at knifepoint, and tried to kill her. He actually cut her. But the director didn't want to end with the young white man. Since the segment was about juvenile crime, I thought ending with the juvenile who had committed the worst crime was really chilling. I felt that if the director ended with the image of the black man, he was consciously making the "face of crime" black, and I would have to quit. On the day we screened both versions for the executive producer, I placed my shoulder bag on the back of my chair "just in case." Fortunately, the executive producer, who was the big dog in the room, said, "No, no, no." He liked the version that ended with the 17 year old, and that's how it went on the air. My relationship with the director changed at that point . . . and he never hired me again. But I had decided that if the executive went with the older felon whom everyone on the production team recognized had really changed, I would simply get my bag and walk out the door. I had lived in L.A. less than a year, but I was not willing to end the tease that way. I didn't care how much they were paying me because to me it had consequences beyond the cutting room. Sometimes you can't say anything, but you can get up and walk away.

documentary? When you are editing a film about the lives of fictional people, the manipulation of action, dialogue, and performance is to serve the trajectory of an imaginary story. A great deal of time is spent in an editing room tracking the words, actions, and behaviors of each character to make sure they are true to a fabricated world. There is freedom to reshape sound, picture, and performances by any means necessary, in service to that goal.

A documentary or reality-based project will present a different set of rules. So the question remains, how far is too far? When does editing the material take you so far down the road that it is unreal or untruthful? Who decides?

Deciding exactly when to take a stand can be a very complicated dilemma, especially when you are young in your career. You may not have the luxury of being able to speak up easily or to walk away from a situation, but it does not mean that your instincts are wrong.

BOX 11.4 SAM POLLARD

Award-winning producer, director, and editor Sam Pollard's professional accomplishments as a feature film and television video editor, and documentary producer/ director span almost 30 years. He has received numerous awards for his documentary work. Mr. Pollard edited Spike Lee's films *Mo' Better Blues*, *Jungle Fever*, *Girl 6*, *Clockers*, and *Bamboozled*. Mr. Pollard and Mr. Lee have also co-produced documentaries for the small and big screen: *When the Levees Broke*, *If God Is Willing and da Creek Don't Rise*, and *Spike Lee Presents Mike Tyson*, a

FIGURE 11.5 Sam Pollard. Courtesy of Terilyn Shropshire.

biographical sketch for HBO for which Mr. Pollard received an Emmy. *Four Little Girls*, a feature-length documentary about the 1965 Birmingham church bombings, was nominated for an Academy Award.

Sam Pollard explains how he learned to express his own ethical position:

I think when you edit anyone's film you run into always ethical challenges. Because sometimes, and particularly more in documentaries than narrative films, you are always concerned about what a person said in the actual interview and what will it be edited down to. How far do you cross that line? How far do you go where what they said becomes unreal or not truthful? Now, I have been in situations with directors where sometimes you work on a scene, and the directors say, "I want the person to say this," and you will turn to the director and say, "Well, that is not the way it really happens. Are you sure you want to do that?" When I was a younger editor, I would be very obstinate, very difficult about wanting to tell the truth, and

I would fight tooth and nail with directors and producers about it. Which would sometimes lead to big screaming and yelling matches. Now what I learned in my years of experience is that if the director of the documentary wants me to do something that I feel ethically isn't correct, I try to be as clear and concise in articulating the why not—why you should not do that. Some directors will say, "I don't agree with that, I'm not going to change it." But, I will always say at a certain point, "This is how this should be, and this is my point of view about it and I've said that, and I want you to know that's how I feel."

AN INTERVIEW WITH LANE BAKER, EMMY-NOMINATED EDITOR

TS: As of this publishing, "Frankenbite" has not made its way into the Merriam-Webster dictionary, but term is commonly used in the world of reality-based programs. "Frankenbiting" refers to the practice of cutting and manipulating sound bites from a person's interview to manufacture what appears to be a fluid, natural thought. I asked Lane Baker to describe "Frankenbiting" in the realm of reality-television.

BOX 11.5   LANE BAKER

FIGURE 11.6   Lane Baker. Courtesy of Alonya Eisenberg.

Lane Baker realized his passion for editing while earning a BA in Cinema/ Television at the University of Southern California. Lane went on to further his studies with an Editing Fellowship at the American Film Institute. Afterward, Lane worked as an assistant editor on feature films, and eventually transitioned to editor on the popular TV series *Survivor*. Over the next decade, this and other reality series such as *The Apprentice*, *Hell's Kitchen*, and *Breaking Pointe* added to his professional experience in the quickly growing genre and earned him a total of five Emmy nominations. In between working on reality TV shows, Lane has also worked on a number of low-budget features including *Dead Tone*, *Nite Tales*, and *The Night Before*.

LB: So this is a term that is used almost every day, and it is a verb or noun. "That is a terrible Frankenbite, we have to take that out," or, "We'll just Frankenbite something." It's just part of the lingo. I don't know anyone who feels that it is wrong to Frankenbite if the essence of what is being said matches the essence of the story. So, if a person feels a certain way or thinks a certain way, but they don't articulate it very well, perhaps they don't say it in a concise way: no one has a problem with going into other interviews, pulling phrases to make a coherent thought based on what the character thinks and feels. What I think that people don't do typically, that I can recall, is say, "You know what, we are going to create a fictional story because we can Frankenbite, we have this ability. We are just going to make these characters say these outrageous things that we just invented." They don't do that because, if it doesn't have the rest of the reality to support it, then it feels really fake.

TS: But, then again, who decides what is too much or what is too far?

LB: The editor and the producer decide what is too far.

TS: So initially, you may put something together or Frankenbite, but then, in playing it back, you will say, "Oh, this is just too much?"

LB: That doesn't happen very often [laughs] but sometimes, I think, if it is too big of a stretch in the context of the story, they won't do it. If it feels like it is just out in left field, they will say no because it doesn't fit the rest of the show.

TS: And from the standpoint of the person who said it? If they are watching the show and they say, "I never said that"? Essentially, whatever they say on camera can be recut however the show chooses to use it for their programming purposes?

LB: Yes, and that is sometimes used to create a sense of suspense. On a show where contestants help dictate the story—it's an elimination, for example. If their interview bites are giving away the story, we might have to play with stuff to make things seem a little more vague, a little less decisive, and I don't have an ethical issue with that because regardless of whether or not the character goes home saying, "They made it seem like I didn't know what I was going to do, or that I was conflicted, and I really wasn't that conflicted. I kind of already knew." But at that point, I feel like the characters are not necessarily people, they are characters in a show that are based on real people. I think that we have to tell a compelling story the best we can, and I don't have an ethical issue with that.

The realm of reality television can raise some ethical considerations for an editor. Usually, the editor is working within a set of rules that has already been established by the show-runners or the network. They are not necessarily shaping a story toward a point of view, but creating what will be compelling, provocative entertainment for the viewers. Lane describes the world of television reality as often portrayed in two categories: docusoap and reality competition.

Whereas a docusoap is structured around real-life scenarios being played out in a soap opera-like style (e.g. the *Real Housewives* series), a reality competition is based on a subjective judgment. "How well can you sing a song?" "Are you the best chef?" "How well do you perform a task?"

So what happens when a contestant's character or personality does not translate to interesting entertainment on the screen? What if one contestant brings more comedy or drama to the situation, or fits in the demographic the show is seeking? While these decisions are usually dictated by executives who have creative control, it is the editor who must execute the decisions. This may include changing or skewing the cut in a particular way that may appear to favor another person.

LB: We might look at the materials as editors and say, "Well this person did fantastic," but that is not the end result. And the person who won the competition: perhaps we would not pick them as the winner based on the footage we have to look at, yet we [are] obligated to make one person look like they deserved it and one look like they didn't. And we always try to the best of our ability to make things look close because that is more dramatically interesting when it is like a horse race. Sometimes, we have to balance things out in the cut, depending on the results. So if someone looks great in the cut, but they lost, we have to make them look not so great. If someone doesn't look so great in the footage that we have to work with, yet they won, we have to find ways to build them better and make it look like it is merited. It's just part of the job. Regardless whether you like or not, it not your decision, but you do have to execute it.

WHEN THE FINISH LINE MOVES

As the end of the editing process approaches, an editor may be asked to re-cut a scene that the Motion Picture Association of America (MPAA) has determined to be too graphic, sexually provocative, or violent in nature to receive the desired rating. In television, it is the Standards and Practices department of the network that will determine if a scene is too strong to air. How do you rethink the footage in a way that maintains the intent and essence of the story while addressing the required changes to tame or soften the scene?

In the film I edited, *Love and Basketball* (2000), the lead character Monica loses her virginity to her childhood friend, Quincy. When the rating boards reviewed the sequence, they deemed the scene too strong for the desired PG-13 rating despite there being no nudity or graphic elements in the scene. After back and forth conversations with the representative from the MPAA, we were told that part of the issue was the visual point at which it appears Monica transitions beyond the pain of her first sexual experience to relaxing into the moment. Setting aside the female sociopolitical ramifications of this issue, the bottom line was that if we wanted to receive a rating that permitted the desired demographic of young women to have access to this story, we were going to need to change the scene. Despite our initial reluctance to re-cut the scene, the director and I created a version with which we were happy.

More often than not, you can make a cut that stays true to the emotional intent of the scene and passes the rating board's scrutiny. Making an adjustment for non-creative reasons to a scene that is working is, however, not one of my favorite editorial pursuits, and I rarely ever feel it results in a better cut. I approach the task as another obstacle to overcome in the overall mission to deliver the best film. In some cases, it involves re-juxtaposing or changing an angle, adjusting a sound effect, or using visual effects to help make a graphic element more visually acceptable. In the end, the decision to adjust content for a particular rating is made by the filmmakers and the producing partners, and facilitated by the editor.

YOUR INNER COMPASS

In this chapter you have been introduced to the various creative, political, and ethical "what ifs?" an editor may face during the postproduction process. Each project will present different challenges, but how you overcome them will ultimately prepare you for your next pursuit. In the end, the ethical dilemmas you may encounter in service to the story will define your career journey as you move forward.

TAKE HOME POINTS

- As editor, you are the story's advocate and the early audience for the material. Communicate and collaborate in service to that responsibility.
- As the story evolves through the editing process, you must be receptive to the inevitable changes that will occur. Overcome your attachment to what exists and be open to other possibilities.
- Prepare yourself to navigate the unpredictable politics that are part of every editing room. Trust your voice and internal governor to guide you through the more ethically challenging situations.
- The best ethical advice any editor can give you is: pay attention to what you are feeling and what your instincts are telling you. It is important for you to have your individual opinion, even if it is not in sync with others.
- You are in the room to offer perspective with a balance of ego and humility. You have to live with the decisions you make. Practice discretion and be respectful of other collaborators'/artists' perspectives.
- It is crucial to be honest with your creative collaborators. Be forthright about what works, and what doesn't.

NOTES

1   Trade publications are always a great resource for beginners. *Cinema Editor: The Magazine for Film & Television Editors, Assistants and Post-Production Professionals*, for example, is available online for a very reasonable fee at www.cinemaeditormagazine.com/
2   Completion bonds are often used to insure that a feature film will get completed. It is a financial contract that insures a given project will be completed even if the producer runs out of money, or any measure of financial or other impediment occurs during the production of the project.

BIBLIOGRAPHY

Betancourt, M. (2016). *Beyond spatial montage: Windowing, or the cinematic displacement of time, motion, and space.* Burlington, MA: Focal Press.

Bowen, C. J., & Thompson, R. (2013). *Grammar of the edit* (3rd ed.). Burlington, MA: Focal Press.

Gordon, A. D., Kittross, J. M., Merrill, J. C., & Babcock, W. (2011). *Controversies in media ethics* (3rd ed.). New York, NY: Routledge.

Hampton, H. (Executive Producer). (1987–1990). *Eyes on the prize* [Motion Picture]. Public Broadcasting System.

Harris, K. M. (2006). *Boys, boyz, bois: An ethics of black masculinity in film and popular media.* New York, NY: Routledge.

Lemmons, K. (Director) (1997). *Eve's Bayou* [Motion Picture]. Trimark Pictures.

Lumet, S. (1996). *Making movies.* United States: First Vintage Books Edition.

Murch, W. (2001). *In the blink of an eye: A perspective on film editing* (2nd ed.). Los Angeles, CA: Silman-James Press.

Ondaatje, M. (2002). *The conversations: Walter Murch and the art of editing.* London, UK: Bloomsbury.

Perebinossoff, P. (2008). *Real-world media ethics: Inside the broadcast and entertainment industries.* Amsterdam, Netherlands, & Boston, MA: Focal Press.

Poitras, L. (Director). (2014). *Citizenfour* [Motion Picture]. HBO Films/Radius-TWC.

Prince-Bythewood, G. P. (Director). (2000). *Love and basketball* [Motion Picture]. New Line Cinema.

Chapter 12

Case Study in Regulation and Censorship in Indian Cinema

K. Hariharan

ABSTRACT

Historical and cultural contexts are always reflected in media regulation. Definitions of what requires regulation, and approaches to regulation vary from country to country. Regulation can be in the form of censorship as in the case of India's Central Board of Film Certification (CBFC) presented here; or as in the U.S. Motion Picture Association of America (MPAA) ratings system. This chapter offers a study of complexities in media regulation in India, the world's largest democracy.

Media regulation and censorship are always influenced by historical, cultural, and social sensitivities. As a way of securing or promoting their vision of co-existence in diverse pluralistic societies, government authorities engage in media censorship.

This type of governmental intervention is often at odds with the interests of media creators and proponents of freedom of expression. However, most agree that certain controls or limits generally serve the public good. But who decides how much control? Who defines what is in the best interests of the public?[1]

Further complicating media regulation today is the pressure of globalization and the emergence of new technologies. The internet continues to stay one step ahead of regulatory agencies because of the lack of a clear national location, loose forms of control, and elusive and evolving technology.

In some countries, technological innovation has generated potential markets that can only be opened up by relaxing old forms of regulation and providing new, more welcoming regulatory frameworks. In this way new technologies challenge rationales for certain regulations while introducing needs for new forms of regulation.

BOX 12.1 *CHARLIE HEBDO* AND THE BATTLE OVER FREE SPEECH

FIGURE 12.2   Around 50,000 people marched in a unity rally in Strasbourg, France, on January 11, 2015 in response to the attacks on the satirical magazine *Charlie Hebdo*. Credit: Hadrian/Shutterstock.com.

On January 7, 2015, in Paris, France the entire world was shaken by the murderous attack on the journalists of the French satirical magazine *Charlie Hebdo*. This magazine had featured, among many other satirical cartoons, caricatures of Prophet Mohammed, the Pope, and other religious figures in bizarre poses. Despite verbal and written warnings issued by Islamic groups, the magazine continued with their expressions which were considered "blasphemous" by some Muslims. When the offices of *Charlie Hebdo* were attacked and journalists killed, there was an international outrage and demonstrations in support of the magazine's freedom of expression saying that such violence was not the right way to express dissent. *Charlie Hebdo* was criticized in at least some spaces around the world—and even in some prominent U.S. media outlets such as CNN—for being culturally insensitive toward a minority group that is discriminated against in France. The attack on the magazine was clearly wrong, but were journalists too quick to valorize *Charlie Hebdo*?

In a recent interview, the celebrated novelist and Booker Prize winner Salman Rushdie said, "A question I have often asked is, 'What would an inoffensive political cartoon look like?' 'What would a respectful cartoon look like?' The form requires disrespect and so if we are going to have in the world things like cartoons and satire, we just have to accept it as part of the price of freedom" (Padmanabhan, 2012). The assumption Rushdie makes is that satire as a style of humor is comprehensible to all global citizens. This is not the case. Satire requires a certain level of education and familiarity with a distinctive style of political humor. George Orwell's *Animal Farm* is not required reading in all parts of the world.

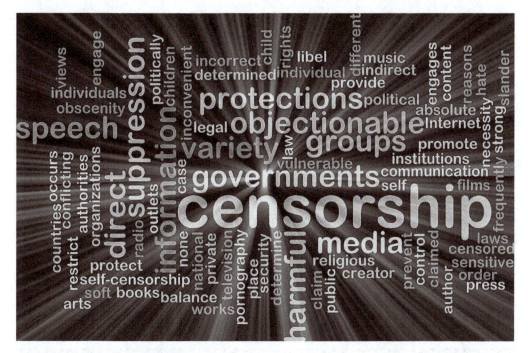

Urgent ethical questions regarding media regulation include the following:

- Who determines which content needs regulation?
- Should all forms of media expression be legally permissible?
- How are ethical boundaries determined for provocative films, violent television programs, and incendiary internet media content?
- Who is responsible when media programs fuel hate and encourage violence?
- How much regulation and constraint is acceptable in a democratic society?

A BRIEF OVERVIEW OF THE SCOPE OF INDIAN MEDIA

The scope of Indian media is vast. There are over 823 television channels broadcasting programs in 18 different languages. Of these, 125 are pay-channels telecasting narrative films, apart from soaps and documentaries, to about 312 million television sets (Press Trust of India, 2010). While almost every middle-class Indian family has media in the home, even in remote Indian villages dozens of villagers gather regularly in courtyards to enjoy the few televisions in their localities.

BOX 12.2   REASONS FOR MEDIA REGULATIONS

According to noted media scholar Denis McQuail (2010), the main issues of public concern for regulation are:

- The protection of public order and the security of the state.
- Maintaining respect for public mores in matters of taste and decency.
- Achieving benefits for the public sphere in terms of information flow, access, diversity and public participation.
- Maintaining cultural standards and supporting the national or regional culture and language.
- Respecting human rights of expression and protection from insult and prejudice.
- Preventing harm to society, especially by way of harm to children and young people from undesirable content.
- Protecting and advancing the national economic interest in media and communication industries.

FIGURE 12.3   India. Credit: Rakchai Duangdee.

FIGURE 12.4　Neon-lit movie theater in Jaipur, India. Credit: Regien Paassen/Shutterstock.com.

More than 1,250 films are screened in India annually. Some 13,000 cinemas nationally sell over four billion tickets at an average cost of 35 rupees (equivalent to 50 U.S. cents).

Unlike many developing countries, over 85 percent of India's movie theaters thrive by screening locally made films from India instead of movies from abroad. This gives Hollywood cinema a very small window to expose their productions.

Along with movie theaters and television, India has over one billion cellular phones that are capable of downloading and distributing all kinds of messages and programs via the internet.

Every film screened in a public movie theater or broadcast on an Indian television channel must display a clearance certificate from the Central Board of Film Certification (CBFC). The cost of getting a film certified is minimal. Given the extraordinary costs of international film production, the cost of regulation is not a burden to Indian filmmakers. Regulation and censorship, however, often pose ethical dilemmas and consequences.

CENSORSHIP IN INDIA

The Central Board of Film Certification originated under the Indian Cinematograph Act of 1952. Before that, it was known as the Censor Board and was instituted by the British in 1920.

Responsibility for Censor Board administration was held by the Inspector General of Police in Bombay, Madras, and Calcutta. After 1947 this board became a central government organization known as the Central Board of Film Censors, which has been loved and hated by people in and out of the media ever since.

Right from its inception under British colonial rule in 1920, the Censorship Board tried to conceal a clear political agenda: weeding out any form of nationalist propaganda or

BOX 12.3   *THE MESSENGER OF GOD* (2015)

As I am writing this piece in 2015, this venerable institution (the CBFC) has been rudely shaken by the resignation of its chairperson, Dr. Leela Samson, and several of the board members under allegations of bureaucratic interference and corruption at high levels. The appointment of Dr. Samson, a classical Bharata Natyam danseuse with no connection to the Indian film industry, as its chairperson was hailed as a curious but healthy decision seven years ago under the previous regime of the Indian National Congress Party.

The reason for this turmoil is indeed worth noting. The film which stirred the hornet's nest was called *The Messenger of God*. The film was produced, directed, and enacted by a self-appointed god-man-cum-rock-star named Gurmeet Baba Ram Rahim Singh of a Punjabi religious sect called Saccha Dhed Sauda. With several dances and fights, the film is as inane as several other Bollywood films but its audacious self-proclamations about religion and truth seem to have rudely shaken the CBFC members. Added to this, the religious head also has several civil and even criminal cases pending against him. So when the CBFC refused certification, the producers decided to take it up with a higher Appellate Tribunal. Surprisingly, they certified and passed the film with no questions asked and cleared the film for release. Unfortunately for this tainted "god-man," not a single theater was willing to screen the film to cash in on the controversy. The film opened weeks later and obviously the media had lost interest in this work. Since there were no celebrities involved to provide some juicy gossip, the film was a damp squib at the cash registers. The audiences had obviously moved on to newer pastures in the same way our low-profile danseuse chairperson Dr. Samson and her entourage also moved on.

This is indeed a brilliant instance which showcases the relation between law, ethics, and tolerance at play in India. The Indian judicial system overrode the ethics proposed by its own "autonomous" certifying body but the audience simply could not tolerate the inanity of a self-styled god-man using cinema as a medium for proselytizing his sectarian politics. The new government had to somehow put the house in order. So, a new board was set up swiftly; now under the chairmanship of Pahlaj Nihalani, a Bollywood film producer and staunch supporter of the ruling BJP party. In its wake, the real time-tested political colors of such an organization has been revealed to an entire nation. Will they make a sharp "right" turn as desired by their political bosses?

anything subversive of the colonial powers in charge. The censorship scissors fell in those days on a sizeable number of films from Hollywood and Europe whose criticism of colonial rule in the wake of the Great Depression in the 1930s was not digestible for the Raj. The atrocities committed by the colonial rulers on a non-violent struggle led by Mahatma Gandhi and his followers hit headlines in the print media and newsreels of the developed world, and the British tried to ensure that none of those reels reached the masses in India where the local media was virtually in its infancy.

One must therefore realize the contradictory impact of the Censorship Board's actions on Indian audiences when they watched the advancements of technology and international news produced by the British via an equally sophisticated cinematographic apparatus. But the subversive quality of the native narratives of Indian cinemas was a kind of virus that the British could not see under any of their powerful microscopes.

The pre-1947 cinema of India relied on a heavy diet of old mythological stories which, to the untrained eyes of the British, looked like inane costume dramas; but to the discerning eyes of Indian audiences, they had all the allegories of a freedom movement revealed in full splendor. In the characterization of the mythical heroic characters, Indian audiences could see the struggles of their own leaders. And the melodramatic form in which these films were

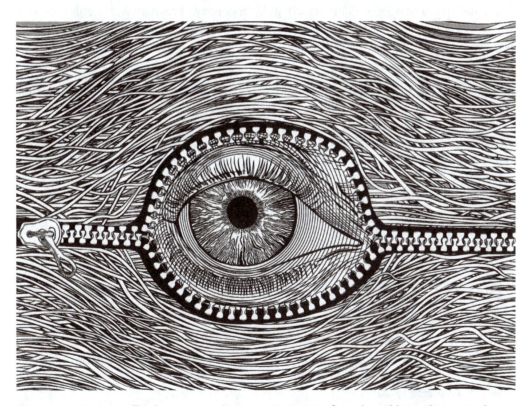

FIGURE 12.5 Despite official attempts to keep certain content from the public, audiences and creators can open up a way of communication by using culturally specific codes. Credit: RYGER.

constructed, replete with poetic dialogues and songs, provided the perfect foil to conceal the truth while actually revealing the realities of a powerful yet widespread independence movement.

The effects of the counter-cultural ethics of the untrained film producer were far stronger than all the propaganda waged by the British establishment.

This subversion intuitively employed by filmmakers across India changed drastically with the coming of Independence. No longer were filmmakers willing to couch their social criticism under the garb of mythology. Instead they switched to a very vibrant critique of the incompetence of the new Indian State and its four estates; namely, the Executive, Judiciary, Legislature, and the Press itself.

Although the newly constituted Central Board of Film Censors was a governmental body, it consisted largely of people who were also appreciators of the new cinema. They trained their microscopes and scissors only on explicit sexuality and harsh political comments. By and large, they were all very receptive to the idea that cinema should play a crucial role in the building up of a larger set of national ethics and social decorum. In the process, scores of Hollywood films were refused certification on the basis of explicit displays of sex and violence which could "harm" the innocence of the Indian minds.

At the same time, the Censor Board was not tolerant toward films which portrayed the Indian nation in a poor light. Films depicting abject poverty of rural masses or cruelty toward women by a patriarchal society were condemned. They even objected to films showing fanciful extremes: women portrayed as "bar dancers," or men indulging in gunfights and violence.

Occasionally, films did slip through some of the regional censor boards and were later greatly appreciated by Indian audiences. These films stood out like sore thumbs for the government's own poorly defined policies.

The question soon cropped up: Could filmmakers be sufficiently objective to monitor their own creative content? Doubts about filmmaker objectivity led to the decision that Censor Board members would be chosen from the "lay" people—those with no vested interest in the film or media industry. It was also decided that there should be one woman on the Censor Board, and representation from various religious backgrounds apart from the Hindu majority.

This 1952 approach at inclusivity was considered extremely progressive. However, the fact that one could get appointed and placed on this select jury made it a highly coveted

BOX 12.4   FILM CLASSIFICATION CATEGORIES IN INDIA (CBFC, 2015)

U   Unrestricted Public Exhibition
UA   Unrestricted Public Exhibition – but with a word of caution for parental discretion required for children under 12
A   Restricted to adults
S   Restricted to any special class of persons

position. In Censor Certification Centers across India, local ruling politicians selected their favorite cronies; getting them appointed to seats of ethical judgment. Politics thus crept into the corridors of the censorship board via appointees who were neither interested in cinema nor in anything remotely called "ethical values." Quite a few of them even managed to convert their membership into a brisk "commercial" activity via the backdoor—accepting bribes and pay-offs in exchange for their votes. The ethical issues here lie in the selection of the Censor Board members, not just in the decisions relating to specific films.

The Supreme Court of India declares:

> Film censorship becomes necessary because a film motivates thought and action and assures a high degree of attention and retention as compared to the printed word. The combination of act and speech, sight and sound, in semi-darkness of the theatre with elimination of all distracting ideas, will have a strong impact on the minds of the viewers and can affect emotions. Therefore, it has as much potential for evil as it has for good; and has an equal potential to instill or cultivate violent or bad behavior. It cannot be equated with other modes of communication. Censorship by prior restraint is, therefore, not only desirable but also necessary.
>
> (CBFC, 2015)

The reality is that governmental Censor Board decisions emerge from typical individuals assessing filmic narratives from an upper-middle-class perspective. This then, goes on to enforce a set of ethical scenarios within which the "ideal spectator" (innocent, honest, and virtuous) has to be constructed.

When members of the Censor Board watch a film in the darkened theater they assume by default, a general audience position, enjoying the film as they laugh, cry, or even get exasperated like a common member of the audience. The moment the screening is over and the lights come on, they come out of that shell and pass judgments on what should be retained and which portions need to be censored. When I ask them why and how they transform into another personality, they often reply, "But is that not our duty as members of the Censor Board? We cannot just sit back and say that all is well!"

THE FUTURE

In India, we believe that true liberty is enshrined in the practice and respect for diversity and pluralism.

Pluralism is undoubtedly here to stay as populations migrate across the globe in the name of trade and employment, and in search of safety and security. The world is certainly growing flatter, and national boundaries are becoming harder to police. Yet strong identities keep cropping up as we witness growing inequalities between the haves and have-nots. Through the centuries, popular culture has played a vital role in reconciling the differences between the visions spelt out by the privileged and the expectations expressed by the masses. A formidable challenge for the current generation of media creators is how best to revise old forms of regulation and create new codes to address current concerns.

FIGURE 12.6 An array of media microphones awaits Indian Prime Minister Narendra Modi at his press conference at the Rashtrapati Bhavan, the presidential residence in New Delhi on May 20, 2014. Credit: arindambanerjee/Shutterstock.com.

In India, stepping into the field to ameliorate differences and keep the peace is the CBFC, establishing a code of conduct and a rating system to placate divergent groups.

BOX 12.5 *ALL-INDIA-BAKCHOD* (2015)

Governmental regulation is often empowered when impending doom is felt by the executioners on either side of the firing line. Such an ethic can get complicated when "vulgar" or "obscene" programs originate on the internet via YouTube. Recently a three-hour program called *All-India-Bakchod* went viral and had over a million instant viewers. The program was ordered to be taken down by the government who felt that such a show was akin to pornography. This "roast" program was modeled on typical American comedy shows where celebrities are called on stage and put through abusive conversations in the name of humor. The producers of the program expressed their apologies for a program which was full of expletives and sexist remarks that played to the gallery—but episodes are still available on YouTube. How does one classify ribaldry and its subsequent distribution in the age of internet? How do we expect the audience of a nation like India to express their "tolerance" in such cases?

Controlling some of the censorship certification decisions are aged custodians of a modern society who often do not seem to understand that ethics and morality work within a very dynamic framework that requires lots of social dialogue. Be it the power houses in the sprawling corporate Hollywood studios, or the slimy distributors gulping cups of sugary tea in dingy back lots of Indian cinema houses, their dream of somehow controlling the minds of the paying audiences is the same.

Attempting to understand conflicts within the CBFC, the India-based film producing community, and the self-appointed guardians of "public" taste and sensitivities is not an easy undertaking. Each dimension is vast and complicated by historical, cultural, and religious factors.

Buddha first confronted such complexity 2,500 years ago and placed a very simple solution on record. At first, the Buddha suggested that one should recognize the powers of our intellect (Buddhi) as superior to our instinctual/spontaneous responses. He extended this concept further: we should therefore create a set of cultural constructs (Dharma) and take recourse in them. The third—but very crucial—tenet of Buddhism is that we should then let the community (Sangha) accept these constructs before we take refuge in it.[2] With these simple aphorisms, the Buddha and his followers spread across the Eastern world and

BOX 12.6 *INDIA'S DAUGHTER* (2015)

The British documentary, *India's Daughter*, told the story of a brutal gang rape that took place on September 16, 2012, in Delhi, India. Produced and directed by Leslee Udwin for the BBC, the documentary included on-camera interviews with family and friends of the victim, as well as with the rapists. The village of the victim is clearly identified, as are the homes of the rapists. All are visually identified.

India's Daughter was banned in India. The BBC and the international press suggested that this was once again an example of India's lack of press and media freedom. Indian Prime Minister Narendra Modi's interviews made it clear to the BBC that the ban was not a question of freedom of expression. He identified three reasons leading to the Indian government's decision to ban the telecast:

1. The identity of the rape victim should not be revealed, which would have happened had the interview been allowed to be telecast.
2. The legal case against the five accused rapists was ongoing and the telecast features an interview with the person who was alleged to have committed the crime. Telecasting this could impact the judicial process.
3. It is our responsibility to ensure protection of the victim. If we had allowed the telecast to happen, we would have—in effect—violated the dignity of the victim.

This example clearly illustrates ethical dimensions of government regulation of the BBC telecast (Kapoor, 2015).

established a wonderful platform for cooperation among a variety of religious positions, from fertility cults to paganism, within a highly settled agricultural economy.

Could the solution to some of the issues discussed in this chapter come back to education? Unless and until India can have a vibrant and well-structured curriculum on the ethics and aesthetics of film and other media integrated into the syllabi of schools and colleges, the nation can only resort to ad hoc measures to resolve the various conflicts that will soon engulf all communication in the future. For now, there is no doubt that the CBFC has to reinvent itself as a more democratic institution.

THE TROUBLE WITH VISHWAROOPAM (2013)

Should all forms of media expression be legally permissible? Who decides the correct and ethical boundary when it comes to provocative films, violent television programs, and incendiary internet media content? Who is responsible when media programs fuel hate and encourage violence?

Let us now take a concrete example. This is a film called *Vishwaroopam* (*The Universal Saga*) by Kamal Hassan, one of the most popular star/directors in the Tamil cinema in south India. He is acknowledged by most Indian audiences and critics as one of the most intelligent film personalities whose films are also accessible and easy to understand. In 2013, he produced this film about an Indian military agent who infiltrates a Taliban terrorist training camp in Afghanistan to find out more about one of its dreaded warlords. He befriends them all, and at the opportune moment, reveals their whereabouts to American forces and has their hideout blasted out. He escapes, but does not realize that the warlord has also managed to survive the attack and is presently planning a dastardly attack on innocent civilians in New York. The hero, now disguised as a traditional Indian dance teacher, tracks the warlord down in New York and defuses the dangerous bomb; thus saving thousands of innocent lives.

The CBFC saw the film and gave it a "clear" certificate. Release dates were announced, publicity banners put up, and prints dispatched to theaters all over India for the release on January 25, 2013. The problem started when a small number of Muslim activists in Chennai (formerly Madras) demanded a private screening of the film. Kamal Hassan acceded, and they saw the film in his own home theater. Late that very evening they petitioned the chief minister of Tamil Nadu, Jayalalithaa Jayaram, saying they felt that the portrayal of Muslims was extremely prejudiced. They expressed that Tamil Muslims would be deeply hurt and might even resort to open arson and violence if the film was allowed to be screened. Sensing trouble, the chief minister had the district collectors announce a restraint on all theaters selected for screening the film.

Technically the CBFC's writ was not challenged as it was a "restraining order" and not a ban. But, the entire nation saw the CBFC's mandate disgraced. The Tamil film that was dubbed and released in all the other states of India was disallowed in its own linguistic zone. A distressed Kamal Hassan lashed out at the government, and a full-blown media war was launched. Almost every channel had the Muslim activists spelling out their grievances and counter groups arguing against them. The ethical arguments are extremely interesting to note. First, the Muslim representatives expressed that it was extremely hurtful to hear terrorists speak Tamil; thus creating an impression that the Tamil Muslims were somehow involved. The film supporters retorted back stating that this was a "Tamil" film, not an Afghani film, and the very same film had been dubbed in Hindi and Telugu for screening in other Indian theaters. So should the Muslims of the other states also express their grievance and ask for a ban? Next, it was argued that each time the terrorists fired their guns, they uttered a war cry invoking their God saying, "Allahu Akbar." This objection was countered with the point that when Hindu fanatics are shown on the screen, they too invoke their God's names. When asked why they did not protest when American films like *Zero Dark Thirty* or *Argo* with similar themes were screened in the same theaters, they looked lost and said they had not heard of such films at all! The meta-talk in that answer was the fact that, if they had protested against those Hollywood films, nobody, not even in their Muslim fraternity, would have bothered to listen to them. Soon the arguments stretched out into how Muslims in India were being targeted as minorities and lumped together with other anti-national elements. In this entire ruckus, Chief Minister Jayalalithaa saw an opportunity to gain some brownie points with a Muslim community she had long neglected, and the television channels saw a chance to boost their own performance with some solid TRP (television rating points) gains—all in the name of keeping up and redefining the virtues of a secular democracy!

After two weeks of such diatribe on all channels, Kamal Hassan had to accede to removing the invocation of the prophet's name in some parts, and the film was allowed to be screened. It was also clear to everyone that this entire exercise was one way of seeking instant limelight by a fringe group; and film celebrities were the softest target available for such a strategy. The protest was not really rooted in a committed cause but only to gain some kind of visibility at no cost whatsoever! This was not the first time that the CBFC's authority was diluted by local vested interests. There are at least ten other films which had to be pulled out of screens, or were voluntarily withdrawn by theater owners even though they had the certified prints. Prominent among them was the Tom Hanks starrer *The Da Vinci Code* (2006), which was attacked by all the Indian Christian churches for "distorting" the story of Jesus. The CBFC had passed this film, but theater owners chose not to screen the film for fear of incurring damages by the mobs outside. Recently a delightful comedy called *PK* (2014) about Indian god-men and their shamanic worlds incurred a lot of protests by right-wing fanatics who felt that it was insulting and hurtful to Hindu religious sentiments. Fortunately, the overwhelming success of this film in a Hindu-dominated nation like India was enough to shout them all down, and the film has continued uninterrupted.

TAKE HOME POINTS

- Regulation is always influenced by historical, cultural, and social sensitivities. Understand the purpose of regulations before attempting to challenge and resist them.
- The tension between media regulation and freedom of expression is inevitable. Understand the impact of what you create on potential audiences. Anticipate cultural and religious sensitivities.
- Self-regulation requires thoughtful consideration of ethics and human rights. It requires asking good questions and being a good journalist when attempting to understand context.

- Government censorship can be a tool for preventing incendiary, provocative media from being circulated. In attempts by governments to secure peaceful co-existence in diverse, pluralistic societies, media censorship is sometimes needed.

NOTES

1   There are many examples of government attempts to regulate artistic work that some may interpret as controversial and provocative. On May 22, 2015, at the Venice Biennale, an installation of a mosque by Christop Buchel, an Icelandic artist, was shut down by local authorities. The installation was set up in an old church, officially allocated as "artistic" space by the Biennale organizers. When government authorities realized that the art installation was attracting Muslim worshipers, the city became intolerant, much to the ire of the large numbers of artists who had assembled there from all over the world. How does one deal with ethics, law, and the spirit of tolerance in an economic world that is rapidly growing flat but developing a political reality that is moving all of us "hapless citizens" back to the crusades?
2   The ideals at the heart of Buddhism are collectively known as the "Three Jewels," or the "Three Treasures." These are the *Buddha* (the yellow jewel), the *Dharma* (the blue jewel), and the *Sangha* (the red jewel). It is by making these the central principles of your life that you become a Buddhist.

BIBLIOGRAPHY

Affleck, B. (Director). (2012). *Argo* [Motion Picture]. Warner Brothers Pictures.

Barendt, E., Lustgarten, L., Norrie, K., & Stephenson, H. (1997). *Libel and the media: The chilling effect*. New York, NY: Oxford University Press.

Bhat, T., & Khamba, G. (Directors). (2015). *All India bakchod: On air with AIB* [Motion Picture]. Star Network/ Star World India/Star Plus.

Bigelow, K. (Director). (2012). *Zero dark thirty* [Motion Picture]. Columbia Pictures.

Brunetti, A., & Weder, B. (2003). A free press is bad news for corruption. *Journal of Public Economics, 87*(7), 1801–1824.

Bubnova, N. (2016). Russian media: Struggling against new controls. In W. A. Hachten, & J. F. Scotton (Eds.), *The world news prism: Digital, social and interactive* (9th ed.) (pp. 99–118). Malden, MA: Wiley-Blackwell.

Castells, M. (2001). *The internet galaxy*. Oxford, UK: Oxford University Press.

Central Board of Film Certification. (2015). Ministry of Information and Broadcasting, Government of India. Retrieved from: http://cbfcindia.gov.in/html/uniquepage.aspx?unique_page_id=6

Cottle, S. (2011, July 01). Media and the Arab uprisings of 2011: Research notes. *Journalism, 12*(5), 647–659.

Freedom House. (2011, September). License to censor: The use of media regulation to restrict press freedom. (Karin Deutsch Karlekar, Ed.). *Freedom House*. Retrieved from https://freedomhouse.org/report/special-reports/license-censor-use-media-regulation-restrict-press-freedom

Hachten, W. A., & Scotton, J. F. (2016). *The world news prism: Digital, social and interactive* (9th ed.). Malden, MA: Wiley-Blackwell.

Hamelink, C. (2000). *The ethics of cyberspace*. London, UK: Sage.

Hassan, K. (Director). (2013). *Vishwaroopam* [Motion Picture]. PVP Cinema/Balaji Motion Pictures.

Hirani, R. (Director). (2014). *PK* [Motion Picture]. UTV Motion Pictures.

Howard, R. (Director). (2006). *The Da Vinci code* [Motion Picture]. Columbia Pictures.

Kapoor, M. (2015, May 08). PM Modi finally talks about why "India's daughter" was banned in India! *India Times*. Retrieved from: www.indiatimes.com/news/india/pm-modi-finally-talks-about-why-indias-daughter-was-banned-in-india-232512.html

Leslie, L. Z. (2000). *Mass communication ethics: Decision making in postmodern culture*. Boston, MA: Houghton Mifflin.

Lester, P. M. (1996). *Images that injure: Pictorial stereotypes in the media*. Westport, CT: Praeger.

MacKinnon, R. (2009). China's censorship 2.0: How companies censor bloggers. *First Monday, 14*(2).

Mcdonald, K. M. (1999, June). How would you like your television: With or without borders and with or without culture – a new approach to media regulation in the European Union. *Fordham International Law Journal, 22*(5), 1991–2023.

McQuail, D. (2010, February 09). *Module 2: Unit 11: Media Regulation*. Leicester, UK: University of Leicester. Retrieved from: www.le.ac.uk/oerresources/media/ms7501/mod2unit11/page_16.htm

On line Desk. (2015, May 07). 3 reasons given by prime minister Modi justifying ban on "India's daughter." *The New Indian Express*. Retrieved from: www.newindianexpress.com/nation/3-Reasons-Given-By-Prime-Minister-Modi-Justifying-Ban-on-India's-Daughter/2015/05/07/article2802270.ece

Padmanabhan, M. (2012, October 8). There is no right not to be offended. *The Hindu*. Retrieved from: www.thehindu.com/opinion/interview/there-is-no-right-not-to-be-offended/article3969404.ece

Phillips, P., & Project Censored (1999). *Censored, 1999: The news that didn't make the news—the year's top 25 censored stories*. New York, NY: Seven Stories Press.

Pool, I. de Sola. (1983) *Technologies of freedom*. Cambridge, MA: Harvard University Press.

Press Trust of India New Delhi. (2010, October 05). 23.77 mn DTH subscribers by June 2010. *Business Standard*. Retrieved from: www.business-standard.com/article/technology/23-77-mn-dth-subscribers-by-june-2010-trai-110100500228_1.html

Rahula, W. (1974). *What the Buddha taught: Revised and expanded edition with texts from suttas and dhammapada*. New York, NY: Grove Press.

Singh, G. R. R. (2015). *The Messenger* [Motion Picture]. Hakikat Entertainment Ltd.

Stanig, P. (2015, January). Regulation of speech and media coverage of corruption: An empirical analysis of the Mexican press. *American Journal of Political Science, 59*(1), 175–193.

Thompson, K. (Ed.). (1997). *Media and cultural regulation*. London, UK, & Thousand Oaks, CA: Sage.

Udwin, L. (Director). (2015). *India's daughter* [Motion Picture]. BBC Storyville. Distributed by Berta Films.

Williams, B. (2015). *Obscenity and film censorship. An abridgement of the Williams report*. Cambridge, UK: Cambridge University Press.

Chapter 13

Copyright and the Right to Copy

Annette Danto and Tami Gold

ABSTRACT

For the general public as well as individual artists, there are many questions about copyright law, individual rights of ownership, and fair use. Copyright is a legal term with ethical implications. We are looking at copyright through an ethical lens. Discussions with two copyright lawyers highlight the legal and ethical dimensions of copyright law and fair use.

Media-makers wear many hats—that of artist, poet, activist, and also that of someone who understands legal and ethical considerations. Copyright laws are rules that protect our own work as well as the work of others.[1] These laws protect intellectual and creative property produced by writers of short stories, musicians, photographers, graphic artists, filmmakers, and novelists. We want to encourage you to understand and respect the principles expressed in these laws.

Copyright law imposes legal obligations. As media-makers, we want our work to have the broadest exposure and largest audiences. Adhering to copyright laws is a way of ensuring this.

COPYRIGHT-PROTECTED MATERIAL

When coming up with an idea for a project, many look to other sources such as short stories, plays, and novels for inspiration and ideas. Adaptations of others' works require permission before proceeding with production. Obtaining permission should happen before and not after the media project is created.[2] If you avoid securing the rights to others' copyright-protected material, and plow forward with your production, you will not be able to sell and distribute the completed project. In some situations, film festivals require a signed waiver attesting that you have acquired all the material in your film legally. If you have not done so, the film will not be screened publicly.

BOX 13.1 FAIR USE

In its most general sense, fair use is any copying of copyrighted material done for a limited and "transformative" purpose, such as to comment upon, criticize, or parody a copyrighted work. Such uses can be made without permission from the copyright owner. In other words, fair use is a defense against a claim of copyright infringement. If your use qualifies as a fair use, then it would not be considered an illegal infringement ("Charts and tools," n.d.).

Seeking permission also applies to documentary. Developing a documentary based on a specific historic moment might require archival material to tell the story effectively. You must find out, before beginning production, how to access the rights to license the footage, illustrations, and photographs necessary to tell this story. Perhaps the material is not available or the license fees are costlier than anticipated. All this needs to be researched during preproduction, as it will have an impact on your fundraising, budget, and ability to tell this story.

While there is no guarantee you will get written permission, it is your responsibility to understand these legal and ethical practices. You must go to the copyright holder(s) or publishers to request written permission to use the material.

As you begin to create your own work, you will understand the importance of ownership, especially as you seek credit and payment for your own creations.

In certain situations, you may not need to request written permission if the fair use doctrine applies. Before you claim fair use, make sure your use falls within its parameters.

Bending the requirements of fair use to avoid compensating artists is unethical. If we choose to use someone else's work, we need to identify whether or not it is copyrighted and then enter into a licensing agreement with the person who owns the license and copyright. If we choose to apply fair use, we need to do so legitimately and honestly.

An ethical concern for filmmakers is not only how we use copyrighted material from others, but also how people use our copyrighted material. In both situations there are laws, and there are ethics. The Box 13.2 is an example where the legal and ethical considerations are at odds. This illustrates a situation where a student cited fair use as justification for copying and re-editing a filmmaker's work. In this case, the student citing fair use did not take into consideration the impact on the filmmaker.

Respecting the work of other artists is an ethical fundamental. We can sometimes resolve copyright transgressions through

FIGURE 13.1 Sometimes legal and ethical considerations are at odds. Credit: rnl.

BOX 13.2   LIFE AND DEBT (2001)

Imagine discovering that someone re-edited your documentary into two separate versions and posted them on YouTube. This happened to documentary director Stephanie Black. Her 87-minute documentary, *Life and Debt*, was re-edited by a sociology student at a Midwestern college, then posted on YouTube with two alternative running times: 40 minutes and 20 minutes. The student received over 20,000 views in one month.

The filmmaker contacted YouTube directly and submitted a "copyright takedown notice" for the edited versions. YouTube informed the director that the student had responded to the takedown request stating: "I would like to counter the company that requested this. I believe the material should be considered 'fair use.' I used it for a sociology project, which makes the two videos in question 'educational content.'"

YouTube informed Stephanie Black that her only recourse to enforce the "takedown" would be for the filmmaker (Black) to provide evidence within ten days that she filed an action seeking a court order against the counter-notifier to restrain the alleged infringing activity. Only once this lawsuit was filed, would they take down the YouTube postings.

FIGURE 13.2   Photo Still from *Life and Debt*. Directed by Stephanie Black. www.lifeanddebt.org. Courtesy of Stephanie Black.

At that point Black decided to contact the student directly having been provided her contact information for the court order. She spoke with the sociology student who expressed surprise at the call, stating that she thought it was okay to re-edit an existing documentary if it was for educational purposes. The student claimed to have studied from a copyright textbook that, in this context, it was acceptable to copy and revise someone else's work. The conversation between the two led to the student agreeing to take down the re-edited YouTube versions.[3]

discussion and conversation rather than resorting to legal actions. It is good to keep the Golden Rule in mind: *Do unto others as you would have them do unto you.*[4]

THE HUMAN DIMENSION

> You are collaborating most with the people in front of the camera . . . If you have tricked them into being in your film, that is a violation of media ethics.
>
> George Stoney (Danto, 2011)

Before you can proceed with copyright registration for your own work, you need to obtain necessary clearances from the people appearing in your media project.

Generally speaking, everyone you film (except for those appearing incidentally or in the background) should be asked to sign a Personal Release Form. This will protect you against legal issues and gives you permission to use the video and sound of the person for commercial and non-commercial purposes. It also gives the person who is participating in your film the right to decide if they want to be in this production. A Personal Release Form is a legal document.

On-camera personal releases are legally binding if the person who is agreeing to be part of your film states their name, contact information, date, and film title they are agreeing to be in. They must include that they are giving permission to the filmmaker to edit the footage however they want, as long as it remains loyal to the truth.

Release forms offer an opportunity to recognize the agency of the people in front of your camera. Respect their right to understand what it means to participate in your media project. Where and how will the film or documentary be screened? Are there any safety considerations related to protecting the identities of your subjects? The release form provides a window for human communication. Use this window to explain what it means to have one's story shared with the public.

While editing a documentary, filmmakers need to ask themselves: Did I fairly represent the people in my film? This is not only a legal consideration, but fundamentally for the filmmaker, an ethical one. Misrepresentation of truth and of a personal or political story can seriously impact someone's life. This cannot be minimized.

One thing filmmakers can do a better job of is explaining the implications of signing a release form. Participants are often unaware of what it means to agree to be featured in a

BOX 13.3   ERRORS AND OMISSIONS LIABILITY INSURANCE

Errors and Omissions Insurance protects companies and individuals against claims made by clients (individuals and or companies) for inadequate work or negligent actions. For publishers, broadcasters, and other media-related entities, there is a specific type of E&O insurance that covers infringement of copyright, defamation, invasion of privacy, and plagiarism. All media-makers must certify in writing to the broadcaster, cable company, or any other type of corporation that intends to license your work, that all graphics, photographs, and other visual elements, every frame of video, and all music and sound have been properly licensed and that you have full legal right to use all the material in your documentary and or dramatic film.

film or documentary. It is the responsibility of the filmmaker and filmmaking team to carefully go over all aspects of what signing the release form means for the distribution of the work. Identifying someone on camera can, in certain instances, jeopardize safety and well-being. This is very true in cases involving abuse, neglect, or political violence. Protecting the well-being of your subjects is critically important, and an ethical responsibility that needs to be carefully considered while reviewing the release form and explaining it to the people involved.

PROTECTING YOUR WORK

> Laws might be different from country to country but the ethical underpinnings of media practice remain the same wherever you are working.
> Andrew Lund, filmmaker and lawyer (personal communication, December 27, 2015)

Registering your media project with the U.S. Copyright Office is a good idea if you believe your work may be copied without your permission. There is another reason to register your copyright, which is to establish a chain of title. Distributors, studios, and networks all require registration for this purpose as well as for enhancing protection against infringers.

Registration is a simple and relatively inexpensive process.[5]

Your name should only be put in the copyright notice if you are the sole owner of copyright. If there are joint owners of copyright, all owners' names should appear.

The copyright logo gives notice to the public that you own your video, short film, or web post. The logo should be seen at the beginning of the project or at the end. You should also include the logo on any and all packaging that contains your material.

DISCUSSION WITH JAIME WOLF

Jaime Wolf is a founding partner of the law firm of Pelosi Wolf Effron & Spates LLP in New York City. He is a graduate of Yale University and the Columbia Law School, and is the

BOX 13.4 INTELLECTUAL PROPERTY

Intellectual property in the United States has become increasingly more important in the last decade. The right to own the products of one's genius is not a new concept. With the arrival of the digital age though, it has become much harder to remain in control of one's intellectual property. Intellectual property rights protect a work of art, and also preserve one's right to monetary gain.[6]

FIGURE 13.3 Be sure to place a copyright logo on your media: © Your Name (date of first publication). Credit: iconswebsite.

vice chairman of the Board of Yaddo, a retreat for artists in Saratoga Springs, NY. He represents creative people and companies in a variety of fields.

Why is copyright relevant to media-creators today?

There has been a lot of chatter out there over the past decade about how copyright law has ceased to be relevant. While it's true that copyright laws—and copyright lawyers—have struggled to keep pace with technological advances, copyright law remains quite relevant.

A U.S. copyright registration remains an artist's most powerful weapon against people and companies that make infringing use of the artist's work. Many artists labor under the false notion that copyright registrations no longer serve an important purpose. That's probably because a minimum level of copyright protection attaches as soon as an artwork is created. So artists have come to believe that they really don't need to take any action to protect their work.

What are the specific advantages to a media creator of copyright?

Copyright registration in the United States has significant advantages. The most significant is this: an artist cannot be awarded lucrative statutory damages and attorneys' fees in the United States unless s/he registered the copyright in the United States before the infringement took place (or within three months of the first authorized publication). Statutory damages can range from $750 to $30,000 for each infringement, and up to $150,000 per infringement if the infringement was "willful."

You may never bring a lawsuit in your life. But if you are an artist and you can wield a credible threat of enforcing these kinds of penalties, then that puts you in a very powerful position. If you just go with the flow and don't obtain a timely copyright registration, you would be forced to demonstrate "actual damages" from an infringing use. Actual damages are notoriously difficult to establish.

And, frankly, once an infringer's attorney hears that the artist didn't obtain a copyright registration, the artist's case is often not taken seriously at all.

Applying for U.S. Copyright registration remains quite affordable. It doesn't cost much to gain the maximum level of copyright protection for your artwork. I encourage all of my clients to register their work with the US Copyright Office.

What is the Digital Millennium Copyright Act and is it relevant to media creators today?

Copyright registrations come in very handy when trying to enforce the provisions of the Digital Millennium Copyright Act (DMCA).

BOX 13.5   HOW TO APPLY FOR U.S. COPYRIGHT REGISTRATION

There are two steps in the application for copyright registration—fill out the form; and send it in along with a check and copies of your work to the U.S. Copyright Office. You can also complete the application online. When your work receives copyright registration with the U.S. Copyright Office, you are making a public record. Information you provide on your copyright application is available to the public and will be available on the Internet.

Many filmmakers choose to register their works because they want to have their copyright on the public record and have a certificate of registration. Registered works may be eligible for statutory damages and attorney's fees in successful litigation. The practice of sending a copy of your own work to yourself is sometimes called a "poor man's copyright." But there is no provision in the copyright law regarding this type of protection. It is not a substitute for registration.

The DMCA law provides for a quick and easy way for a copyright owner to get infringing material removed online. There is no registration requirement to take advantage of the DMCA, but if the infringer decides to challenge the takedown you only have 14 days to bring a lawsuit or the infringing material can remain up until the matter is settled. Unfortunately, even if you spent a lot of money to expedite the registration process, there is no guarantee it will be completed in time, and for U.S. copyright owners, you can't sue without it. So it pays to have registered before launching an assault against an infringer under the DMCA.

Either way, a takedown notification or "cease and desist" letter will always have much more impact if it is backed up by an actual U.S. copyright registration. It shows that the artist knows her rights and is serious about enforcing them. This can send a powerful message to an adversary.

The DMCA essentially exempts online service providers ("OSPs") such as YouTube, Instagram, Tumblr, and many others from liability for copyright infringements caused by their users.

So if somebody rips off your video, photo, or article and posts it online without your OK, the OSP that runs the site on which it's posted will be exempt from liability if they take certain actions spelled out by the DMCA. For example, if the OSP receives a proper DMCA takedown notice of an infringing use on its network, the OSP must "[respond] expeditiously to remove, or disable access to, the material that is claimed to be infringing" (17 USC §512(c)(1)). By doing so the OSP will avoid being held liable for the actions of its users.

If you post something to an OSP and it's removed under the DMCA but you feel that your use of the copyright owner's content was done with the owner's authorization or constitutes "fair use," the DMCA provides an equally simple method for restoring your posting.

If you believe that you have a right to publish your allegedly infringing work, the DMCA provides for a "counter-notice" mechanism to put your page back up. A counter-notice, which you send to the OSP after they inform you that they've taken your page down is easy to fill out and file. After the OSP gets this counter-notice from you, it forwards a copy of your counter-notice to the copyright owner who sent the takedown notice and informs them that the OSP will restore access to the removed material in 10 business days.

Of course, if you file a counter-notice, you had better feel confident of your legal position. Otherwise, by causing the OSP to re-post your content, you may be virtually asking the copyright owner to sue you.

So the DMCA takedown notice is an effective way to combat content thieves. Compared to the money- and time-gobbling machinations required to obtain an injunction to remove infringing content from the Web, a DMCA takedown notice is a breeze. It's simple, speedy, and can be drawn up by a copyright owner without the help of a lawyer.

But if you're on the receiving end of a DMCA takedown notice, you may not be quite so sanguine about it. The OSP's takedown of your content will be swift and the result can be quite jarring. All record of "page views," "likes," and similar measures of your post's popularity may vanish in an instant.

Large media companies concerned about constant, widespread piracy of their content, have dedicated substantial resources to identifying online infringements and swiftly filing

DMCA takedown notices. Some assign clerical staff to the task. Others have gone so far as to program bots to sniff out presumed infringements and automatically shoot out takedown notices. This method seems to work well enough for the large media companies, but it is also purely mechanical. The notices take no account of whether the party posting the content has any right to do so.

Recently in the case of *Lenz v. Universal Music Corp.*,[7] popularly known as the "Dancing Baby" case, the 9th Circuit Court of Appeals (a very important court in California) held that a party filing a DMCA takedown notice must engage in a legal analysis of the alleged infringer's right to post the content. If, for example, the individual posting the copyright owner's content is engaging in a First Amendment-protected "fair use" (e.g., let's say they are using content for the purpose of parodying it), then the copyright owner is supposed to hold its fire.

It's too early to tell whether this legal analysis requirement will result in more nuanced usage of the DMCA weaponry. Cynics are predicting little change. After all, the 9th Circuit is asking the party who fervently wishes to torpedo an adversary's posting to weigh the adversary's rights. An outbreak of fair-minded analysis may not be on the cards.

Do entertainment lawyers ever really think about ethics? In what ways do law and ethics intersect?

Lawyers in the United States are bound by codes of professional ethics. These so-called "canons" of ethics are detailed rules governing how lawyers may practice law. The canons of ethics discuss how lawyers are supposed to deal with their clients, their adversaries, and their colleagues. Common problems such as how to handle potential conflicts of interest and what to do when a client fails to pay are explained in great detail.

But while lawyers have fairly clear rules for how to conduct themselves in at least a minimally ethical fashion, in my experience clients rarely turn to their lawyers seeking ethical guidance.

Most often we see clients asking their lawyers to assess the range of options presented by a particular situation. Put another way, instead of asking counsel "What should I do?" they ask "What can I do?"

When I am asked to provide a menu of options, do I take the opportunity to point out which options seem to me to be wrong or perhaps just ethically unsavory? Of course I do. Do clients always choose the most ethical course of action? Of course they don't, although I have been blessed with wonderful clients whose ethical compass needles most often point in what seems to me to be the right direction.

When trying to protect one's intellectual property or creative work, what are the ethical issues a media-creator needs to be aware of?

Working in the field of intellectual property is similar in many ways to working in the field of real property (i.e., real estate). Sometimes a person will ask a landowner whether she may cross the owner's property on foot, say for the purpose of bird watching. Other people may want permission to cross the owner's property with a convoy of trucks for the purpose of hydraulic fracturing of a neighbor's land. The landowner must decide when it's in his interest to say "yes" or "no," and that decision may well include a calculation about the common good as well.

Similarly, the intellectual property owner must try to calculate the benefits and burdens of a particular situation, hopefully in the context of the common good. For example, visual artists are often asked for permission to use images they created in advertisements. The artist will need to decide whether the license fee being offered is worth their while. They may ask themselves whether being seen in the ad will benefit or harm their career. And they'll certainly want to see the proposed ad and understand who the advertiser is. If the advertiser is, say, an oil company that has recklessly caused immeasurable damage to the environment, the artist may decide she wants no part in promoting their agenda at any price.

I feel that it's important for journalists, filmmakers, and all other creative people to remember that the Golden Rule of "Do unto others as you would have them do unto you" applies in a very concrete way to intellectual property. That's because every creative person is potentially both an infringer and a victim of infringement.

DISCUSSION WITH NEIL ROSINI

Neil Rosini's practice focuses on content clearance for broadcast, publication and online distribution, copyright, rights of publicity and defamation matters, content and software relating to website and mobile platform uses, and online privacy issues. He also mediates disputes in the entertainment industry including disagreements among artistic collaborators.

Do ethical obligations largely overlap with legal obligations?

In my view, the scope of your ethical obligation to stay within the law when it comes to copyright infringement depends primarily on what the law is. Generally, if what you propose to do is legal, then it's usually ethical (provided it doesn't have unjust effects on individuals or groups notwithstanding its legality, which seems relatively rare).

But what if the line of illegality is not well drawn, such as when a new technology arrives that the law has not yet fully addressed? In those instances, in my view, risk assessment rather than ethics comes to the fore. What do existing laws and past decisions have to say about the likely risk of doing x or y? Where do x and y fit on the spectrum of likely risk? Are you comfortable with that risk? If you make a choice that risks copyright infringement, but laws and court decisions don't say definitively that the choice you're making is illegal, then I don't think it's unethical to make that choice.

When Napster first launched, it made file-sharing possible among individual users that essentially eliminated the need to pay for recordings of music they obtained from total strangers. Although doing so applied a new technology that had not been tested in the courts, did the lack of that legal precedent make Napster legal—or ethical? At the time, I didn't think so because based on legal precedents that did exist, I didn't think it was plausibly legal. It turned out it wasn't and judges who considered that technology did not wrestle much with the question. Napster acted both illegally and unethically.

Whether use of copyrighted works without permission is legal or not often is not so clear cut. In another example, Google launched a project to copy into a database, millions of copyrighted books in university libraries for the purpose, they said, of aiding research by making the texts available for massive word searches. This too was a new technology. When authors of books whose works were scanned into the database sued Google to prevent them from making those copies without first obtaining permission from (and compensating) the authors, it wasn't at all clear who would win that contest. Courts have found Google's database to be justified under law. Even if that were not the case, in my view it was not unethical for Google to have tested the law because its actions plausibly fit within legal bounds.

What is Fair Use?

Both the Napster and Google cases were decided against a backdrop of the limits of "fair use," which is a copyright law principle that permits the use of copyrighted works without permission and without compensation under limited circumstances. The fair use principle is derived from the purpose of having a copyright law at all: to benefit society. The thinking goes that society benefits from constant origination of new creative works and with human nature what it is, the best way to give creators incentive to create new works is to give them a legal monopoly during the term of copyright. Copyright's primary purpose is not to compensate creators, but by giving them an exclusive opportunity to earn money from their creations, copyright hopes to benefit society both during the term of copyright and after, when a work enters the public domain.

But copyright law also recognizes that to benefit society, the legal monopoly shouldn't be inviolate even during the term of copyright. Fair use eliminates the creator's exclusive rights under very limited conditions during the term of protection.

Copyright gives authors a remedy against infringers, helps authors earn a living, and motivates authors to create new works (thereby benefiting society). This is not to say that "fair use" shouldn't become more and more expansive in a digital age as an exception to the general rule that the copyright owner enjoys a monopoly of rights. I think the Google case illustrates this: copyright law is still relevant, but the fair use exception in that case prevails.

Should Google contact the authors or whoever holds the copyright? Is this a legal question or ethical one?

In the circumstances of the Google library-copying case, and in most others, I think that any ethical obligation is coextensive with a legal one. If Google isn't legally required to contact authors (and according to court decisions, it isn't), then I don't see any ethical obligation to do so. In fact, if Google had to haggle with millions of authors, it would be so impractical as to make the Google book archive impossible, undermining the purpose of copyright to benefit society.

BOX 13.6 FAIR USE QUESTIONS FOR MEDIA-MAKERS

Media-makers who wish to put a clip in a documentary from someone else's film as fair use, should ask themselves the following five questions:

1. Why precisely is this clip being used? Be as rigorous as possible. The more limited the identified purpose, the more likely fair use standards will be satisfied.
2. Is the function of the clip in your documentary different from the purpose of the original work? If so, fair use will be easier to establish. This is sometimes referred to as the "transformative" test. For example, if the clip comes from a news report that documents an event, it would not be transformative to borrow the clip simply to document the same event. A different purpose would be served, however, if the clip is used to show that the event was the subject of news coverage; or that a particular public official was involved in the event; or as part of a historical sequence (e.g., to show how cultural attitudes changed over time); or to support an argument or thesis.
3. Can the clip be placed into a context of commentary or criticism in the documentary? Social, political, and cultural criticism might be the clearest category of transformative use. Show a short clip and then comment on it. (Even easier to defend: show a short clip while running audio commentary over the clip.)
4. What's the minimum you need to borrow to satisfy the limited purpose you've identified for using the clip in your documentary? The less material you take the better. This is not only a quantitative test (measured in the number of seconds borrowed) but also a qualitative test (don't take the best part of someone else's work if it can be avoided). For example, to establish that a particular actor appeared in a film, you don't need to borrow an entire scene or the best joke or the most famous dialogue; you probably don't even need the audio. You will be tempted to borrow more than you absolutely need in order to make your documentary more enjoyable. Resist that temptation.
5. Is the borrowed clip in your documentary principally for its inherent entertainment value? If so, that cuts against fair use. Also, do not use borrowed material for creative flourishes or in order to take advantage of someone else's distinctive editing. And keep the clip's original audio and video in synch. Supply your own entertainment value if you don't want to license it.

Reproduced with permission from Neil Rosini from his website: www.fwrv.com/articles/101008—fair-use-demystified.html

FIGURE 13.4   Credit: master_art.

It might have been a good case to understand the legal bounds, but is this the main factor in how the courts evaluated this case? Where does intellectual property come into play?

In this instance, intellectual property = what copyright protects. As I understand the Google project, they don't make available an entire book if it's still copyright-protected. Instead, they allow the book to be word-searched and then make snippets of text available. The courts have found this to be a "fair use"—an exemption from the general copyright monopoly that still would apply, for example, to the right to publish a book or make a film from it. In Google's case they argued that what they did was a fair use that benefits society and deserves to predominate over the author's monopoly—and Google has won.

SHARING YOUR WORK

What is Copyleft?

The term "copyleft" is a play on the word copyright. It uses copyright law, but flips it over to serve the opposite of its usual intent. Copyleft is a type of rights-licensing that is based on the understanding that a more open sharing of intellectual property benefits the economy and society as a whole. A copyleft license ensures that the public has the freedom to use, modify, extend, and redistribute the work rather than restricting such freedoms. By using this license, the copyright holder grants irrevocable permission to the public to use the work in any manner that they please—with the very important caveat that all derivative works and uses must also be distributed using a copyleft license, that is, they must also be free and completely accessible to the public.

FIGURE 13.5   Copyleft is a type of rights-licensing that is based on the understanding that a more open sharing of intellectual property benefits the economy and society as a whole. Credit: Yuriy Vlasenko.

What is Creative Commons?

Creative Commons is a non-profit organization founded in 2001 that promotes the sharing and use of creativity and knowledge through free legal tools. The organization's objective is to create different types of licenses with the goal of increasing the amount of creative, educational, and scientific research available to the public for free.

Creative Commons has a set of copyright licenses and tools which add flexibility to the traditional "all rights reserved" designation established by copyright law. These tools give everyone from individual creators to large institutions a standardized way of taking a "some rights reserved" approach that reserves some of the protections of copyright while allowing other uses without the need of a license.

A media-maker can choose the specific terms of a license from a variety of options and control how their work is used. They can let the public have full access of the copyrighted material or place certain limits on how the public can use the work. The popular photo-sharing website Flickr, for example, allows members to use creative commons licensing for their images.

Creative Commons and copyleft have valuable implications when a media-maker decides that the content of the product is more important than ownership and/or profit.

FIGURE 13.6 Creative Commons has a set of copyright licenses and tools which add flexibility to the traditional "all rights reserved" designation established by copyright law. Credit: Sarycheva Olesia.

TAKE HOME POINTS

- When using material from any other source, always give the citation—always!
- When you ask original creators for permission to adapt a pre-existing short story, graphic novel, play, novel, make sure you keep a copy of all email correspondence showing that the creator/owner agreed to let you use the material.
- Always treat other media-makers work with respect—if the material is copyrighted, and if you want to use it, and if fair use does not apply, then ethical and respectful practice entails contacting the media-maker, and obtaining a license to use the material. This often means paying a fee.
- Take the time to familiarize yourself with basic copyright law, rules, and regulations.
- If we, as artists, find people using our work and not applying fair use legitimately, then this needs to be confronted. As filmmakers and media-makers, we would not want someone to bend the requirements of fair use as a way of avoiding compensating us as artists for our work.
- We are collaborating most with the people in front of our cameras. What are they getting out of participating in the project and do they fully understand the implications of

appearing on camera? Always thoroughly explain how and where the media will be screened as part of asking people to sign release forms.

NOTES

1   Legal questions and concerns are geographically specific, so it is important to supplement the core ideas we discuss here with research pertaining to the country in which you are working. For example, American citizens traveling outside of the United States and American media producers distributing their work outside the United States, need to understand they are subject to that country's laws; not those of the United States. In terms of ethics, however, treating others respectfully is universal and not determined by geography.

2   Contacting the owner of the material and requesting permission to adapt the material requires some negotiation. The advice and guidance of an entertainment lawyer can be very helpful in negotiating this process. In New York and elsewhere, there are voluntary organizations such as Volunteer Lawyers for the Arts that provide free or low-cost legal consultations.

3   Personal communication with Stephanie Black, the director of *Life and Debt* (2001), on October 30, 2015.

4   This so-called golden rule is stated in a variety of ancient texts about behavioral precepts (including the New Testament, Talmud, Koran, and the Analects of Confucius). Among the earliest appearances in English is Earl Rivers's translation of a saying of Socrates (Dictes and Sayings of the Philosophers, 1477): "Do to others as thou wouldst they should do to thee, and do to none other but as thou wouldst be done to."

5   Go to www.copyright.gov for detailed information and instruction about how to copyright your work.

6   In the United States, the first form of intellectual property law was patent law. In 1790, Congress passed the first patent laws. These laws were modeled after European, patent common law. Before Americans had the right to their intellectual property, it belonged to the King of England. If colonists wanted the rights to their inventions, they had to petition the state or "the governing body of the colony" (Bellis, n.d.).

7   Lenz v. Universal Music Corp. 572 F. Supp. 2d 1150 (N.D. Cal., 2008).

BIBLIOGRAPHY

About the licenses. (n.d.). *Creative Commons*. Retrieved from: https://creativecommons.org/licenses/

Aufderheide, P. (2007, August). Fair use put to good use: 'Documentary filmmakers' statement' makes decisive impact. *International Documentary Association*. Retrieved from: www.documentary.org/content/fair-use-put-good-use-documentary-filmmakers-statement-makes-decisive-impact

Bellis, M. (n.d). *The 212th anniversary of the first American Patent Act*. Retrieved from: http://inventors.about.com/library/weekly/aa073100a.htm

Bernard, S. C., & Rabin, K. (2009). *Archival storytelling: A filmmaker's guide to finding, using, and licensing third-party visuals and music*. Burlington, MA: Elsevier Press.

Black, S. (Director). (2001). *Life and debt* [Motion Picture]. Tuff Gong Pictures.

Center for Media & Social Impact, School of Communication, American University. (2015, February). Dangerous documentaries: Reducing risk when telling truth to power. *Center for Media & Social Impact*. Retrieved from: www.cmsimpact.org/dangerousdocs

Charts and tools. (n.d.). *Stanford Copyright & Fair Use Center*. Retrieved from: http://fairuse.stanford.edu/charts-and-tools/

College Art Association. (2015, February). Code for best practices in fair use for the visual arts. *Center for Media & Social Impact*. Retrieved from: www.cmsimpact.org/fair-use/best-practices/fair-use-visual-arts

Copyright & fair use. (n.d.). *Stanford Copyright & Fair Use Center*. Retrieved from: http://fairuse.stanford.edu/

Danto, A. (Director). (2011). *Reflections on media ethics* [Documentary]. San Francisco, CA: Forwardintime.com.

Documentary filmmakers' statement of best practices in fair use. (n.d.). *Center for Media & Social Impact.* Retrieved from: www.cmsimpact.org/fair-use/best-practices/documentary-filmmakers-statement-best-practices-fair-use

Greenleigh, I. (2014). *The social media side door: How to bypass the gatekeepers to gain greater access and influence.* New York, NY: McGraw-Hill.

Johnson, T. (2015, July 29). Filmmaker says unearthed songbook proves "Happy Birthday" is in public domain. *Variety.* Retrieved from http://variety.com/2015/music/news/filmmaker-says-unearthed-songbook-proves-happy-birthday-is-in-public-domain-1201552544/

Johnson, T. (2015, September 22). "Happy Birthday" not under copyright protection, judge rules. *Variety.* Retrieved from http://variety.com/2015/biz/news/happy-birthday-song-public-domain-copyright-1201600319/

Litman, J. (2001). *Digital copyright: Protecting intellectual property on the Internet.* Amherst, NY: Prometheus Books.

Mickelsen, J. (n.d.). Answers to common intellectual property questions for the independent documentary filmmaker. *Center for Media & Social Impact.* Retrieved from: www.cmsimpact.org/fair-use/related-materials/documents/answers-common-intellectual-property-questions-independent-docu

Postigo, H. (2012). *The digital rights movement: The role of technology in subverting digital copyright.* Cambridge, MA: MIT Press.

Rabin, K. (2008) The ethics of archival use: a roundtable discussion. *International Documentary Association.* Retrieved from: www.documentary.org/content/ethics-archival-use-roundtable-discussion

Stim, R. (2010, October). What is fair use? *Stanford Copyright & Fair Use Center.* Retrieved from: http://fairuse.stanford.edu/overview/fair-use/what-is-fair-use/

The campus guide to copyright: From creative commons to fair use. (n.d.). *VideoBlocks Education.* Retrieved from: http://offers.education.videoblocks.com/campus-guide-creative-commons-fair-use?utm_campaign=Fall%202015%20Copyright%20Guide%20Ad&utm_medium=google&utm_source=cpc

Chapter 14

Digital Distribution Ethics

Mobina Hashmi

ABSTRACT

This chapter outlines the ethical considerations at two levels of distribution: infrastructure and practice. The regulatory, technical, and economic infrastructures for distribution are shaped by assumptions about the public good, efficiency, and profit that allow certain kinds of media to gain wide circulation while other kinds of media struggle to reach an audience. Through analysis of a range of case studies, this chapter also explores how considerations of audience, cultural contexts, and financing shape media producers' distribution practices.

> Analysis of distribution is the key to liberating communication in the twenty-first century.
> Sean Cubitt (2005, p. 209)

> Content is king, but distribution is queen and she wears the pants. It's not nearly enough to create a good piece of content. You have to understand how content spreads across the web.
> Jonathan Perelman, Buzzfeed (Himler, 2013)

At the age of 19, Gary Brolsma became an internet superstar. In 2004, Brolsma, an average teen living in New Jersey, uploaded a brief low-resolution video of himself enthusiastically lip-syncing and bopping along to a Romanian pop song. Once the website newground.com linked to the video on its home page, it became a sensation. Within a couple of months, the video had two million hits, and, as of early 2016, it has almost 23 million views on YouTube.

Eight years later, in 2012, Korean pop star Psy's music video "Gangnam Style" received one million views a day on YouTube and went on to get 2.5 *billion* views in three years. It not only became one of the most shared videos in countries across the world, it also inspired thousands of tribute and parody videos from groups as diverse as Mongolian soldiers, cheerleaders for the football club Crystal Palace, and young Saudi men.

This is the face of digital distribution today. Or, at least, one of its faces: the viral video.

Digital distribution is vast and varied: it includes video streaming sites like Hulu, Netflix, iTunes, and Amazon; websites with user-generated content like reddit, indymedia, and Funny or Die; Web 2.0 platforms like YouTube, Twitter, Instagram, and Facebook; and hybrid websites like Buzzfeed which features user-generated content, serious original journalism, and content aggregation—most notoriously in "listicles" that circulate far and wide on social media.

In this new environment, we *all* act as distributors when we share, like, retweet, or forward digital content.

With so much content available—hundreds of hours of new video uploaded to YouTube every minute, tens of thousands of hours of television and film on Netflix, thousands of news sites from all over the world, millions of blogs—the scarcest commodity today is viewer attention. As a creator of media content, your biggest challenge is not getting your work distributed; it is getting it noticed.

CHANNELING THE FLOW: DISTRIBUTION STRUCTURES AND PRACTICES

> Keeping information and ideas out of public circulation is equally a function of distribution. Both promoting and denying circulation confer wealth and power, introducing disjunctures, deferrals, omissions and selections that restructure and reorganize both content and audience activity.
>
> Sean Cubitt (2005, p. 200)

Distribution is what brings audiences or users into contact with content.[1] Distribution decisions thus hinge on the following very basic ethical questions: Who is your project for? Who do you hope will see it? Who do you think will be able to see it? And who might see it that you didn't intend it for?

We used to think about distribution as the last stage in the production process; the moment when the "completed" project goes out into the world and is exhibited for an audience. Contemporary forms of digital distribution fundamentally altered this paradigm. Thinking about distribution begins right when a project is still in the concept stage.

But while production, distribution, and exhibition may have converged in practice, it still helps to make analytic distinctions between these stages.

Distribution structures are not ethically neutral. They place constraints on the options available to media-makers looking for an audience. For example, public access television represents an ethic that values public participation and democratic access to the means of media creation, whereas a premium cable channel like HBO is a commercial enterprise that values aesthetic quality and limits access. One is not ethically superior to the other, but they do represent different visions of the public good.

As a media-maker, you have to balance the distribution options available to you with the ethical implications of your choices. In other words, you have to simultaneously keep the following two issues in mind:

- The choices already encoded into the physical and regulatory structures of distribution.
- The consequences of specific modes of distribution.

Despite all the hype around "disruptive technologies" and claims that everything has changed, the traditional structures of distribution persist. They may not be as dominant as they once were, but it is important to recognize continuities as well as change, especially since many of the same media corporations own both old and new forms of distribution. I end with a brief discussion of alternative distribution options.

MOTION PICTURE AND TELEVISION DISTRIBUTION

Some of my film scholar friends who live in small university towns make trips to New York City to see new independent, alternative, or foreign-language films that are not playing at their local multiplex. Only some feature films get national distribution exhibition. Access to this expensive and coveted form of distribution is controlled by a few powerful gatekeepers: the major studios (distributors) and the major theater chains (exhibitors).[2]

Just as independent movie producers can have a hard time getting wide distribution, independent exhibitors can find themselves locked out of the distribution of high-profiled films. For example, Look Cinemas, an independent theater in Dallas, protested to the major studios when an AMC theater got to exhibit the third *Hunger Games: Mockingjay, Part I* (2014) because of an existing—and possibly unethical—agreement with the distributor (Verrier, 2015). Being excluded from major distribution networks can mean that these independent theaters struggle economically, thus further reducing the exhibition options available to independent filmmakers.

The picture looks similar across the globe. In Korea, for example, as of 2009, five main exhibition companies controlled 77 percent of theater screens (Jin, 2012).

Television distribution was organized in a similar way until the early 1990s. In the United States, the big three broadcast networks—NBC, CBS, and ABC—had a lock on national distribution through their network of affiliate stations and were able to dictate highly unequal terms to both television producers and exhibitors.[3] In other countries like the U.K., India, China, Brazil, and Nigeria, broadcast television was controlled by either a state-run or a state-sanctioned monopoly.

Starting in the 1980s though, broadcast networks around the world were challenged by new modes of distribution: cable came into its own as a medium and—not restricted by the requirement placed on many broadcasters to act in the public interest—opened up a whole new universe of distribution options for original productions as well as a new afterlife for old television programs and films that had been out of circulation for decades.

One important, but often overlooked, consequence of the rise of cable television in the United States was that cable operators were required to offer "public access" channels; one or more channel that would be open to any resident who wanted to air any kind of content. If you live in the United States, find out about your local public access channel. Many offer classes and have free or low-cost production equipment that you can use. Your work can then be distributed locally to all cable subscribers.

Today, traditional film and television distributors are both being challenged by upstart digital distributors like Netflix. Starting in the late 2000s, Netflix began offering an online streaming service. Now you could watch films and television programs at your own convenience and without having to make a trip to the video store. Netflix—quickly followed by Amazon—has recently moved into television and film production as well. Interestingly, Netflix is itself becoming a major global distribution company. From its origin as a United States-based mail rental company, it now has digital services in 60 countries with planned expansion in 2016 to another 130 countries (Villareal, 2016).

Faced with declining audiences and shrinking revenues, traditional film and television companies have themselves developed online distribution options. Hulu, for example, is a streaming service that is co-owned by the parent companies of NBC, Fox, and ABC.

International Distribution

Some of the most vigorous debates in international media distribution have to do with concerns about American media imperialism. Films and television programs are commodities, but they are also expressions of cultural identity. France was an early and loud critic of American influence and, like many other countries, places limits on foreign media content (Katsarova, 2014). The European Union also has quotas for foreign media content and provides subsidies for domestic media production.

As a media-creator, you need to be aware of how distribution is organized across different markets and media formats. For example, big media conglomerates like Sony or Disney have subsidiaries and enter into partnerships and co-production deals with local media companies in countries around the world. In these instances, they are often responsive to local conditions and can provide new distribution options for media-creators in those regions (Christophers, 2009; Oren & Shahaf, 2013). China, for example, has strict content quotas for foreign content, but allows greater distribution access for companies that partner with Chinese media producers (Curtin, 2007).

The global box office, which was projected to hit $40 billion in 2015, has seen most of its growth in international distribution, which now accounts for almost three-quarters of revenue while the North American market stagnates (Faughnder, 2015). The film market in China, for example, grew by 50 percent to a staggering $6.8 billion in 2015 (Lang, 2015). The importance of the global market means that Hollywood films are more likely to be shot in countries that require local production as a prerequisite for gaining distribution, more likely to feature stars from countries with big movie-going audiences, and more likely to show a slightly greater acknowledgment of different cultural sensitivities.

Breaking the Distribution Window

A few media companies—the United States-based Disney, Comcast, Universal, and Viacom; the German company Bertelsmann; and the Japanese company Sony—control the vast majority of global media flows.[4] In recent years, Google—which owns both YouTube and Blogger—has joined this list.

They put together complex deals determining "distribution windows": where, when, and for how long a film is made available to various publics in the theater, streaming, on premium cable, pay-per-view, on airplanes and in hotels, on DVD, etc.

FIGURE 14.1 From its beginnings as a U.S. mail-order DVD rental store in 1997, Netflix has become a leader in online video streaming with services available, or planned, in 190 countries as of 2016. Credit: Twin Design/Shutterstock.com.

They coordinate a film's release internationally or in staggered releases in smaller and bigger markets. In other words, the distribution company—with the help of its marketing and publicity arms—can make or break a film. It is not uncommon for a blockbuster to have a publicity budget that is as much as 50 percent of its production budget.

These windows which used to be carefully staggered to maximize revenue at each stage—first-run theatrical distribution, pay-per-view, DVD and streaming, premium cable— are now converging. For example, Netflix released director Cary Fukunaga's film *Beasts of No Nation* (2015) in theaters and online simultaneously instead of keeping to an industry average of about 80 days for the theatrical window (Fanelli, 2015).

As you will see a bit later in this chapter, digital distribution offers many more options for beginners. But if you are interested in going the traditional route, Elliot Grove, the founder of Raindance, a U.K.-based film festival, suggests being prepared to negotiate multiple deals for distribution in different countries and on different platforms; recognizing that the bigger the distributor, the more control you will have to give up; and, accepting that revenue will be slow in coming (Grove, 2015).

Marketing, Publicity, and Access: The Politics of Representation

As the creator of a motion picture, you have to learn about the economics of distribution deals and about the degree of control you will have over how the film is marketed.

Newcomers often have to sign over control of their creation to the distributor in exchange for royalties.

One troubling ethical consequence of licensing your work to a distribution company is that you will very likely not have control over how it is publicized—even if you are a well-known figure.

The movie *12 Years a Slave* was one of the most critically acclaimed films of 2013 and went on to win the Oscar for Best Picture making its director, Steve McQueen, the first black director of an Oscar-winning film. Italian publicity posters for the film in Italy prominently featured the two white male stars—Brad Pitt and Michael Fassbender—while the image of the black lead actor, Chiwetal Ejiofor, was reduced to a small corner. An article in *Forbes* magazine, playing devil's advocate, argued that the decision not only made marketing sense, but was also ethically defensible: "Moreover, if more people seeing *12 Years A Slave* is not only financially beneficial to Summit Entertainment [the overall distributor] but arguably a morally just cause to get more people to see the picture, then is not what BIM [the Italian distribution company] attempted perhaps a necessary evil?" (Mendelsen, 2013).

The poster was pulled from circulation, but it caused embarrassment to the film's actors and producers. BIM Distribuzione apologized for creating the posters while Lionsgate Films (the studio) distanced itself saying, "The *12 Years a Slave* theatrical posters featuring Brad Pitt and Michael Fassbender that were recently released in Italy were unauthorized and were not approved by any of the producers or licensers of the film" (Variety Staff, 2013).

Motion picture distributors have power because they often provide financing. Thus, their views on what will or will not have wide appeal carry considerable weight in determining whether a picture will be "greenlit" or not. In this process, pictures with minority casts or with casts centered on white women are discriminated against because of industry lore that such films will not appeal to a large audience. These beliefs stay in place despite repeated examples of films featuring white women such as *Bridesmaids* or films with a majority black cast such as *The Perfect Man* that significantly outperform box office expectations (Stewart, 2012, 2015; Mendelsen, 2015; McClintock, 2011).

DIGITAL MEDIA AND SELF-DISTRIBUTION

If distribution in the pre-digital era was a carefully controlled and standardized process with clear bottlenecks and gatekeepers, digital distribution is marked by anxiety and excitement; by uncertainty, and opportunity as media technologies, industries, and genres converge.

Changes in distribution are inextricable from changes in our understandings of intellectual property and the role of copyright. It is easy to forget the intense debates on the ethics of digital distribution around peer-to-peer services in the late 1990s and early 2000s. Services like Napster, Gnutella, and LimeWire first made it possible for people to directly share music files and—if you were patient—films online. Legal challenges from the music industry for copyright violations under the newly minted Digital Millennium Copyright Act drove Napster into bankruptcy, but the model it pioneered has become the norm today—thanks to improvements in digital rights management (DRM) technology and exponential increases in internet bandwidth and speed.

The power of traditional distribution structures is being challenged by new platforms for digital distribution that enable "disintermediation," which simply means cutting out the middle man—the distributor. Web 2.0 platforms offer a range of distribution options directly to content creators: anyone can upload content to YouTube, and anyone can view that content; Twitter, Instagram, and other social media platforms leave it up to users to build a distribution network by cultivating followers; and Amazon offers distribution through its Kindle Direct Publishing service, but takes a cut of the royalties from authors.

In addition to the commercial options listed above, there are a number of public, non-profit, or activist digital distribution networks such as Witness, Indymedia, and Frameline. Websites and blogs such as the India-based *Kafila* or the investigative journalism site *The Intercept* create spaces for dialogue, debate, and the circulation of ideas—as well as content—that is shut out of or marginalized in mainstream media.

A Series of Tubes: The Ethics of Internet Infrastructures

Control over the infrastructure of the internet has been a contentious issue since the mid-1990s and led to a protracted struggle between internet service providers, content providers, and public advocacy groups over what became called "net neutrality." This is the principle that all traffic over the internet—whether it is a livestream from a protest or Netflix's latest original series—should be treated equally, that is it should be accessible to users at the same speed. Net neutrality is absolutely fundamental to keeping the internet a democratic space because otherwise certain content providers—MSNBC, for example—could get preferential treatment by paying ISPs such as Comcast (also MSNBC's parent company) for faster speeds while the website hosting your independent feature keeps buffering.

The net neutrality debate mobilized Americans as few other regulatory debates had because it was so clearly about ethical issues of fairness, access, and transparency. Public figures weighed in, and more than four million people left comments on the FCC's website, motivated in part by comedian John Oliver's call to his viewers to take action (Oliver, 2014).

In late February 2015, the FCC finally affirmed the principle of net neutrality in its "Open Internet" rules, saying: "The open Internet drives the American economy and serves, every day, as a critical tool for America's citizens to conduct commerce, communicate, educate, entertain, and engage in the world around them" (Federal Communications Commission, 2015).

Despite this recent move, the United States remains behind the global curve in recognizing broadband internet access as a public right. In 2009, Finland became the first country to declare that all citizens had a legal right to have access to broadband internet and its capital, Helsinki, has free mobile hotspots (Johnson, 2009). A number of other countries and cities across the world also have policies based on the belief that broadband access is a right; and if the market does not provide this access, the government should.

Of course, internet access does not ensure that citizens have unrestricted access to content. Singapore, for example, does ensure internet access for citizens, but it also censors certain kinds of content such as pornography. The Chinese government keeps its citizens behind the "great firewall of China," controlling ISPs and limiting how search engines work. Companies such as Google have been criticized for placing their profits above the ethical principles of

BOX 14.1 THE LABOR AND ENVIRONMENTAL COST OF DIGITAL MEDIA

The incredible ease of digital consumerism allows us to ignore the physical infrastructure that supports digital distribution. A number of news stories in 2014 about Amazon's labor practices described the intense monitoring and demanding pace for workers at its many warehouses (Cadwalladr, 2013; Head, 2014). We have to ask ourselves if we want to support such practices.

In a similar vein, we cannot ignore the incredible amounts of e-waste—old cell phones, computers, tablets, and other electronic devices—that are shipped to dumps in developing countries in Africa and Asia (Vidal, 2013). This e-waste is rich in toxic substances ranging from mercury and lead to arsenic and is exported to countries with less restrictive environmental policies such as Ghana. Aside from the highly questionable ethics of exporting the costs of our consumer decisions, this practice can also mean that sensitive private information on these devices can be recovered and used. So before you rush to buy the latest version of a phone or a camera that you don't really need, stop to consider what will happen to the old one that you discard.

free speech by accommodating censorship requests from China. And, in Pakistan, the Supreme Court issued an order in September 2012 banning YouTube because the site hosted the blasphemous video "Innocence of the muslims" ("Senate body seeks legislation," 2015). The ban—which many simply bypassed by using proxy sites—was lifted in early 2016 following an agreement with Google that would allow the Pakistani government to block certain content (Wilkes, 2016).

U.S. government control over digital content has happened through copyright law rather than censorship. The Digital Millenium Copyright Act (DMCA), passed in 1998, has become the key legislation for digital distribution. The DMCA protects digital intellectual property through prohibiting the creation of technologies that enable circumvention of DRM or digital rights management even if the technologies are not actually used for that purpose. In other words, the DMCA makes it more difficult to create and distribute pirated material.

Abundance and Access: Rhetoric or Reality?

If broadcast television was defined by "scarcity," the internet is defined by "abundance." Publishing or distribution can require as little effort as free registration on a website. We can easily access films, television programs, advertisements, government documents, newspapers, magazines, novels—all with a click or two and all on the same device. Although the distribution bottleneck has been unclogged, the role of distributors remains central. With so many options, the scarce commodity now is viewer attention and engagement and what distribution platforms and companies promise is the publicity and marketing that will bring your content to the attention of the audience.

FIGURE 14.2 Innovative marketing: A mural for Netflix's original television series *Orange Is the New Black* in the culturally influentially neighborhood of Williamsburg in Brooklyn. Credit: Leonard Zhukovsky/Shutterstock.com.

Mainstream digital distributors encourage viewer participation as a way of building audience interest in potential projects. Netflix, for example, allows viewers to vote for pilots of television programs that they want to see produced instead of such decisions being made solely by industry executives.

Digital platforms certainly offer an abundance of distribution and viewing options. However, the ethics of such abundance and access are not uncomplicated. The easy distribution and circulation of content online combined with the emergence of new genres of online content such as "listicles" (numbered compilations of popular images, tweets, etc.) and programs such as Storify creates ethical challenges not just around copyright, but also around citation, acknowledgment, and intellectual labor.

We create the content on social media. What Terranova (2000) calls "free labor"— writing reviews, making funny videos, posting analyses on blogs, live tweeting breaking news, writing code, archiving, digitizing, and curating content—is most often done because we enjoy doing it, and we do it voluntarily. But, economic models for social media depend on this kind of unpaid labor to generate revenue that is not shared with content creators.

In 2014, a collective of women of color wrote an online essay called "This tweet called my back."[5] In it, they announced a strike:

> We are Black Women, AfroIndigenous and women of color who have organized a
> social media Blackout. We are your unwaged labor in our little corner of the internet that
> feeds a movement. Hours of teach-ins, hashtags, Twitter chats, video chats and phone
> calls to create a sustainable narrative and conversation around decolonization and
> antiblackness.
>
> (Collected Authors, 2014)

The authors, who are identified only by their Twitter handles, draw our attention to how the
work they do on social media platforms—education, analysis, political commentary, activism,
journalism, and organizing—is simply appropriated by journalists, bloggers, scholars, and
activists working in more established and legitimized settings. They receive neither acknowledgment, nor economic reimbursement: "Never mind that we are constantly a full month ahead
of the news cycle and that our frameworks mysteriously appear in a rash of articles and essays
after we hammer them out publicly on digital mediums" (Collected Authors, 2014).

Social media platforms have enabled previously isolated and marginalized voices to be
heard in a broader public space and have allowed members of minority communities to come
together to build their own digital spaces. As we see from the example above, the openness
of these spaces can lead to surveillance and exploitation as well. Your ethical responsibility
as a social media user is to actually enact your belief in the importance of consent, respect for
others, and critical self-reflexivity every time you think about how to retweet or post a link.
Are you driving traffic to websites that participate in the exploitation of unpaid labor? If in a
position of relative privilege, are you opening up distribution options for marginalized voices,
or are you using their work to enlarge your own network? The answers to these questions are
not at all clear because digital distribution is not a linear process. That is, it is not the case that
content moves in a straight line from creator to distributor to exhibitor to audience member;
instead, we see the constant recirculation of content in widening networks of distribution.
Thus, you need to think in each instance about where the line between exploitative work and
work that enhances visibility should be drawn.

Financing Digital Media Production

Motion picture or television production has traditionally been funded, at least partly, through
licensing deals with distributors. These deals put the distributor at an advantage because they
control access to the audience and have the resources and knowledge and access to successfully
publicize the motion picture or television program.

Crowdfunding websites such as Kickstarter or Indiegogo which are two of the better-
known ones have become popular as ways of bypassing industry gatekeepers. One digital
distribution success story is that of writer, director, actor, producer Issa Rae who received
widespread critical acclaim for her YouTube series *The Misadventures of Awkward Black
Girl*. Initially self-funded, Issa Rae turned to Kickstarter after the series got some good buzz.
After it became a hit, she got a seat at the table with established television producers such as
Shonda Rhimes and HBO (Wagmeister, 2015).

YouTube is undoubtedly the biggest avenue for digital self-distribution. It began in 2005
with the call to "broadcast yourself." Ten years later, in 2015, YouTube had over a billion

users, hundreds of billions of views, and over 300 hours of content uploaded every minute, and is available in 76 languages with more than 80 percent of views coming from countries other than the United States (Statista, 2016; YouTube, n.d.).

A number of ordinary people have become stars—and millionaires—through their self-produced and self-distributed YouTube series. One of the biggest such stars is PewDiePie, a young Swedish man, whose channel has more than 40 million subscribers. On average, YouTube offers its content partners $2 to $5 per 1,000 views in exchange for placing advertising before or over their content. PewDiePew earns millions of dollars through his short videos. But, YouTube takes about 45 percent of advertising revenue generated by user content (Bateman, 2016). Furthermore, for every YouTube star who makes it big, there are tens of thousands of others who are trying to make a living as a social media content producer. YouTube begins to look suspiciously like a traditional media distributor. In some ways it is, but it is important to remember that it also offers a space for people who have no interest in making money to share content.

Like Blogger, one of the biggest blogging platforms, YouTube is owned by Google. When you upload content to YouTube and Blogger, or if you are browsing the internet while logged in to Google, you are sharing your digital information with Google (Gillmore, 2014). The same holds true of Facebook. When we create, share, or view digital content, we are also sharing data about our digital habits. This data—which circulates in the all-important distribution network of advertisers, marketers, and software companies—crucially shapes the kinds of media we have access to as well as having obvious implications for the degree of control we have over our privacy (see Chapter 9 in this book for more on government surveillance of citizens). When we think about social media distribution, we have to keep in mind that our information—and that of our audience—is also being distributed in ways that are not transparent or within our control. As Christine Choy mentions in Chapter 2, one of the ethical questions this poses for us: What will you do when you are the one collecting this information?

ALTERNATIVE DISTRIBUTION NETWORKS AND COLLECTIVES

It is important to recognize that independent and alternative distribution practices and networks have always existed alongside—and in many cases in opposition to—mainstream distributors. Specialized social, political, cultural, and religious distribution networks have emerged to distribute media—books, music, films, television programs, news stories—that are either of interest only to smaller communities, or that are simply not attractive economic propositions for larger distributors.

Non-profits and collectives like Women Make Movies, New Day Films, Deep Dish Television, and Newsreel are among the best-known alternative distributors. Access to these networks varies: Women Make Movies, for example, accepts films for distribution through an application process while Deep Dish Television has relationships with a wide range of activist media organizations and individuals. Deep Dish primarily provides satellite distribution to public-access stations across the country, and has acted as a distributor for the alternative media collective Paper Tiger TV and for journalist Amy Goodman's show *Democracy Now*.

Distribution means connecting points of production with points of exhibition that may be far removed in time and space. Thus far, I have focused on the temporal aspects of distribution; the ease and speed with which we can share content. However, the spatial aspect of distribution is equally important. Local distribution connects audiences with media that are being produced within their communities and offers the chance to enhance public life in that community. Public access cable channels are the best example of this in traditional media; and neighborhood blogs are examples of digital solutions to the decline of local newspapers.

The same principle of making media accessible to local audiences informed the call for a New World Information and Communication Order (NWICO) in the 1970s. Endorsed by the United Nations, NWICO was intended to create contra-flows of news from and between countries in the "global South" to counteract the dominance of the big press agencies of the "global North" such as the Associated Press (AP), Reuters, and Agence France Presse (AFP). The ethical purity of this call was significantly complicated by the international politics surrounding it: many of the developing countries that championed NWICO were run by dictators or had authoritarian governments (Mattelart, 1994, pp. 179–184).

Finally, distribution networks for educational media are a vital and important alternative to mainstream media. In the United States, the Media Education Foundation is well known for its catalog of educational documentaries on a range of media issues. Other well-known educational media distributors include PBS and the now-defunct Cable in the Classroom. Internationally, the United Nations—through its various agencies, notable UNESCO—funds educational media production and initiatives. For example, *Sexto Sentido* (Nicaragua, 2001–2005) was an "edutainment" telenovela that focused on issues of HIV awareness and risks (Howe, 2008). It was produced by the NGO Puntos de Encuentro as part of a broader media education strategy and proved to be effective in raising teen awareness of these issues.

FIGURE 14.3 The U.N.'s World Press Freedom Day, celebrated on May 3, is an opportunity to remind people of the importance of an independent press. Credit: Mattz9o

DISTRIBUTION DECISIONS

Decisions About Audiences

New distribution technologies offer media-makers many more options for how to reach and build relationships with audiences. The obvious advantages are those offered by mainstream sites like YouTube that enable beginners to actually make money from their uploaded videos. But, you should also think creatively about using distribution to strengthen community ties and amplify minority voices.

Decisions about Authorship and Financing

The model of authorship that you use will have an impact on the kinds of distribution (and funding) that you can get for your project. If you

BOX 14.2   IMPARJA TV

FIGURE 14.4   An Australian stamp from circa 2001 commemorates Outback Services. Credit: rook76/Shutterstock.com.

Lisa Parks (2005) describes how the Imparja TV, a satellite television network run by and for Aboriginal Australian communities, used the distribution technology in creative ways to reach different audiences at different times. Regular programming on Imparja included standard fare such as syndicated American television series. But local communities were also able to filter this satellite feed and insert local content. And, "during the satellite downtime Imparja became a relay center for the circulation of Aboriginal dreaming videos, many of which contained sacred performances considered unsuitable for outsiders' eyes" (Parks, 2005, p. 65). The same distribution technology that brings a range of commercial media to audiences was imaginatively used to help maintain community and tradition in concert with rather than in resistance to new technologies.

> ## BOX 14.3   TWO MODELS FOR COLLABORATIVE AUTHORSHIP: *18 DAYS IN EGYPT* (2011) AND *STAR WARS UNCUT* (2010).
>
> The project *18 Days in Egypt* (2011) is a crowd-sourced, collaborative documentary that, on its web page, invites Egyptians to participate: "You witnessed it, you recorded it. Now, let's write our country's history. Join 18 Days In Egypt in documenting Egypt's ongoing revolution." It explicitly recognizes that we are all documentarians. With their camera phones, social media apps, blogs and video cameras, millions of people documented the uprising in Egypt and their own role in it. Such projects have to decide on a balance between text and process; and the balance between distribution and circulation. The role of the "viewer" also changes and becomes more demanding.
>
> Another well-known project is *Star Wars Uncut* (2010/2014), which is a "crazy fan mashup remake" of the first two films in the franchise. Anyone can claim 15 seconds of the film and then re-create those 15 seconds using any genre they wish. The result is—for fans at least—an exciting and playful recreation of the film that is also an impressive showcase for fan creativity.

choose to make a crowdsourced or collaborative work, you will most likely need to go with a Creative Commons license that enables you to define your intellectual property rights in a more flexible manner. A crowdsourced project that can circulate freely and encourages audiences to become collaborators can garner you a dedicated—and even sizable—audience. However, major distribution companies require much more stringent copyright and authorship clearances since the work is intended for profit rather than community sharing. Thus, your best bet for financing will probably be crowdfunding or applying for grants.

Decisions about Viewing and Consumption Choices

As members of networked publics, our viewing and consumption can have a much more direct impact on content creators than was the case with traditional media.

Social media has emerged as an incredibly important medium for holding public officials accountable and for enabling public debate where ordinary people hold each other accountable. It is your responsibility to think about if you want to engage in such conversations and how to conduct yourself in these spaces.

Think about the ethical consequences of your creative and technological decisions at all stages of media creation. In particular, always remember that what you create will affect not only your life but also those of the people you collaborate with in the process of making media, the people who are the subjects of your project, and the people who will engage with your work. Distribution, as the final stage in this process, has its own ethical considerations, but it also reveals the results of the decisions you have made throughout your journey from conception to completion.

BOX 14.4   TWITTER SHAMING

We are all distributors when it comes to social media. The phenomenon of what we can broadly call "Twitter shaming" most clearly illustrates the ethical complexities of whether or not to recirculate material on the internet. One of the most notorious instances of Twitter shaming was the story of Justine Sacco, a young woman whose thoughtless racist tweet linking Africa with AIDS went viral while she was on an 11-hour flight from New York to Cape Town, South Africa. By the time she landed, her life had changed: her feed was filled with tens of thousands of angry tweets, her name was everywhere, and she lost her job (Ronson, 2015).

TAKE HOME POINTS

- Distribution is so much more than content delivery: it is the creation of a relationship between audiences and media-makers.
- Think about how your distribution choices can support the creation of a more equitable public sphere where all voices can be heard.
- Different distribution infrastructures allow varying degrees of access, privacy, and control for both media-makers and audiences. Your choice of distribution platform carries with it your implicit ethical endorsement of its commercial, social, and political uses.
- Who is your intended audience? Your distribution decisions determine whether the people you want to have access to your work will actually be able to access it.
- A distribution deal with a major company can mean a potentially huge audience. But it can also mean giving up control over how your creation is marketed and promoted. Think through the ethical consequences of this decision.
- As a member of social media publics, think about the impact of your decision to post or share content on the lives of the subjects of that content.

NOTES

1 In a nutshell, distributors either own or have contractual agreements with a range of exhibition venues—for example, movie theaters, broadcast and cable television, streaming services, and hotels. They can thus get media content to audiences. They license content from media-makers: the distributor gets temporary ownership of the content and the rights to the revenue it generates in exhibition; and, the media-maker gets a percentage of this revenue. If you are a beginner or do not have an established reputation, your percentage of the profits will be small.

2 See Fox (1992) for an analysis of the Paramount decision, the Supreme Court case in 1948 that broke the big film studios' grip on distribution and exhibition, and on the reemergence of vertical integration in the film industry in the decades that followed. Today, the top five U.S. theater chains—Regal, AMC, Cinemark, Carmike, Cineplex—control the majority of screens and have distribution deals with the big movie studios granting them "clearance": the exclusive rights to a film in a particular area. For more recent analysis of how

the industry is structured, the University of California, Santa Barbara's Media Industries Project (www.carseywolf.ucsb.edu/mip) has excellent analyses and resources on all aspects of digital distribution.

3   For example, the practice of "deficit financing" meant that producers of television programs were forced to license their programs at prices lower than the actual cost of production, leaving them with a deficit that they could only recoup if the program successfully made it to the second distribution window of off-network syndication.

4   For more on this see, Cubitt (2005) and Acland (2003).

5   The authors were identified by their Twitter handles: @tgirlinterruptd, @chiefelk, @bad_dominicana, @aurabogado, @so_treu, @blackamazon, and @thetrudz.

BIBLIOGRAPHY

Acland, C. R. (2003). *Screen traffic: Movies, multiplexes and global culture*. Durham, NC: Duke University Press.

Anzaldúa, G., & Moraga, C. (Eds.). (1983). *This bridge called my back: Writings by radical women of color*. New York, NY: Kitchen Table Press.

Appadurai, A. (1996). *Modernity at large: Cultural dimensions of globalization*. Minneapolis, MN: University of Minnesota Press.

Barret, E. (Director). (1999). *Stranger with a camera* [Documentary]. United States: PBS.

Bateman, D. (2016, January 3). So you want to be a social media star? Some are "barely scraping by." *Thestar.com*. Retrieved from: www.thestar.com/business/2016/01/03/so-you-want-to-be-a-social-media-star-some-are-barely-scraping-by.html

Cadwalladr, C. (2013, November 30). My week as an Amazon insider. *The Guardian*. Retrieved from: www.theguardian.com/technology/2013/dec/01/week-amazon-insider-feature-treatment-employees-work

Castells, M. (2000). *The information age: Economy, society, and culture* (Vol. 1: *The rise of the network society*) (2nd ed.). Malden, MA: Blackwell.

Christophers, B. (2009). *Envisioning media power: On capital and geographies of television*. Lanham, MD: Lexington Books.

Collected Authors. (2014, December 13). This tweet called my back. Retrieved from: https://modelviewculture.com/pieces/thistweetcalledmyback.

Cubitt, S. (2005). Distribution and media flows. *Cultural Politics, 1*(2), 193–214.

Curtin, M. (2007). *Playing to the world's biggest audience: The globalization of Chinese film and television*. Berkeley, CA: University of California Press.

Curtin, M., Holt, J., & Sanson, K. (Eds.). (2014). *Distribution revolution: Conversations about the digital future of film and television*. Berkeley, CA: University of California Press.

Fanelli, W. (2015, March). Four major theater chains are boycotting Idris Elba's latest film, here's why. *Cinema Blend*. Retrieved from: www.cinemablend.com/new/Four-Major-Theater-Chains-Boycotting-Idris-Elba-Latest-Film-Here-Why-70131.html

Faughnder, R. (2015, December 30). $40 billion in global box office? Thank China and "Star Wars." *Los Angeles Times*. Retrieved from: www.latimes.com/entertainment/envelope/cotown/la-et-ct-global-box-office-20151231-story.html

Federal Communications Commission (2015, March 12). Report and order on remand, declaratory ruling, and order. FCC 15-24. Retrieved from: https://apps.fcc.gov/edocs_public/attachmatch/FCC-15-24A1.pdf

Fox, Kraig G. (1992). Paramount revisited: The resurgence of vertical integration in the motion picture industry. *Hofstra Law Review 21*(2). Retrieved from: http://scholarlycommons.law.hofstra.edu/hlr/vol21/iss2/6

Gillmore, D. (2014, April 18). As we sweat government surveillance, companies like Google collect our data. *The Guardian*. Retrieved from: www.theguardian.com/commentisfree/2014/apr/18/corporations-google-should-not-sell-customer-data

Grove, E. (2015, July 5). 10 distribution basics. Retrieved from: www.raindance.org/10-film-distribution-basics/

Havens, T. (2006). *Global television marketplace*. British Film Institute.

Head, S. (2014, February 23). Worse than Wal-Mart: Amazon's sick brutality and secret history of ruthlessly intimidating workers. *Salon*. Retrieved from: www.salon.com/2014/02/23/worse_than_wal_mart_amazons_sick_brutality_and_secret_history_of_ruthlessly_intimidating_workers/

Himler, S. (2013, July 9). Content is king, distribution is queen. *Forbes*. Retrieved from: www.forbes.com/sites/peterhimler/2013/07/09/content-is-king-distribution-is-queen/#2715e4857a0b34435f324b11

Howe, C. (2008). Spectacles of sexuality: Televisionary activism in Nicaragua. *Cultural Anthropology*, 23(1), 48–84.

Jin, D. Y. (2012, August). Transforming the global film industries: Horizontal integration and vertical concentration amid neoliberal globalization. *International Communication Gazette, 74*(5), 405–422.

Johnson, B. (2009, October 14). Finland makes broadband access a legal right. *The Guardian*. Retrieved from: www.theguardian.com/technology/2009/oct/14/finland-broadband

Katsarova, I. (2014, December). An overview of Europe's film industry. European Parlimentary Research Service. PE 545.705. Retrieved from: www.europarl.europa.eu/RegData/etudes/BRIE/2014/545705/EPRS_BRI%282014%29545705_REV1_EN.pdf

Lang, B. (2015, December 31). Box office reaches record $11 billion thanks to return of "Star Wars," "Jurassic Park." *Variety*. Retrieved from: http://variety.com/2015/film/box-office/2015-box-office-record-star-wars-jurassic-park-1201670278/

Mattelart, A. (1994). *Mapping world communication: War, progress, culture*. Minneapolis, MN: University of Minnesota Press.

McClintock, P. (2011, May 15). "Bridesmaids" rocks weekend box office with $24.6 Million opening. *Hollywood Reporter*. Retrieved from: www.hollywoodreporter.com/news/bridesmaids-rocks-weekend-box-office-188509

Mehta, J. (Producer), & Elayat, Y. (Producer). (2011). *18 days in Egypt* [Documentary]. Available at: http://beta.18daysinegypt.com/

Mendelsen, S. (2013, December 31). In "defense" of the Brad Pitt "12 Years A Slave" posters. *Forbes*. Retrieved from: www.forbes.com/sites/scottmendelson/2013/12/31/in-defense-of-those-brad-pitt-12-years-a-slave-posters/#2715e4857a0b42e47e494bee

Mendelsen, S. (2015, September 8). Box office: Don't be surprised when *Perfect Guy* scores big this weekend. *Forbes*. Retrieved from: www.forbes.com/sites/scottmendelson/2015/09/08/box-office-dont-be-surprised-when-perfect-guy-scores-big-this-weekend/

Oliver, J. (Producer). (2014, June 1). *Last week tonight with John Oliver* [Television Broadcast]. New York, NY: HBO.

Ong, A. (1999). *Flexible citizenship: The cultural logics of transnationality*. Durham, NC: Duke University Press.

Oren, T., & Shahaf, S. (Eds.). (2013). *Global television formats: Understanding television across borders*. New York, NY: Routledge.

Parks, L. (2005). *Cultures in orbit: Satellites and the televisual*. Durham, NC: Duke University Press.

Pugh, C. (Producer). (2010/2014). *Star wars uncut* [Motion Picture]. Available at: www.starwarsuncut.com/about

Ronson, J. (2015, February 12). How one stupid tweet blew up Justine Sacco's life. *The New York Times Magazine*. Retrieved from: www.nytimes.com/2015/02/15/magazine/how-one-stupid-tweet-ruined-justine-saccos-life.html?_r=0

Senate body seeks legislation to lift YouTube ban. (2015, September 15). *Dawn.com*. Retrieved from: www.dawn.com/news/1207132

Statista. (2016). Hours of video uploaded to YouTube every minute as of November 2014. Retrieved from: www.statista.com/statistics/259477/hours-of-video-uploaded-to-youtube-every-minute/

Stewart, D. (2012, April 30). Why *Think like a man* topped the box office again and *The five-year engagement* bombed. *Jezebel*. Retrieved from: http://jezebel.com/5906275/why-think-like-a-man-topped-the-box-office-again-and-the-five-year-engagement-bombed

Stewart, D. (2015, September 14). Movies with black casts are winning at the box office right now. *Fusion*. Retrieved from: http://fusion.net/story/196936/movies-with-black-casts-are-winning-at-the-box-office-right-now/

Terranova, T. (2000). Free labor: Producing culture for the digital economy. *Social text*, *18*(2), 33–58.

Variety Staff. (2013, December 23). Lionsgate vows to recall Italy's "12 Years a Slave" poster focusing on Brad Pitt. *Variety*. Retrieved from: http://variety.com/2013/film/news/italys-12-years-a-slave-poster-favors-brad-pitt-over-black-star-1200990875/

Verrier, R. (2015, March 17). AMC, Dallas theater clash over rights to screen new movie releases first. *Los Angeles Times*. Retrieved from: www.latimes.com/entertainment/envelope/cotown/la-et-ct-look-cinemas-dispute-20150316-story.html

Vidal, J. (2013, December 14). Toxic "e-waste" dumped in poor nations, says United Nations. *The Guardian*. Retrieved from: www.theguardian.com/global-development/2013/dec/14/toxic-ewaste-illegal-dumping-developing-countries

Villarreal, Y. (2016, January 7). Netflix announces huge global expansion, adding 130 more countries to its service. *Los Angeles Times*. Retrieved from: www.latimes.com/entertainment/envelope/cotown/la-et-ct-netflix-global-expansion-20160107-story.html

Wagmeister, E. (2015, October 15). HBO greenlights comedy series "Insecure" from YouTube star Issa Rae. *Variety*. Retrieved from: http://variety.com/2015/tv/news/insecure-hbo-issa-rae-series-order-comedy-1201619196/

Wilkes, T. (2016, January 18). Pakistan has lifted its 3-year ban on YouTube after launching its own censored version. *Reuters*. Retrieved from: www.businessinsider.com/r-pakistan-lifts-ban-on-youtube-after-launch-of-own-version-2016-1

YouTube. (n.d.) Statistics. Retrieved from: www.youtube.com/yt/press/statistics.html

Index

Page numbers in italics refer to figures.